The Ultimate Shrimp Book

Other books by Bruce Weinstein

The Ultimate Ice Cream Book

The Ultimate Party Drink Book

The Ultimate Candy Book

The Ultimate
Shrimp Book

*More Than
650 Recipes
for Everyone's
Favorite Seafood
Prepared in
Every Way
Imaginable*

Bruce Weinstein
and Mark Scarbrough

WILLIAM MORROW
An Imprint of HarperCollins*Publishers*

To David Weinstein and Lisa Aiello

and

Rick and Catherine Colvin

For forgiving impediments to the true mind of marriage
when we could only admit them

HarperCollins books may be purchased for educational, business, or sales promotional use. For information please write: Special Markets Department, HarperCollins Publishers Inc., 10 East 53rd Street, New York, NY 10022.

FIRST EDITION

Designed by Mary Austin Speaker

Printed on acid-free paper

Library of Congress Cataloging-in-Publication Data

Weinstein, Bruce, 1960–
 The ultimate shrimp book : more than 650 recipes for everyone's favorite seafood
prepared in every way imaginable / Bruce Weinstein and Mark Scarbrough.—1st ed.
   p. cm.
 Includes index.
 ISBN 0-06-093416-6
 1. Cookery (Shrimp) 2. Shrimp. I. Scarbrough, Mark. II. Title.

TX754.S58 .W45   2002
641.6'95—dc21

                                                     2001044512

CONTENTS

ACKNOWLEDGMENTS

Countless thanks to these who made this book possible:

Harriet Bell at Morrow. A doyenne of publishing: quick-witted, savvy, and relentlessly fair.

Susan Ginsburg at Writers House. The rarest of agents, a friend.

Beth Shepard at Lisa Ekus Public Relations. Apparently the one media agent in the world who'll take limitless phone calls.

Carrie Weinberg at Morrow. Energy beyond bounds in a publicist with the media's attention.

Dixie Blake at Ocean Garden in San Diego. Such generosity, with both product and knowledge. Dixie, you're the queen of the sea. You made this book easy.

Karen Ferries at Morrow. Not only an ace editorial assistant but a woman with trustworthy ideas about Asian cooking.

Annie Leuenberger at Writers House. Unflappable, simply unflappable.

James Haggerty at Morrow. How can someone say yes so many times?

Kate Stark and Mark Landau at Morrow. Simply put, they make books move.

Roberto de Vicq de Cumptich, Leah Carlson-Stanisic, and Mary Speaker. Impeccable design sense, far exceeding everything else out there.

Beatriz da Costa. A photographer whose sophisticated style makes shrimp mouthwatering, even after we've eaten 700 pounds of it.

Judith Sutton. A copyeditor with a fine-mesh sieve for manuscripts.

Ann Cahn. A production editor who followed this book from manuscript to bound book with incredible care.

Karen Lumley. A production manager who kept us on schedule.

Juli Vitello at Home Matters. A tireless executive producer who's also a fine supporter.

Lynn Sadofsky and Jennifer DiLullo at Gotham TV. What a hilarious day we had, filming two guys in a cramped Manhattan kitchen.

John Boyajian at Boyajian, Inc. For his generosity with outstanding oils and vinegars.

Neil Silverman at DeLonghi. For their generosity with a deep fryer.

Marcos Rodriguez at Alba Specialty Seafood Company. For holding shrimp for months and delivering it at a moment's notice.

Marianne Macy. Not only did she eat almost every dish in this book—and manage to stay TV-thin—but her endless support of us has made this book, quite literally, possible.

Alethea Worden, Patricia Clough, David Sisson, Scott Stevens, and Carol Altes. How did we ever end up with such good friends with such good taste?

Danny Diaz and Andrew Mackhanlall. Great sports, even in the face of the cameras.

Justin Schwartz. How rare, that a first start could become a friendship.

Lucy and Mickey Shoeff. For a lifetime of home-cooking advice.

Kyoko Yagi. A friend for years, and a font of knowledge about the intricacies of Japanese cooking.

Rainey Day and John Irwin. How could we ever thank you enough for offering us your country home so we could finish this book and still stay sane? May the birds live cat-free.

INTRODUCTION

Fried, steamed, or barbecued? In the end, it doesn't matter, because everyone's crazy about shrimp. It's the world's most popular fresh seafood. (Only canned tuna surpasses these little crustaceans.) U.S. cooks and consumers ate 963,000,000 pounds in 2000. And to think shrimp was bait a century ago.

When you bite into a perfectly prepared shrimp, its meat sweet and moist, you may wonder why it deserved all the health-scare press it got in the 1990s. While admittedly high in cholesterol, shrimp actually contributes to better ratios between LDL (bad cholesterol) and HDL (good cholesterol). Shrimp also lowers triglycerides in the blood. And a quarter-pound serving has only 80 calories, with less than 1 gram of fat.

Over the last year, we've been on a quest for the new-and-different and the tried-and-true. We tasted a stew of shrimp and pastis at a country hotel in Provence. In Denver, far from either coast, we found an authentic Japanese country restaurant, serving the finest tempura this side of Kyoto. And one spring night, we wandered from one Queens diner to the next, searching for the consummate example of that East Coast staple, shrimp scampi.

As you may have noticed, *The Ultimate Shrimp Book* is part of an ongoing series that includes *The Ultimate Ice Cream Book*, *The Ultimate Party Drink Book*, and *The Ultimate Candy Book*. "Shrimp?" friends asked when we started. "How does that fit with the others?"

Easily. Shrimp is fun food, party food: quick, simple, and satisfying.

In this book, there are standards you probably haven't thought of in years, like Shrimp Thermidor and Shrimp à la King. There are also plenty of modern favorites, like Popcorn Shrimp and Kung Pao Shrimp. And there are some surprising treats, like Black Pepper Caramel Shrimp, a Vietnamese delicacy. As in all the *Ultimate* books, these basic recipes are pushed to new heights with variations. Once you master a basic recipe and some of the variations, try making up your own variations. That way, shrimp, the ultimate fun food, will be as fun for you to make as it is to eat.

Shrimp:
The Skinny

In this chapter, we'll follow shrimp through their culinary life. Along the way, we'll address a few health concerns, tell you how to "size" shrimp, and offer tests for freshness.

FROM THE OCEAN TO THE MARKET

Ah, the Pleasures of the Sea!

They're fast growing few. The Sea of Japan, once teeming with shrimp, is now almost barren. The mangrove swamps of Malaysia, the habitat for some of the world's best shrimp, are being eradicated to satisfy the world's hunger. And industrial contaminants have pushed Atlantic shrimping as far north as Greenland.

All is not lost. In 1990, there were no shrimp farms in the United States. Today, they constitute a thirty-five-million-dollar industry. They're sprouting up even faster in Central and South America, a gold mine for fledgling economies.

That said, there are still a few pockets in the ocean where shrimp are caught wild, where the harvest is nondestructive. The best lie off the Baja Peninsula. The white shrimp found there are the yardstick against which most farmed shrimp are measured.

Fresh Shrimp Probably Aren't

Almost every shrimp available in North America and Europe, whether wild-caught or farmed, was flash-frozen the moment it was harvested. Unless you live within fifteen minutes of the ocean, or are fortunate enough to live near a Chinese community where shrimp are sold live from saltwater tanks, never-frozen shrimp simply aren't available.

Actually, that's the good news. Flash-freezing ensures a shrimp's freshness—as do certain chemicals. The FDA permits two additives. Sodium tripolyphosphate preserves the moisture content of shelled shrimp. Like beef or chicken, shrimp meat dehydrates when it's exposed to the air. Bathing it in sodium tripolyphosphate allows a thin, gelatinous, moisture-sealing coating to form around the meat. But if you're leery of such chemistry, or are on a low-sodium diet, buy shrimp in their shells and peel them yourself.

Sodium bisulfite, the second additive, eliminates black spot (or melanosis), a natural condition caused by a digestive enzyme that runs amuck in the meat once the shrimp's killed. In the initial stage, the enzyme causes black dots; in more advanced cases, black rings. Black spot is not harmful, just unsavory—and a pretty sure indication that the shrimp has been mishandled during processing.

For most of us, sodium bisulfite, like sulfites in red wine, presents no problems. But if you're allergic to sulfites, you'll most likely react to it. To get around it, buy organic or nonadditive shrimp (*organic* is the industry term; *nonadditive* the governmental one in the United States and Canada). To guarantee that your shrimp are chemical-free, ask to see the box they were packaged in. Your fishmonger should be happy to let you have a look.

One surefire way to avoid problems is to buy shrimp exactly the way your fishmonger does—frozen, in 3- or 5-pound boxes. You may find these in the freezer cases of gourmet supermarkets, or you can ask your fishmonger to sell you one directly. You'll end up with perfect shrimp, sealed in a double layer of protective ice (called *double glazing*). If you're lucky enough to land one of these boxes, they should be thawed for 2 to 3 days in your refrigerator, on a lipped baking sheet to catch the runoff. Yes, with 5 pounds, you might have more than you want, but you can always use what you need for the recipe, then steam the rest (see page 180) and keep them in the freezer in a freezer-safe bag. Refreezing is the safest way to store shrimp once you've cooked them; never refreeze raw shrimp.

"Off with Their Heads!"

Although we North Americans may cry it, we're the only ones who do. Around the globe, shrimp heads are a delicacy.

In Manhattan's hopping Chinatown, during spring and fall, the dim sum parlors are buzzing every Sunday morning with shrimp and hot peppers, fresh from the fryer. Each shrimp, no more than three inches long, is deep-fried—head, feelers, legs, tail and all. Pure magic, all crunch.

If you're lucky enough to find shrimp with their heads on, buy 50% more than the recipe calls for (the head accounts for about that much weight). You can cook them whole, and your family can snap off the heads and suck out the juices, just as they do with crawfish in New Orleans. Or you can snap off the heads before cooking and save them in your freezer to make fish stock.

FROM THE MARKET TO YOUR REFRIGERATOR

Use Your Nose and Eyes

To tell if shrimp are at their peak, just smell them (ask your fishmonger to hold up a handful). They should have little odor, just a hint of the sea, clean and bright.

A shrimp should *not* smell like

Ammonia or rotten eggs: it's undoubtedly old.
Chlorine: Washing shrimp in chlorine to kill bacteria is legal, but not acceptable.
Gasoline: the harvesting trawler was leaking fuel into its belly.

After you've smelled the shrimp, look at them—and beware two ominous colors. Avoid a shrimp that's dark pink around its shell segments. Yes, some are pink by nature (see page 4)—but that's a rosy translucence in the meat itself. If a shrimp looks warmly pink just at the shell segments, or if it is unevenly pink on one side but not the other, chances are it's been defrosted under warm water, and is thus partially cooked. Or, worse yet, it's been improperly preserved, the chemical decay actually cooking the meat.

A shrimp should also not appear dusty yellow, especially around its neck (that is, the fleshy part exposed outside the shell, just where the head was snapped off). Yellowing is an indication of excessive sodium bisulfite (see page 1). The meat will be rough, like sandpaper. Tell your fishmonger to quit playing mad scientist in the back.

Size Matters

But it doesn't mean anything. There's no governmental standard for sizing shrimp. "Jumbo," "large," "colossal" are just marketing words, some accurate, some quaint, some window dressing. For the purposes of this book, shrimp are broken into three categories, each designated by about how many shrimp make up 1 pound (or about 450 grams).

Large	12 to 15 per pound
Medium	35 to 40 per pound
Small	more than 55 per pound

Always buy shrimp from a market that sells them sized per pound. But there is no institutional standard among markets. You may not find "large" shrimp that are exactly 12 to 15 per pound—yours may be 10 to 12 per pound. Fortunately, we're not playing roulette. Close enough counts.

A Shrimp by Any Other Name . . .

. . . would still be a shrimp. But that doesn't tell you what kind it is. So let's first deal with three terms that add to the confusion:

Prawns In most of North America, a prawn means any large shrimp (usually 15 or fewer per pound). But in Great Britain, a prawn is any medium or large shrimp (35 or fewer per pound). And in the Pacific Northwest and Alaska, a prawn is a large freshwater shrimp. In the end, *prawn* is a term bandied about recklessly, a fearful thing for any gourmand or home cook to encounter. It is not used in this book.

Gulf Shrimp This used to mean any shrimp caught wild off the Texas coast, once the sole source for the U.S. market. Slowly, the term has morphed into a feel-good moniker for any shrimp from a warm-water locale. Unless you live in Galveston, Texas, the label's probably just window dressing.

Scampi *Scampi* is a Venetian word for a small clawed lobster that's now so rare, it's almost gone the way of the dodo. In Italy, what are still called scampi are for the most part the original scampi's close cousin: the nine- or ten-inch Norway lobster, a crustacean with large pinchers. (Norway lobsters are also called Dublin Bay shrimp, not because they were caught there, but because in the 1700s, fishing boats from Norway would enter Dublin Bay loaded with them.) But in most of the United States, *scampi* no longer refers to any particular crustacean at all, but rather to a preparation: baked or broiled in oil or butter with garlic. In this book, in deference to U.S. fashion, the term refers only to the preparation.

With these three confusing terms out of the way, how are shrimp classified? Quite simply, by the water they live in: fresh water, cold (salt-) water, or warm (salt-) water.

Freshwater shrimp are far larger than the shrimp available in most grocery stores. They can grow to be a foot long, weighing well over a pound, and are shipped live, like lobsters. Those from the Americas have blue shells; those from Asia are yellow with brown stripes. Since freshwater shrimp constitute less than 1 percent of the U.S. market, no recipe in this book calls for them. Should you find one, boil up a pot of salted water, dump the shrimp in live, and boil for 8 minutes. Melt the butter, and have yourself a rare feast with a loaf of crusty bread.

Cold-water shrimp are tiny crustaceans, often called *baby shrimp* (or *salad shrimp* or *bay shrimp*). Although they usually run over 100 to the pound, small is not young—these shrimp take four years to mature before they can be harvested off Greenland or Alaska. They arrive in the freezer section of your supermarket shelled and precooked.

Many of the recipes in this book that call for *small shrimp* (warm-water ones over 55 per pound) allow you to substitute *cold-water (or baby) shrimp*. However, the taste of small warm-water shrimp is sweeter, more, well, shrimpy than their cold-water cousins.

Warm-water shrimp are the standard. These are the shrimp we normally find in our grocery stores and gourmet markets. They are classified by color when raw—any of them can be used for the recipes, provided the size is right.

White shrimp are the most common in the United States, wild-caught or farmed. They have grayish-white shells, are moderately sweet, and turn a pale pink when cooked.

Brown shrimp once rare, are becoming more prevalent because of farming trends in Mexico. These shrimp have a taupe cast to their shells; the cooked meat turns a very pale pink, sometimes only in streaks. Brown shrimp are often tangier than white.

Pink shrimp, a Caribbean variety, are always caught wild. When cooked, they turn a brilliant pink and are far sweeter than any other variety. However, since they swim vigorously in the ocean, they can also be a bit tough.

Black shrimp, sometimes called *tiger shrimp*, are an Asian delicacy introduced to North America in the early '80s. They are known by their black stripes, sometimes with blue tinges around their legs. They are most likely the largest warm-water shrimp available in your market.

What About Rock Shrimp?

This deep-water cousin of the white shrimp is always sold peeled and cleaned—its shell is too tough for the home cook to tackle. More like crayfish than standard shrimp, rock shrimp are firmer and more toothsome. No basic recipe in this book calls for them, but some variations do.

What About Canned Shrimp?

Canned shrimp were first mass-produced to give the troops quick wartime meals; after World War II, they were mass-marketed for a world before modern shipping. No recipe in this book calls for canned shrimp. Its tinny taste will compromise the final dish.

FROM YOUR REFRIGERATOR TO YOUR TABLE

Haste Doesn't Make Waste

Shrimp are best eaten the day they're bought, or at most the day after. Let's say, however, that you've bought a pound of shrimp, and your partner comes home from work and says, "Tonight I'm taking you to the Four Seasons."

(It could happen.) You don't say, "But I was going to make Shrimp Remoulade." But you also don't need to throw out the shrimp. Instead, follow the recipe for steamed shrimp (see page 180), cool them, dry them, and then freeze them, first on a nonstick cookie sheet, much as you might freeze berries. Later, you can store them in the freezer in a freezer-safe bag.

The Dirty Work (Or, How to Peel and Devein a Shrimp)

If a shrimp must be peeled for a recipe, there's no getting around it. But should it be deveined? That's a matter of opinion. The black, brown, or green so-called vein that runs through a shrimp isn't a vein at all. It's the digestive tract, often full of sand and other impurities the shrimp picked up as it went about its shrimpy business. Some farm-raised shrimp have next to none; large shrimp pick up more, simply because of their size. In the end, small and medium shrimp can be deveined as a matter of preference, but large shrimp should always be deveined.

To peel a shrimp: Turn it so that the small legs are facing you. Using your thumbs, gently pry the shell loose, starting in the middle of the body and pulling out. The shell should now be loose, attached just at the end of the tail.

Some recipes in this book ask you to *leave the final segment of the tail shell intact*. To do that, gently tear the shell at the last segment, just before the tail fins. The loosened shell should fall off, leaving the tail segment intact.

Other recipes ask you *to peel a shrimp completely*. To do that, pinch the loosened shell at the farthest end of the tail, just at its tip, and pull in a steady, gentle motion—never jerk. The meat should come clean from the shell.

To peel and devein a shrimp: The dark vein will often be sticking out from the neck (or fleshy end) of the shrimp. To remove it, hold the shrimp in one hand and gently pull the vein out with the thumb and forefinger of your other hand. If the vein does not come out easily or completely—or if it's not visible—use scissors or a sharp paring knife to cut down the back curve of the shell (opposite the little legs), cutting into the shrimp to a depth of only about ⅛ inch. Start cutting at the fleshy end and stop just before you reach the last segment of shell near the tail. Gently open the slit with your fingers and run the shrimp under cold water to remove the exposed vein. Then peel off the shell, removing it completely or leaving only the last tail segment intact, as indicated by the recipe.

Some kitchenware shops sell long-handled deveiners that are good for digging out the sandy bits, although they split the shrimp open just as scissors or a knife would. If you use one of these newfangled tools, carefully follow the instructions on the package—otherwise, you'll tear the meat to shreds.

Now That You Have Fresh Shrimp, What Can Possibly Go Wrong?

In truth, not much. The only real problem is overcooking. If shrimp are rubbery or decidedly tasteless, they're probably overcooked. But that's just the flip side of the good news. Shrimp are easy, fast, and tasty. They're done in two or three minutes in a saucepan over high heat. In a world of rush, they're the ultimate comfort food.

USING PRECOOKED SHRIMP

While fresh shrimp are the standard, precooked medium or large shrimp, sometimes called *cocktail shrimp*, as well as precooked cold-water *baby* shrimp, can be the next best thing. These chilled shrimp are usually available at the fish counter, or in bags in the market's freezer section.

Of course, uncooked in-their-shell shrimp make better dishes. In stir-fries, the raw shrimp add flavor that you lose when you use precooked shrimp. In most cases, freshly boiled shrimp have a sweeter, brinier taste than precooked. Nevertheless, when you're dead tired because you had to write that report for the zillionth time, or worn out from the carpool circuit, precooked shrimp fit the bill for a quick supper everyone will enjoy. If you buy these precooked miracles to use in recipes, remember two things:

1. Cocktail shrimp often have a small tail segment left on, for easy handling in a shrimp cocktail. If you're using them in a recipe that calls for completely peeled shrimp, you'll need to remove that end bit of shell.

2. Since they're precooked, you obviously don't need to cook them. The recipes will show you how to skip ahead if you're substituting.

Check out these recipes, which allow you to substitute precooked shrimp, either cocktail shrimp or tiny cold-water (baby) shrimp.

Recipes that can be made with precooked cocktail shrimp
À la King • Bell Pepper • Bengalese Stew • Black Pepper Caramel • Bon Bon • Bruschetta • Cashew • Cocktail (see Easy Shrimp Cocktail variation) • Diane • Fra Diavolo • Garlic Sauce • Maki • Newburg • Paprikash • Penne à la Vodka • Pesto • Phyllo Pillows • Portuguese • Rémoulade • Salad Niçoise • Sushi • Tuscan White Bean • Vegetable Stir-fry • Wraps

Recipes that can be made with precooked, cold-water (baby) shrimp
Cakes • Curry • Dip • Fried Rice • Fritters • Lo Mein • Noodle Soup • Puffs • Quiche • Salad • Soufflé

Ingredients
and Equipment

INGREDIENTS

In the main, the recipes in this book call for standard pantry items. But because there's a wide range of regional specialties here, some ingredients may be new to you. Many of them are available in the Asian or Mexican or Indian sections of larger supermarkets. But if you're having a hard time locating them, you can always order them by mail from outlets listed in the Source Guide (page 239).

Bean Thread Noodles

These milky-white noodles (*fen si* in Chinese, also called *cellophane noodles*) are made from ground mung beans, the mature beans of what we call bean sprouts. Unfortunately, bean thread noodles are available only dried in North America, and they must be soaked before use. Place them in a large bowl, cover with boiling water, and allow them to soak until they become transparent, about 15 minutes. Drain them and rinse under cold water.

Chile Powder

Commercial chile powder is made by blending dried chiles with oregano and cumin. The recipes in this book, however, call for *pure chile powder*, which contains only dried ground chiles. Sometimes it is labeled with the type of chile in the package, sold as perhaps ancho chile powder or pasilla chile powder. Pure chile powder is available in Latin American markets and sometimes in the Mexican section of large supermarkets.

You can also make your own with dried chiles. Remove the stems, cut the chiles open, and scoop out the seeds. Grind the pods in a spice grinder, with a mortar and pestle, or in a coffee grinder. Store tightly covered in a dark, cool place for up to 3 months. (To remove any lingering chile powder from a coffer grinder, fill the grinder with rice; process the rice to a fine dust, and discard.)

Chili Oil

Popular in Asian cuisine, this fiery flavoring oil is *not* for frying. Used as a condiment, it adds a splash of heat, like Tabasco sauce, but is sweeter and more aromatic. Chili oil is often made with a nut-oil base, such as walnut or peanut. (If you have nut allergies, read the label carefully.) Because of the nut oil, chili oil goes rancid quickly—keep it refrigerated, for no more than to 2 months.

As chiles themselves vary in heat levels, so do chili oils. (*Chili* is the spelling used on most labels.) As a general guide, but not a rule, Chinese and Vietnamese versions may be milder; Thai and Malaysian, hotter. The recipes in this book use chili oil sparingly, but you can always set a bottle on the table so others can spice the dish more heavily.

Clam Juice

If you don't want to make your own fish stock (see page 11), bottled clam juice (the runoff from canning clams) can be a quick fix. Some brands have a slight amount of sediment, which comes from improperly cleaned clams; always buy clam juice in glass bottles, and check the bottom for residue. If necessary, you can strain clam juice through a double layer of cheesecloth. Never save leftover juice—it can go bad in less than a day, even refrigerated.

Clams and Mussels

Use clams and mussels the day you buy them. Store them in a large bowl in your refrigerator, with moistened paper towels lining the bowl and laid loosely over the top. Never store them in an airtight plastic bag—they will suffocate. Their shells must be scrubbed with a stiff brush under cold water to get rid of grit. Mussels must also be *debearded*—that is, the wiry "hairs"

protruding from the shell must be pulled out just before you're ready to cook them. Never use a clam or mussel that is open and unyielding before you cook it. (If you tap it and it closes, it's just taking in the air.) And discard any clams or mussels that don't open during cooking.

Coconut Milk

This milk-like liquid is made by pressing coconut flesh with water, sometimes the "water" from inside the coconut. Canned coconut milk is now sold in its regular full-fat way, and in a newer low-fat version, usually made by squeezing the coconut and water mixture a second time. You can use either for the recipes in this book, but don't substitute cream of coconut, which is a sweetened coconut purée, good for desserts or frozen drinks.

To prepare your own coconut milk, pierce two of the dark eyes of a coconut with a chef's knife or clean screwdriver, then drain out any liquid inside. Bake the coconut on a lipped baking sheet in a 375°F oven for 20 minutes, or until the shell cracks. (If it hasn't cracked even after 25 minutes, wrap the hot coconut in a dish towel and bash it in the center with a hammer until it breaks open.) With a sharp paring knife or a clean screwdriver, loosen the meat from the brown shell. Place all the meat in a large heavy saucepan, add 2 cups water, and bring to a boil over medium-high heat. Cover and simmer for 10 minutes. Remove the pan from the heat and cool thoroughly, then pour the coconut mixture into a food processor. Process it for 1 minute, then let it stand for 20 minutes. Strain the coconut milk through a fine-mesh strainer or a double layer of cheesecloth into a medium bowl. Use a wooden spoon to press all the liquid from the pulp. Refrigerate the coconut milk until you're ready to use it. It should keep, covered, for up to 2 weeks.

Curry Paste

Indian curry paste, a thick, spicy red or yellow paste, is available in Indian and some Asian markets, as well as the Indian section of most supermarkets. The best brands are a blend of ghee (clarified butter), curry powder, vinegar, and spices. Cheaper ones use vegetable oil instead of ghee. The red variety is usually hotter and more highly prized—the yellow has been cut with turmeric to make it affordable. Once it's been opened, store curry paste tightly covered in the refrigerator for up to 2 months. You can substitute it for curry powder in equal amounts in soups and stews—it will give the dish a richer texture. But do not confuse Indian curry paste with Thai curry paste, always labeled as such and not called for in this book. Thai curry paste is a fiery mixture of peppers, vinegar, and spices, without any added fat.

Curry Powder

Curry powder is not a single spice, nor even a set blend of spices. It may include cardamom, cayenne pepper, cinnamon, cloves, coriander, cumin, fennel seeds, fenugreek, mace, nut-

meg, sesame seeds, saffron, tamarind, and/or turmeric. Because of chemical reactions among the spices, curry powder goes stale quickly. It should be stored in the refrigerator and used within 2 months. *Madras curry powder,* which relies heavily on cayenne pepper, is very spicy.

Dried Chinese Black Beans

This delicacy should not be confused with the black beans used in Latin American cooking. Dried Chinese black beans are actually soybeans, coated with salt and dried under high heat until they blacken from enzymatic processes. You'll most likely find them in Asian markets. Buy beans in clear plastic pouches— they should be whole, not crushed or powdered. They are used as a flavoring for many dishes, tossed in just at the end. Crush them slightly with the side of a knife or the bottom of a pot to release their flavor.

Dried Red Asian Chiles

Although chiles may seem endemic to Chinese cooking, they aren't. They were actually introduced about two hundred years ago from the Americas, where they've been eaten for over nine thousand years, according to archaeological records. That said, dried red Asian chiles are now necessary for dishes like Garlic Sauce Shrimp or General Tsao's Shrimp. Look for bags of whole chiles, about 2 inches long and dark red. They are usually a mixture of various small chiles, no type taking precedence. If you can't find them in the Asian section of your supermarket, order them from one of the outlets listed in the Source Guide (page 239).

Dried Shrimp

An Asian seasoning, not a time-saver, these tiny head-on shrimp are dehydrated to a brittle crunch. Their taste is rather musky. Only one basic recipe in the book calls for them (Thai Sticky Rice), but they are offered in variations throughout. Use them only as a flavoring additive, never as a substitute for shrimp.

Fish Stock

There's no better base for a shrimp dish than a fine fish stock. Several brands are available in gourmet markets as reductions, usually set in the freezer case alongside the demi-glace. These packaged reductions need to be cut with water—read the label carefully.

Alternatively, you can make your own. Simply save unwanted shrimp shells in your freezer in a freezer-safe bag until you have 1 pound. When you eat other fresh fish, also save the bones in freezer-safe bags until you have 1 pound—or ask your fishmonger to sell you a pound of fish heads, skin, and bones. Place these "remnants" and your shrimp shells in a large pot and fill it with 6 quarts water; add 4 celery stalks, a quartered onion, 3 garlic cloves, 2 bay leaves, and 1 tablespoon

salt. Bring to a boil over high heat, reduce the heat to low, cover, and simmer for 20 minutes, skimming the foam occasionally. Allow the stock to cool in the pot, then strain it through a fine-mesh sieve, or a double layer of cheesecloth. You can save the stock tightly sealed in quart jars or other small containers for up to 4 days in the refrigerator, or in the freezer for up to 2 months.

Fish Sauce

Made from fermented and salted fish skins and innards, fish sauce (*nuớc mắm* in Vietnamese, *nam pla* in Thai, and *fish gravy* on some Hong Kong packaging) is the soy sauce of Southeast Asia. It was originally made to preserve the oily proteins of fish so that people could get basic nutrition during the rainy season, when fishing was difficult. Commercial fish sauce is a salty, briny brew than can be orange, rust, brown, or black. It has a very pungent smell, but it mellows in a cooked dish and creates a subtle background for other tastes. Fish sauce will keep for up to a year in a cool, dry place.

Five-Spice Powder

The blended spices in this powder epitomize Chinese flavor: fennel seed, star anise, Szechwan peppercorn, cinnamon, and clove. Each represents one of the five cosmological elements of ancient Chinese philosophy (water, wood, metal, earth, and fire, respectively).

Flavored Oils

Flavored oils are available in many variations, such as basil oil, black pepper oil, and rosemary oil. Not good for frying or cooking—their taste is compromised by heat—these oils add a special twist to a finished dish.

Ginger

A rhizome (or underground stem), not a root, ginger is from the same botanical family as cardamom and turmeric. Its name comes from a Sanskrit word for horn, perhaps a reference to its shape, but more likely a reference to its alleged aphrodisiac properties. Ginger's first documented use was in about 600 B.C.E. as a medicinal derivative in China, used to treat sexual dysfunctions—an ancient Viagra. Today, it is one of the five "fortunate flavors" in Chinese cuisine (along with scallions, cinnamon, garlic, and red chiles). Ginger is called for in two versions in this book:

Fresh ginger Look for wheat-colored, relatively small stems in the vegetable section of your grocery store. The skin should be papery but smooth. Bigger chunks tend to be fibrous. Unless it's grated on a ginger board, ginger should be peeled with a sharp knife before use. Never substitute ground ginger for fresh ginger.

Pickled ginger Used as a condiment for many Japanese and Chinese dishes, these pieces of ginger have been pickled in wine. Do not buy *red sweet ginger* (also called *preserved ginger*),

which is far sweeter and used as an additive in many Asian desserts.

Herbs

The recipes in this book call for fresh herbs, not dried. In a pinch, you can substitute dried herbs, especially if cooked in a stew, but use only half the amount called for. Replenish your supply of dried herbs frequently—they lose their aroma and develop a tea-like taste that affects a dish's flavor.

Hoi Sin Sauce

Popular in Asian cuisine, this thick sauce is made from soybeans, garlic, sugar, spices, and vinegar. Sometimes, the name is written as one word in the West, although it is indeed two words in Chinese and labeled as such on most Chinese bottles. It is used as a table condiment in China, where it also glazes roast meats. (It's occasionally packaged as *Chinese barbecue sauce with hoi sin.*) Look for brand names such as Pearl River or Ma Ling. *Chee hou sauce* is a stronger version of hoi sin, and it can be used as a substitute if you want a far more pungent taste.

Japanese Bread Crumbs

Called *panko* in Japanese, these dry bread crumbs are coarser than their Western counterparts, partly because they have shortening added. Because of the higher fat content, they make fried shrimp extra crispy. Japanese bread crumbs are also excellent on fried chicken or pork cutlets.

Lemongrass

The sour lemon taste of this tough herb that somewhat resembles a scallion is often associated with Thai cooking, although the plant (a perennial grass) is also indigenous to North America and Australia. To release the oils (including citral, the essential oil in lemons), you must crush the bulb end before you use it. Buy lemongrass stalks that smell peppery and lemony but are not dried out. The fibrous stalks are usually removed from a final dish, because they don't break down and so remain tough. Lemongrass will keep in the vegetable crisper, wrapped in dry paper towels, for up to 4 days. Leftover lemongrass can be used to make a soothing herbal tea, thought in some Thai communities to cure digestive disorders. Lemons are no substitute for lemongrass.

Oyster Sauce

This brewed brown sauce is made from oysters, spices, sugar, vinegar, and soy sauce. Its salty flavor mellows considerably during cooking. It is very popular in southern China, where it is even used as a condiment. Some brands contain MSG—read the label carefully. More expensive brands are less salty. Oyster sauce will keep in the refrigerator, sealed tightly, for up to 2 years.

Pancetta

This Italian bacon is cured with salt and spices but not smoked. Most varieties are pork belly, pressed into a roll. All are sold by weight, sliced. In some recipes, you can substitute Canadian bacon, although the dish's flavor will change considerably. Unused pancetta can be stored in the freezer, tightly wrapped, for up to 3 months.

Paprika

Particularly associated with Hungary, this spice is made from hard red peppers, ground in several go-rounds to a fine powder. In this book, the common burnt-red supermarket variety is called *sweet paprika*. The hotter versions are sold as *hot Hungarian paprika*—they are made by leaving the seeds in the peppers during processing. Paprika should be stored tightly sealed in a cool, dark place for no more than 2 months. If left for longer, it will turn into a dusty-red, flavorless coloring agent—familiar from your aunt's deviled eggs.

Parmigiano-Reggiano

This grainy wheat-colored aged Italian cheese is made from skimmed cow's milk. True *Parmigiano-Reggiano* is always stamped so on the rind. Although "Parmesan" has come to stand for a host of grating cheeses, real Parmigiano-Reggiano is always preferred. And never use pregrated Parmesan cheese, often a tasteless product, sometimes oil-based. Buy a chunk of Parmigiano-Reggiano (aged from 2 to 4 years)—or a wedge of domestic Parmesan (aged up to 14 months)—and grate it yourself as you need it.

Peanut Oil

This clear, golden oil is pressed from peanuts, which are not nuts at all, but legumes. Peanut oil has a high smoke point (that is, it can be heated to a high temperature without burning), so it's perfect for stir-frying. Unfortunately, some people are allergic to peanuts; you can substitute vegetable oil for peanut oil if necessary, but the dish will be far less aromatic.

Prosciutto

An Italian ham, prosciutto is seasoned with salt and spices, pressed, and air-dried, not smoked. Don't use ham as a substitute. Any leftover prosciutto can be eaten with melon, figs, or nuts as an appetizer—but it should be used within a day of purchase.

Saffron Threads

These stigmas of a purple crocus, used in the ancient world exclusively as a dye, are the modern world's most expensive spice. Saffron has a delicate, musky taste, wholly its own, although it's often—mistakenly—replaced with turmeric in North America. Saffron's harvest is labor-intensive, each crocus yielding only three tiny stigmas, gathered by hand. Saffron is sold in threads (the whole stigmas) or as a powder (the crushed stigmas). Only the threads are called for in this book, because the powder is often cut with turmeric.

Sesame Oil

The pressed oil from the world's oldest spice, sesame oil is available in two forms: a golden oil (sometimes called *untoasted*), and a dark brown oil (sometimes called *toasted*). The latter, a flavoring oil used to finish dishes, is the only kind called for in this book.

Soy Sauce

In ancient China, soy sauce was governmentally sanctioned as one of the essentials for life—not ever for sale—along with firewood, rice, vinegar, and tea. Back then, soy sauce was a light-colored salty liquid with preserved soybeans mixed in. Today, the soybeans have been pressed out—they are first fermented in a flour and water paste, then squeezed to release all their liquid. Soy sauce comes in two versions: light and dark. Light soy sauce is saltier than dark but has a softer taste. It's sometimes sold in Asian markets as *superior soy sauce*. Dark soy sauce is aged longer and has a more pungent taste. Complicating the matter, *low-sodium soy sauce,* produced principally for the West, is sometimes called *light* or *lite* soy sauce—but it will also be marked *low sodium* somewhere on the bottle.

Straw Mushrooms

Popular in Asian cooking, these small mushrooms are so named because they once grew exclusively in the straw used to dam rice paddies. Once in a great while, these loose-capped mushrooms are found fresh in Asian markets. More commonly, they are sold canned in the Asian food section of supermarkets. They should be drained thoroughly before use.

Szechwan Peppercorns

Not peppercorns at all, these are the dried berries of a plant in the prickly ash family. The astringent Szechwan peppercorns are best bought in clear packets. Select those with peppercorns that are red or brown; avoid black berries.

Tabasco Sauce

This hot red sauce, fermented for 3 years, is made from vinegar, spices, and Tabasco peppers.

Vermouth

This fortified wine, made with herbs, is available in two varieties: *dry* with a white label, and *sweet* with a red. Dry vermouth is bracing; sweet has a caramel taste. Both are called for in this book; they are not interchangeable. The word *vermouth* comes from the German word for wormwood, which was its principal flavoring until it was declared a toxic substance in the nineteenth century.

Vinegar

Because the natural sweetness of shrimp cries out for balance, there are a host of vinegars called for in the recipes in this book.

Black vinegar (or black rice wine vinegar) This staple in Chinese cooking is made from glutinous rice. It's dark and smooth, somewhat similar to well-aged balsamic vinegar, but interchangeable only in a pinch. In a real emergency, you can substitute Worcestershire sauce and cut the amount of soy sauce in the recipe in half.

Balsamic vinegar This highly prized Italian vinegar is made from the juice of Trebbiano grapes. It's aged for anywhere from a few weeks to decades, and priced accordingly.

Cider vinegar Made from fermented apple cider, this vinegar has a strong, sharp taste with a pleasant, fruity finish.

Rice wine vinegar This is a generic term for any number of Chinese vinegars. Basically, it's a clear, smooth vinegar made from a fermented rice and grain mixture. White wine vinegar is an acceptable, albeit more astringent, substitute.

Sweetened Chinese vinegar (or sweetened black vinegar) Like black vinegar, this dark vinegar is made from glutinous rice, but it has sugar and star anise added. Highly aromatic, use it only as a final flavoring agent.

White wine vinegar Don't confuse this delicate vinegar with standard distilled white vinegar. White wine vinegar has a lighter, more pleasing finish.

Wasabi Paste

Made from what's often called Japanese horseradish, this thickened paste has a sharp, hot taste. The paste is available ready-made in tubes or small jars, but it can also be prepared by stirring drops of water into dried wasabi powder until the mixture resembles wet cement. Some Japanese believe that wasabi stimulates the appetite, aiding digestion.

EQUIPMENT

Most of the recipes in this book can be made with standard kitchen equipment. However, there are a few specialized tools that may require an introduction.

Kitchen Scale
Weighing shrimp with an accurate scale is the sure way to know you have the right amount for the recipe. Digital models are the easiest to clean; just make sure you set the scale for ounces, not grams.

Paella Pan
This large lidless shallow round pan is needed to cook short-grained Bajia or Arborio rice evenly. Cooked uncovered, the rice develops that al dente texture so highly prized in paella.

Shrimp Deveiner
This tool looks like a knife with a long, hook-like blade. Following the path of the vein that runs down the back of the shrimp, simply insert it and pull up, splitting the body and revealing the vein, which can they be pulled out or washed out with water.

Skewers (metal, bamboo, or wooden)
For skewering shrimp, invest in a set of metal skewers (avoid tin or copper ones for health concerns). Disposable bamboo or wooden skewers, available in most supermarkets, are fine substitutes. Soak them in water for at least 20 minutes before using.

Steamer
Bamboo steamer baskets sit on top of a pot or in a wok of simmering water, much like a lid. They can be stacked in multiple layers, then covered, since the bamboo weave allows the steam to circulate through the layers. Bamboo steamers should be lightly oiled before each use. Metal vegetable steamers, on the other hand, are set inside the pot; they have petallike, collapsible lids that help contain or even close over the ingredients. If you use a metal vegetable steamer for dumplings and the like, first oil it lightly. Alternately, you can lay Napa cabbage leaves in the bottom of any steamer to prevent sticking. When using any steamer, make sure the simmering water does not touch the bottom of the steamer basket.

Sticky Rice Steamer
Essential for cooking Thai Sticky Rice, this simple steamer consists of a V-shaped bamboo basket and a deep narrow-necked pot. The rice is soaked, then steamed. (See the Source Guide, page 239.)

Sushi Mat

The bamboo mat allows you to roll sushi with one, simple motion. The technique for using it is given in the recipe for Shrimp Maki. Sushi mats are available in Japanese markets and via mail-order (see the Source Guide, page 239).

Wok

This round-bottomed pan is perfect for stir-frying. Its sides conduct heat up and back into the pan. Some woks require you to hold them over the flame with one hand and stir-fry with the other, a feat of sustained coordination; beginners should probably use a wok that sits on a stable ring over a burner. A few flat-bottom models, such as Le Creuset's, sit directly on the burner. A wok should never be washed with soap and water—the soap will get into the pores and seep back into the food. Wipe the wok out with damp paper towels. If food is crusted onto it, use coarse-grain salt to scrape it off under running water. Set the wok back over high heat and let it get smoking hot to sterilize it.

Shrimp Recipes, A to Z

Shrimp à la King

THE MORE FAMILIAR CHICKEN à la King was most likely created in the 1860s by Chef George Greenwald for Mr. and Mrs. E. Clark King III, proprietors of the chic Brighton Beach Hotel in Brooklyn. The Kings wanted a dish to serve to the Fifth Avenue set who retreated to the country (or eastern Brooklyn) in August. This shrimp version maintains the creamy sauce and mixed vegetables, popularized in the 1950s at Gibson's lunch counters. Although the dish is traditionally served in a puff pastry shell—something you can purchase ready-to-use in supermarket bakeries or unbaked in the freezer section—it's equally good over rice or in a hollowed-out bread bowl. **MAKES 6 SERVINGS**

6 tablespoons (¾ stick) unsalted butter; or 4 tablespoons (½ stick), if using precooked shrimp

1½ pounds medium shrimp (35 to 40 per pound), peeled and deveined, or precooked cocktail shrimp, thawed and peeled

½ pound white button mushrooms, cleaned and quartered

3 tablespoons all-purpose flour

3 cups milk, whole or low-fat, warmed

1 teaspoon Worcestershire sauce

2 dashes Tabasco sauce

1 teaspoon salt

½ teaspoon freshly ground black pepper

One 10-ounce package mixed frozen vegetables (such as peas and carrots), thawed

1. Melt 2 tablespoons of the butter in a large skillet over medium heat. Add the raw shrimp, and cook, stirring often, until pink and firm, 3 to 5 minutes. Transfer to a bowl and set aside. If you're using precooked cocktail shrimp, skip to step 2.

2. Add 1 tablespoon butter to the skillet and set it back over medium heat. Add the mushrooms and cook, stirring often, until they give off their juices and the pan is almost dry, about 5 minutes. Add the mushrooms to the shrimp.

3. Add the remaining 3 tablespoons butter to the skillet and set it back over medium heat. When the butter is melted, add the flour and whisk until well combined. Reduce the heat to low and continue to cook, whisking, for 2 minutes. Do not allow the flour to brown.

4. Slowly whisk in the warmed milk and cook, whisking constantly, until the sauce is thick and smooth, about 1 minute. Whisk in the Worcestershire sauce, Tabasco sauce, salt, and pepper. Continue to cook, whisking constantly, until well combined, about 1 minute.

5. Add the mixed vegetables, as well as the shrimp and mushrooms, to the skillet. Stir until they are well coated and heated through. Serve immediately.

BRANDIED SHRIMP À LA KING Reduce the milk to 2½ cups. Add ½ cup brandy along with the milk. Be careful—the brandy may flame. If it does, cover the pan immediately to put out the fire.

DIJON SHRIMP À LA KING Add 1 tablespoon Dijon mustard with the Worcestershire sauce.

FLORENTINE SHRIMP À LA KING Substitute one 10-ounce package frozen chopped spinach, thawed and squeezed of excess moisture, for the mixed vegetables.

SEAFOOD À LA KING Reduce the shrimp to ½ pound. Cook ½ pound sea scallops, cut in half, with the remaining shrimp. Add ½ pound lump crabmeat, picked over for shells and cartilage, with the cooked shrimp and scallops.

SOUTH OF THE BORDER SHRIMP À LA KING Omit the Worcestershire sauce. Increase the Tabasco sauce to 6 to 8 dashes, and add 2 teaspoons oregano, 1 teaspoon pure chile powder, and 1 teaspoon cumin with it.

SPANISH SHRIMP À LA KING Omit the Worcestershire and Tabasco sauces. Add ¼ teaspoon saffron threads with the milk. Replace the vegetables with one 10-ounce package frozen peas, thawed.

Shrimp Alfredo

IN 1927, DOUGLAS FAIRBANKS and Mary Pickford were on their honeymoon in Rome when a photographer caught them eating a pasta dish of noodles with cheese and butter at a modest trattoria, Alfredo's. The U.S. press picked up the story, and Fettuccine Alfredo became an instant craze—with one difference. A savvy studio publicist didn't want the stars seen eating such simple fare, so cream was added to the reported recipe. We've added shrimp to make this classic even more luxurious. **MAKES 6 SERVINGS**

1 pound dried fettuccine

4 tablespoons (½ stick) unsalted butter

1 pound small shrimp (more than 55 per pound), peeled and deveined

1 cup heavy cream

¾ cup coarsely grated Parmigiano-Reggiano (about 3 ounces)

Salt and freshly ground black pepper to taste

1. Bring 6 quarts salted water to boil in a large pot over high heat. Add the pasta and cook according to the package directions until al dente, usually 6 to 8 minutes.

2. Meanwhile, in a saucepan large enough to cook the shrimp and eventually hold the pasta, melt the butter over medium heat.

3. Add the shrimp and stir to coat them with butter. Add the cream and bring it to a simmer. Cook, stirring frequently, until the shrimp are pink and the cream is slightly thickened, about 3 minutes. Turn off the heat.

4. Drain the pasta and add it to the pan with the shrimp. Turn the heat to medium and cook, stirring and tossing, until the sauce is bubbling and the pasta is well coated.

5. Add the cheese and continue tossing until the cheese is melted and the sauce is smooth, about 1 minute. Add the salt and pepper. Serve immediately.

BLUE CHEESE SHRIMP ALFREDO Reduce the Parmigiano-Reggiano to ½ cup and add ¼ cup crumbled blue cheese (such as Gorgonzola, about 2 ounces) with it.

FOUR-CHEESE SHRIMP ALFREDO Reduce the Parmigiano-Reggiano to ¼ cup, and add ¼ cup grated Asiago (about 2 ounces), ¼ cup crumbled blue cheese (such as Gorgonzola, about 2 ounces), and ¼ cup diced Fontina (about 2 ounces) with it.

ROCK SHRIMP ALFREDO Substitute 1 pound peeled and cleaned rock shrimp for the small shrimp.

SHRIMP ALFREDO BASILICA Add ¼ cup shredded basil with the cooked pasta.

SHRIMP ALFREDO CARBONARA Add 1 cup crumbled cooked bacon (about 6 strips) with the cooked shrimp.

SHRIMP ALFREDO FLORENTINE Add one 10-ounce package frozen spinach, thawed and squeezed of excess moisture, with the cream.

SHRIMP ALFREDO ROMANA Add 1 cup fresh or thawed frozen peas with the cream.

SHRIMP ALFREDO WITH MUSHROOMS Sauté 2 cups sliced button mushrooms in 2 tablespoons unsalted butter in a medium skillet over medium heat until they release their juices, about 5 minutes. Drain and add them with the cooked shrimp.

SHRIMP ALFREDO WITH SUN-DRIED TOMATOES Drain and chop ½ cup sun-dried tomatoes packed in oil. Add them with the cheese.

Bacon-Wrapped Shrimp

THIS DISH WAS ONCE fashionable luncheon fare in Bath, England's upper-crust watering hole. The shrimp bundles were fried in butter and served with dollops of mayonnaise and a healthy glass of sulfured water. You'll probably want to forgo the curative water, but bacon-wrapped shrimp still make an elegant appetizer. For a healthier take on this classic, these delicacies are broiled, but do try the Buttery Bacon-Wrapped Shrimp variation for an old-fashioned delight. There's also a list of suggested dipping sauces following the recipe. **MAKES 8 TO 10 APPETIZER SERVINGS**

20 strips bacon, cut into thirds

60 medium shrimp (35 to 40 per pound), peeled and deveined

8 to 10 metal skewers, or 15 bamboo or wooden skewers, soaked in water for 20 minutes

1. Preheat the broiler.

2. Wrap 1 piece of bacon around a shrimp and thread it on a skewer, piercing the shrimp and the bacon in two places to hold it in place. Repeat with the remaining bacon and shrimp, placing 6 to 8 shrimp on each skewer.

3. Place the skewers on the broiler tray or a lipped baking sheet. Place under the broiler and cook for 5 minutes, turning the skewers once or twice, until the bacon is browned and crisp and the shrimp are pink and firm, about 4 minutes. (You may need to cook the shrimp in batches.)

4. Remove the shrimp from the skewers, and serve hot, with your favorite dipping sauce.

DIPPING SAUCE IDEAS

Barbecue Sauce (page 26) • Chili con queso • Duck sauce • Hoi sin sauce • Mayonnaise (the classic British dip; some even prefer the sweeter "salad cream") • Oyster sauce, diluted by half with water • Plum sauce (available in many Asian markets) • Ranch dressing or Thousand Island dressing (buy a good-quality brand, such as one from the refrigerator section of your supermarket)

BUTTERY BACON-WRAPPED SHRIMP Instead of broiling the shrimp, melt 4 tablespoons (½ stick) unsalted butter in a skillet large enough to hold several skewers. Use bamboo or wooden skewers only, since metal will be too long. Fry the bacon-wrapped shrimp in batches, turning once or twice until the bacon browns and the shrimp are pink and firm, about 4 minutes. This technique can also be used for any of the following variations.

CHEESY BACON-WRAPPED SHRIMP Before wrapping them in the bacon, roll the shrimp in 2 cups freshly grated Parmigiano-Reggiano (about 8 ounces) until well coated.

CRACKED PEPPER BACON-WRAPPED SHRIMP Before wrapping them in the bacon, roll the shrimp in 1 cup cracked black peppercorns until well coated.

ROSEMARY BACON-WRAPPED SHRIMP Before wrapping them in the bacon, roll the shrimp in 1 cup chopped rosemary until well coated.

STUFFED BACON-WRAPPED SHRIMP Place any (or all) of the following ingredients on or around each shrimp before you roll them in bacon.

A thin slice of Cheddar (sharp, aged, or mild)

A slice of pickled or fresh jalapeño pepper

A sliced almond

A thin strip of seeded green or red bell pepper

A thin slice of peeled ginger

Shrimp Balls

YOU'LL NEED TO PLAN ahead for this dish, because the glutinous rice must soak at least 8 hours, or overnight. Glutinous rice, which absorbs twice its weight in water when soaked and cooked, produces the prized sticky coating for these savory appetizers. (Do not substitute long- or short-grain rice.) Serve these toothsome morsels as cocktail-party nibbles or as a side dish for an Asian-inspired menu. Glutinous rice is available in Asian markets and by mail-order (see the Source Guide, page 239). **MAKES 12 PIECES**

1⅓ cups glutinous rice

½ pound small shrimp (more than 55 per pound), peeled and deveined

4 shiitake mushrooms, stems removed and discarded, caps cleaned and finely chopped

1 large egg white

1 teaspoon minced ginger

1 scallion, white part only, minced

1 tablespoon soy sauce

Vegetable oil for the steamer

1. Place the rice in a large bowl and cover with water by at least 3 inches. Set aside to soak for at least 8 hours, or overnight.

2. Line a baking sheet with three layers of paper towels. Drain the rice and spread it evenly on the towels, which will absorb any excess water.

3. Combine the shrimp, mushrooms, egg white, ginger, scallion, and soy sauce in a food processor and pulse 4 or 5 times, scraping down the bowl as necessary. Then process the mixture until a smooth paste is formed, about 1 minute. Transfer to a bowl.

4. Shape tablespoonfuls of the paste into balls and roll them in the rice, covering them completely.

5. Lightly oil the bottom of a bamboo steamer tray. Place the balls 1 inch apart in the steamer tray. Use as many steamer trays as necessary, stacking them on top of one another, to hold all the shrimp balls.

6. Choose a pot that will allow the steamer to rest snugly on its upper rim so no steam will escape. Fill the pot with an inch or so of water and bring it to a simmer. Cover the top of the bamboo steamer, place it over the pot, and steam for 15 minutes. Alternatively, you can use a standard metal vegetable steamer basket. Oil the basket and fill it with as many shrimp balls as will fit in one layer without touching. Place the basket in a pot with ½ inch of simmering water, cover, and steam for 15 minutes. Repeat the process until all the shrimp balls are steamed.

ALMOND SHRIMP BALLS Form each shrimp ball around a blanched whole almond.

CASHEW SHRIMP BALLS Form each shrimp ball around a salted roasted cashew.

DOUBLE SHRIMP BALLS Add 1 tablespoon dried shrimp to the food processor with the shrimp.

FIERY SHRIMP BALLS Add 1 teaspoon chili oil, or more to taste, to the food processor with the shrimp. When forming the balls, stick a hot red pepper (such as a Thai hot pepper or a dried red Asian pepper) into each ball for a handle.

FIVE-SPICE SHRIMP BALLS Add 1 teaspoon five-spice powder to the food processor with the shrimp.

GARLIC SHRIMP BALLS Omit the ginger; add 2 garlic cloves, peeled, to the food processor with the shrimp.

GINGERY SHRIMP BALLS Double (or even triple) the amount of ginger.

NUTTY SHRIMP BALLS Add 1 cup drained canned water chestnuts to the food processor with the shrimp.

SESAME SHRIMP BALLS Add 2 teaspoons toasted sesame oil and 1 teaspoon hoi sin sauce to the food processor with the shrimp.

THAI SHRIMP BALLS Add ½ cup tightly packed basil leaves and 2 teaspoons fish sauce to the food processor with the shrimp.

Barbecued Shrimp

SHRIMP ON THE BARBY. Long before it was a slogan for Australian tourism, it was a staple in Texas. Large shrimp work best because the meat-to-sauce ratio is significantly higher, but you can use medium shrimp (35 to 40 per pound). Thread the smaller shrimp on metal or soaked bamboo skewers so that turning and handling them are easier. The sweet-and-hot barbecue sauce can be made up to 1 week in advance—it's also perfect for ribs, chicken, or burgers. **MAKES 6 TO 8 APPETIZER SERVINGS OR 4 MAIN-COURSE SERVINGS**

FOR THE BARBECUE SAUCE

- 1½ cups ketchup
- 1 large onion, very finely chopped
- ½ cup fresh lemon juice
- ¼ cup cider vinegar
- ¼ cup dark rum (such as Myers's)
- ¼ cup packed light brown sugar
- ¼ cup unsulfured molasses
- 1 tablespoon Worcestershire sauce
- 1 tablespoon dry mustard
- 3 dashes Tabasco sauce, or more to taste
- ¼ teaspoon ground cloves
- ¼ teaspoon liquid smoke (optional)
- Salt and freshly ground black pepper to taste

- 2 pounds large shrimp (12 to 15 per pound), peeled, leaving the final segment of the tail shell intact, and deveined

1. To prepare the barbecue sauce, combine the ketchup, onion, lemon juice, vinegar, rum, brown sugar, molasses, Worcestershire, mustard, Tabasco sauce, cloves, and the liquid smoke, if desired, in a large saucepan over medium heat. Stir until the sugar is completely dissolved and the mixture comes to a simmer.

2. Reduce the heat to low and simmer, stirring occasionally, for 30 minutes, or until the sauce is thickened and the onion is soft. Season with salt and pepper. Allow the sauce to cool before using. (The sauce can be made up to 1 week ahead and kept tightly covered in the refrigerator. Bring it back to room temperature before using.)

3. To prepare the shrimp, light the coals in the barbecue at least 20 minutes before you're ready to cook the shrimp. Or if you're using a gas grill or the broiler, preheat it 5 minutes before you're ready to cook.

4. Transfer half the barbecue sauce to a small bowl for serving with the shrimp; set aside.

5. When the coals are glowing red with a thin covering of ash, place the rack on the barbecue. One or two at a time, hold the shrimp by the tail and dip them into the remaining sauce, then lay the shrimp on the barbecue rack directly over the coals. Cook for 2 minutes, then turn with metal tongs or a spatula, and cook until the shrimp are firm and the sauce is starting to brown, about 2 more minutes. Or, if you're using the broiler, lay the dipped shrimp on a baking sheet and place them 4 inches from the flame. Cook for 2 minutes per side, or until they are firm and the sauce is starting to brown.

6. Serve the shrimp with the reserved barbecue sauce on the side.

BARBECUED SHRIMP-AND-VEGETABLE KEBABS Thread the plain shrimp onto metal or soaked bamboo or wooden skewers, placing a 2-inch vegetable chunk in between each shrimp. Depending on the size of the shrimp, the quantity of shrimp and vegetables on each skewer will vary. Use as many skewers as necessary. Brush the entire kebabs with the sauce before cooking. Vegetable suggestions: thick zucchini slices, eggplant cubes, bell pepper (green, yellow, or red) chunks, sweet red onion quarters, or whole mushrooms.

CHINESE BARBECUED SHRIMP Substitute hoi sin sauce for the ketchup and add 1 teaspoon five-spice powder to sauce.

FIERY BARBECUED SHRIMP Increase the vinegar to ⅓ cup and add ¼ cup finely chopped pickled jalapeño peppers to the sauce.

HONEY BARBECUED SHRIMP Omit the brown sugar and molasses and add ½ cup honey to the sauce.

ISLAND COCONUT BARBECUED SHRIMP Substitute ½ cup lime juice for the lemon juice. Sprinkle the shrimp generously with shredded coconut after dipping them in the sauce. Sprinkle on additional coconut, if desired, after cooking.

PINEAPPLE BARBECUED SHRIMP Add ½ cup canned crushed pineapple, drained, to the sauce.

Beer Batter Shrimp

THIS RESTAURANT FAVORITE IS perfect for a Sunday afternoon ball game or a Friday night bridge party. Other recipes often call for flat beer, but this one calls for fresh beer full of bubbles to lighten the batter. Wheat beers work particularly well. Even some flavored beers, like cardamom-orange–scented Heffeweisse, can add an interesting taste. But avoid fruity or berry-laced brews. **MAKES 6 TO 8 SERVINGS**

8 cups peanut oil or vegetable oil

1 cup all-purpose flour

2½ teaspoons salt

½ teaspoon baking powder

¼ teaspoon freshly ground black pepper

1 large egg, lightly beaten

1 cup beer, at room temperature (but not flat)

2 pounds medium shrimp (35 to 40 per pound), peeled and deveined

1. Pour the oil into a large saucepan at least 4 inches deep and 10 inches in diameter; the oil should be at least 1½ inches deep but reach no more than halfway up the sides of the pan. Alternatively, fill an electric deep fryer with oil according to the manufacturer's instructions. If you're using a pan, clip a deep-frying thermometer to the inside and place the pan over medium heat. Heat the oil to 375°F. Adjust the heat to maintain that temperature while you prepare the shrimp. If you're using an electric deep fryer, set the temperature control to 375°F.

2. Combine the flour, 1 teaspoon of the salt, the baking powder, and pepper in a large mixing bowl. Whisk until well combined. Add the egg and beer and whisk until the batter is completely smooth.

3. Dip 1 shrimp into the batter until it is completely coated. Let any excess batter drip off, then gently slide the shrimp into the hot oil. Repeat with the remaining shrimp, dipping and frying only as many at a time as will fit in the pan in one layer without crowding. Fry the shrimp until lightly golden, 1 to 2 minutes, turning occasionally with metal tongs. Remove the shrimp from the oil and drain them on paper towels.

4. While they're hot, sprinkle the shrimp with the remaining 1½ teaspoons salt. Serve immediately with the dipping sauce of your choice.

EASY DIPPING SAUCE SUGGESTIONS

Most of these can be purchased; the others are easy to make.

Balsamic vinegar • Barbecue Sauce (page 26) • Blue Cheese Dip (page 50) • Bottled pasta sauce • Szechwan Cold Garlic Sauce (page 194) • Duck sauce • Honey mustard • Hot mustard • Italian dressing • Ketchup • Lemon Sauce (page 106) • Malt vinegar • Mango chutney • Peanut Sauce (page 166) • Ranch dressing • Salsa • Sesame Dipping Sauce (page 203) • Tartar Sauce (page 51) • Thousand Island dressing

Bell Pepper Shrimp

SHRIMP WITH BELL PEPPERS is a Chinese-American classic. With its piquant sauce, this simple stir-fry makes a satisfying midweek meal, a quick weekend lunch, or a wonderful addition to an Asian buffet. Remember this trick for a perfect stir-fry: heat the pan before you add the oil. Serve this dish with generous bowls of white or brown rice. **MAKES 4 SERVINGS**

2 tablespoons sherry

2 tablespoons soy sauce

1 tablespoon oyster sauce

1 teaspoon sugar

1 teaspoon freshly ground black pepper

¼ cup canned or homemade chicken stock

1 tablespoon peanut oil

1 scallion, thinly sliced

1 tablespoon minced ginger

1 garlic clove, minced

2 green bell peppers, cored, seeded, and cut into 1-inch pieces

1 pound small shrimp (more than 55 per pound), peeled and deveined, or precooked cocktail shrimp, thawed and peeled

2 teaspoons cornstarch, dissolved in 2 teaspoons water

Toasted sesame oil to taste

1. Combine the sherry, soy sauce, oyster sauce, sugar, pepper, and chicken stock in a small bowl; set aside.

2. Place a large wok or skillet over high heat. When the pan is very hot, add the oil. Swirl to coat the pan, then quickly add the scallion, ginger, and garlic. Cook, stirring constantly, for 10 seconds. Add the peppers and cook, stirring constantly, for 30 seconds.

3. Add the raw shrimp if using, and cook, stirring and tossing with two wooden spoons or long-handled heatproof spatulas, until the shrimp are firm and pink, about 3 minutes. If you're using precooked cocktail shrimp, omit this step.

4. Add the sherry mixture to the wok. Bring the sauce to a boil, stirring occasionally. If you're using precooked shrimp, add them now and stir to heat.

5. Add the cornstarch mixture and stir constantly until the sauce is thickened, about 30 seconds. Take the pan off the heat at once, and serve immediately.

BELL PEPPER SHRIMP WITH ALMONDS Add ½ cup slivered almonds with the raw shrimp.

BELL PEPPER SHRIMP WITH BEAN THREAD NOODLES Soak two 2-ounce packages of bean thread noodles in boiling water for 15 minutes. Drain thoroughly. Use them as a bed for the stir-fry, rather than rice.

BELL PEPPER SHRIMP WITH PEANUTS Add ½ cup unsalted roasted peanuts with the raw shrimp.

BELL PEPPER SHRIMP WITH SAUSAGE Add ½ pound sliced hot Italian sausage, cooked, with the raw shrimp.

CANTONESE BELL PEPPER SHRIMP Increase the garlic to 3 cloves and use ¼ cup thinly sliced peeled ginger.

HOT PEPPER SHRIMP Replace 1 of the bell peppers with a sliced, seeded, and stemmed poblano chile.

RAINBOW BELL PEPPER SHRIMP Use any mixture of peppers: yellow, red, orange, and/or green.

SZECHWAN BELL PEPPER SHRIMP Add 1 to 2 teaspoons chili oil and ½ teaspoon sugar with the scallion. Add ½ pound ground pork with the peppers, and stir and toss for 2 minutes before adding the shrimp.

Shrimp Bengalese Stew

THIS RICH DISH IS a shrimpy take on the ginger-and-coconut-milk stew found in Calcutta's open-air markets. Of course, devout Hindus would never eat shrimp, so to honor that tradition, we offer a vegetarian variation with tofu. Serve this stew on a bed of fragrant rice: jasmine, basmati, or Texmati. **MAKES 4 TO 6 SERVINGS**

3 tablespoons unsalted butter; or 1 tablespoon unsalted butter, if using precooked shrimp

1½ pounds medium shrimp (35 to 40 per pound), peeled and deveined, or precooked cocktail shrimp, thawed and peeled

1 small onion, finely chopped

1 garlic clove, minced

1 teaspoon salt

1½ tablespoons minced ginger

½ teaspoon grated nutmeg

1 tomato, coarsely chopped

¾ cup fish stock or clam juice

½ cup ground almonds

½ cup coconut milk

Juice of ½ lime

1. Melt 2 tablespoons of the butter in a large heavy saucepan over medium heat. Add the raw shrimp, if using, and cook, stirring often, until pink and firm, 3 to 5 minutes. Transfer the shrimp to a large bowl and set it aside. If you're using precooked cocktail shrimp, skip to step 2.

2. Place the pan back over medium heat and add 1 tablespoon butter. Add the onion and garlic; sauté until softened, about 2 minutes.

3. Add the salt, ginger, and nutmeg; cook, stirring constantly, for 30 seconds. Immediately add the tomatoes and cook, stirring constantly, until the mixture thickens slightly, about 2 minutes.

4. Add the fish stock and bring to a simmer. Add the ground almonds and stir until they thicken the sauce, about 1 minute. Immediately add the coconut milk and cook, stirring gently, until the sauce comes back to a simmer. Add the cooked shrimp and cook until the sauce is bubbling and the shrimp are heated through.

5. Remove the pan from the heat, add the lime juice, and stir well. Serve immediately.

CURRIED SHRIMP BENGALESE STEW Omit the ginger and nutmeg. Add 2 teaspoons curry powder with the salt.

SCALLOP AND SHRIMP BENGALESE STEW Add 1 pound scallops, sliced in half, with the raw shrimp.

SPICY SHRIMP BENGALESE STEW Add ½ cup tightly packed, shredded basil and 1 teaspoon chili oil, or more to taste, with the coconut milk.

VEGETABLE AND SHRIMP BENGALESE STEW Add 1 cup diced celery, ½ cup diced carrots, and ½ cup green beans cut into 2-inch segments, with the tomatoes.

VEGETARIAN BENGALESE STEW Omit the shrimp. Add 1 pound silken tofu, cut into ½-inch dice, and one 10-ounce package frozen mixed vegetables, thawed, with the coconut milk.

Shrimp Bisque

THIS BISQUE FOLLOWS THE traditional French preparation, rather than the modern New Orleans version. When first introduced in France in the 1750s, a *bisque* was a shellfish purée added to quail or pigeon soups as a flavor enhancer, much the way pesto is sometimes swirled into Mediterranean soups. In the nineteenth century, French aristocrats began to enjoy this thickener on its own, with cream added, to make it a full course. Serve this creamy, velvety soup with a loaf of crusty bread and a vinegary salad of tomatoes, celery, and toasted pecans. **MAKES 6 TO 8 SERVINGS**

3 tablespoons unsalted butter

1 pound small shrimp (more than 55 per pound), peeled and deveined, shells reserved

6 cups fish stock or 4 cups vegetable stock plus 2 cups clam juice

2 large shallots, minced

2 tablespoons all-purpose flour

2 teaspoons sweet paprika

½ teaspoon grated nutmeg

1 cup heavy cream

2 tablespoons dry vermouth

¼ cup minced chives

1. Melt 1 tablespoon of the butter in a large saucepan or pot over medium heat. Add the reserved shells and cook, stirring constantly, until they turn pink, about 2 minutes.

2. Add the stock, raise the heat to high, and bring to a boil. Reduce the heat to low, cover the pan, and simmer for 10 minutes.

3. Meanwhile, melt the remaining 2 tablespoons butter in another large saucepan over medium-low heat. Add the shallots and cook, stirring constantly, until softened, about 2 minutes.

4. Add the flour to the shallots and whisk until it is completely incorporated into the melted butter. Cook, stirring constantly, for 1 minute. Do not allow the mixture to brown.

5. Strain the shrimp stock into the pan with the shallots and whisk until the soup thickens, about 2 minutes. Add the shrimp and cook until they are pink and firm, about 2 minutes. Remove the pan from the heat.

6. Purée the soup, in batches if necessary, in a food processor or blender until completely smooth. Rinse out the pan, return the soup to it, and whisk in the paprika, nutmeg, and cream. Bring the soup back to a simmer and cook for 5 minutes, stirring often.

7. Remove the pan from the heat. Stir in the vermouth and chives; serve immediately.

CURRIED SHRIMP BISQUE Omit the paprika and nutmeg. Add 2 teaspoons curry powder with the cream.

HERBED SHRIMP BISQUE Omit the paprika and nutmeg. Add 3 tablespoons chopped parsley, 2 teaspoons chopped tarragon, and ½ teaspoon minced thyme with the shallots. If desired, top each bowl of soup with 1 teaspoon (or more) flavored oil, such as basil oil or black pepper oil.

HOT HUNGARIAN SHRIMP BISQUE Omit the nutmeg. Substitute 1 to 2 teaspoons hot Hungarian paprika for the sweet paprika, and add 1 teaspoon dry mustard with the cream.

NEW ORLEANS SHRIMP BISQUE Add 1 teaspoon cayenne pepper with the cream, then add ½ cup diced celery and ½ cup diced green bell pepper; cook, stirring often, for 10 minutes.

SHRIMP BISQUE WITH CLAMS Add 12 medium clams (such as cherrystone or Pacific littleneck), scrubbed, with the cream. Cover and cook over low heat until the clams open, about 7 minutes.

SHRIMP BISQUE WITH MUSSELS Add 1 pound mussels, scrubbed and debearded, with the cream. Cover and cook over low heat until the mussels open, about 5 minutes.

SHRIMP VICHYSSOISE Cook 2 pounds new potatoes, peeled and cut into cubes, in the stock-and-shallot mixture until they are tender, then add and cook the shrimp. Omit the paprika and increase the vermouth to ½ cup. Chill the soup thoroughly, for at least 8 hours. Serve cold in small cups.

Black Bean Shrimp

A STAPLE IN SOUTHERN CHINA, these dried black beans are actually fermented soybeans (page 10). Their pungent, salty taste softens considerably when they are heated in a sauce. Peanut oil also gives this dish its distinctive taste (vegetable oil can be substituted if food allergies are an issue). As with any stir-fry, do all your preparation before you start cooking—the steps move very quickly. Serve this dish over steaming rice or bean thread noodles soaked in boiling water for 15 minutes, or until transparent. **MAKES 4 SERVINGS**

1 pound medium shrimp (35 to 40 per pound), peeled and deveined

1 tablespoon soy sauce

1 teaspoon toasted sesame oil

1 tablespoon sherry

3 tablespoons peanut oil

3 scallions, minced

1 tablespoon minced ginger

1 garlic clove, minced

1 red (or green) bell pepper, cored, seeded, and cut into 1-inch pieces

1 teaspoon freshly ground black pepper

¼ cup dried, salted, Chinese black beans, slightly crushed with the side of a chef's knife or the bottom of a small pot

⅓ cup canned or homemade chicken stock

1 tablespoon oyster sauce

2 teaspoons cornstarch, dissolved in 1 tablespoon water

1. Combine the shrimp, soy sauce, sesame oil, and sherry in a medium bowl. Toss until the shrimp are well coated. Set aside to marinate for 30 minutes.

2. Heat 2 tablespoons of the peanut oil in a large wok or skillet (preferably nonstick) over high heat. When the oil is hot but not smoking, add the shrimp with their marinade and cook, stirring constantly, until pink and firm, about 3 minutes. Transfer the shrimp to a bowl or plate and set aside.

3. Return the wok to high heat and add the remaining 1 tablespoon oil. Add the scallion, ginger, and garlic; cook, stirring constantly, for 20 seconds. Add the bell pepper and black pepper and cook, stirring and tossing constantly, for 2 minutes, or until the bell pepper begins to soften.

4. Return the shrimp to the wok, along with the black beans, chicken stock, and oyster sauce. Stir and toss until the sauce is bubbling and the shrimp are heated through, 1 to 2 minutes.

5. Pour the cornstarch mixture into the wok and stir until the sauce thickens, about 10 seconds. Serve hot.

MANGO BLACK BEAN SHRIMP Add 1 large mango, peeled, pitted, and coarsely chopped, with the bell pepper.

PINEAPPLE BLACK BEAN SHRIMP Add 1 cup canned pineapple chunks, drained, with the bell pepper.

SCALLOPS AND BLACK BEAN SHRIMP Reduce the shrimp to ½ pound and add ½ pound sea scallops, cut in half, to the marinade.

SPICY BLACK BEAN SHRIMP Increase the ginger to 2 tablespoons. Add 1 teaspoon chili sauce, or more, with the black beans.

SWEET BLACK BEAN SHRIMP Omit the oyster sauce, and add 1 tablespoon hoi sin sauce and 1 teaspoon sugar with the black beans.

SZECHWAN BLACK BEAN SHRIMP Add 1 banana, thickly sliced, with the bell pepper. Add 1 teaspoon chili sauce, or more, and ½ teaspoon sugar with the black beans.

Black Pepper Caramel Shrimp

THIS SWEET-AND-HOT SAUCE, a surprising combination of French technique and Southeast Asian sensibilities, has long been considered a harbinger of good luck (and an aphrodisiac) by many Vietnamese. Bowls of fluffy white or nutty brown rice will help cut the heat—but it's best to avoid a rice with an intense aroma, like jasmine, since the point of the dish is the fragrant sauce. **MAKES 4 SERVINGS**

3 tablespoons peanut oil

1 pound medium shrimp (35 to 40 per pound), peeled and deveined, or precooked cocktail shrimp, thawed and peeled

6 garlic cloves, minced

2½ teaspoons freshly ground black pepper

2 tablespoons fish sauce

¼ cup canned or homemade, chicken stock

3 tablespoons Caramel Syrup (recipe follows)

1. Set a large wok or skillet over medium-high heat and allow it to heat thoroughly, about 3 minutes. Add 2 tablespoons of the oil and swirl to coat the pan. Add the raw shrimp, if using, and cook, stirring constantly, until pink and firm, 2 to 3 minutes. Transfer the shrimp to a bowl and set aside.

2. Add 1 tablespoon oil to the wok and set it back over medium-high heat. Add the garlic and cook, stirring constantly, until it begins to brown, about 1 minute. Immediately add the pepper and cook for 10 seconds.

3. Raise the heat to high, add the fish sauce and chicken stock, and bring to a boil. Add the caramel syrup and stir constantly until the syrup dissolves in the sauce, then return the sauce to a boil.

4. Add the cooked shrimp. Toss and stir until the sauce is bubbling and the shrimp are heated through, about 1 minute. Serve immediately.

Caramel Syrup

SINCE THIS SYRUP WILL keep for months, you can make Black Pepper Caramel Shrimp when-ever you want. The syrup is also delightful over ice cream—or mix it in a ratio of one to three with vanilla-flavored vodka for a golden caramel martini. **MAKES ABOUT 1 CUP**

> 1 cup sugar
>
> ⅔ cup boiling water

Place the sugar in a large heavy skillet over high heat and stir constantly until the sugar com-pletely melts and turns amber; it should resemble maple syrup. Immediately remove the pan from the heat and add the water. Be careful: the syrup will boil wildly and splatter when you add the water, so stir in water with a long-handled wooden spoon to avoid burns. Some of the syrup may scize into a hard clump on the bottom of the pan. If this happens, place the pan back over low heat and stir until the caramel is dissolved and the syrup is smooth. Let cool completely. (The syrup can be kept covered at room temperature for up to 3 months.)

BANANA BLACK PEPPER CARAMEL SHRIMP Add 1 large banana, thinly sliced, with the fish sauce.

BLACK PEPPER CARAMEL ROCK SHRIMP Substitute 1 pound peeled and cleaned rock shrimp for the medium shrimp.

BLACK PEPPER CARAMEL SHRIMP AND BEEF Reduce the shrimp to ½ pound, and stir-fry ½ pound thinly sliced top round or sirloin with the shrimp.

CINNAMON BLACK PEPPER CARAMEL SHRIMP Add 1 teaspoon ground cinna-mon with the black pepper.

MALAYSIAN-INSPIRED BLACK PEPPER CARAMEL SHRIMP Add 1 tablespoon tamarind syrup (see Source Guide, page 239) and ¼ teaspoon grated nutmeg with the fish sauce.

SPICY BLACK PEPPER CARAMEL SHRIMP Add 1 green or red bell pepper, cored, seeded, and sliced, with the garlic. Add 2 tablespoons minced ginger and ¼ cup tightly packed chopped basil with the fish sauce.

Bon Bon Shrimp

NORMAN WEINSTEIN, A NEW YORK LEGEND, has led informative and opinionated tours of the Chinatowns in Manhattan and Queens for decades. Years ago, a staple of his Szechwan cooking class was Bon Bon Chicken, a zippy main course that fused East and West. This version is updated a bit—and includes shrimp, of course. Served at room temperature, it is a wonderful summer dinner, a simple luncheon entrée, or even a great midnight snack. **MAKES 4 APPETIZER SERVINGS OR 2 MAIN-COURSE SERVINGS**

Two 2-ounce packages dried bean thread noodles

1 pound large shrimp (about 12 to 15 per pound), peeled and deveined, or precooked cocktail shrimp, thawed and peeled

¼ cup toasted sesame oil

3 tablespoons peanut butter

2 tablespoons soy sauce

2 tablespoons black vinegar

1 tablespoon sugar

1 teaspoon chili oil, or to taste

½ teaspoon freshly ground black pepper, or more to taste

2 large cucumbers, peeled, seeded, and thinly sliced

1. Place the noodles in a large bowl and cover them with boiling water. Set aside to soften for at least 15 minutes.

2. If using raw shrimp, bring 2 quarts salted water to a boil in a large pot over high heat. Fill a large bowl halfway with ice water and set it aside. Add the shrimp to the boiling water and cook until pink and firm, about 5 minutes. Remove the shrimp with a slotted spoon or a strainer; place them in the ice water to chill. Drain the shrimp and blot dry with paper towels. Set aside.

3. Whisk the sesame oil, peanut butter, soy sauce, black vinegar, sugar, chili oil, and pepper in a medium bowl until completely smooth.

4. Drain the noodles and rinse them with cold water. Squeeze them with your hands to remove as much excess water as possible. Place the noodles on a large serving platter. Mound the sliced cucumber on top of the noodles, and lay the shrimp on top. Drizzle the platter with the sauce and serve immediately.

BON BON SHRIMP AND CRAB Reduce the shrimp to ½ pound. Mound ½ pound lump crabmeat, picked over for shells and cartilage, with the shrimp.

BON BON SHRIMP AND SCALLOPS Reduce the shrimp to ½ pound. Mound ½ pound sea scallops, cut in half and cooked with the shrimp.

COCONUT BON BON SHRIMP Whisk ¼ cup unsweetened coconut milk with the sesame oil.

CRUNCHY BON BON SHRIMP Use crunchy peanut butter, and add ¼ cup unsalted peanuts with the sesame oil.

SAVORY BON BON SHRIMP Substitute flavored oil, such as black pepper oil or basil oil, for the sesame oil.

Shrimp Bread Pudding

A RICH, SATISFYING CASSEROLE, shrimp bread pudding can stand on its own as a main course or be served on a buffet with a standing rib roast and steamed greens. It's even good cold the next day. **MAKES 10 TO 12 SERVINGS**

4 cups Court Bouillon (recipe follows), or 2 cups fish stock, plus 2 cups vegetable stock

3 pounds small shrimp (over 55 per pound), peeled and deveined, or medium shrimp (35 to 40 per pound), peeled, deveined, and cut in half

Three day-old 12-inch loaves French bread, cut into 1-inch slices

2 cups whole milk

2 large eggs

2 tablespoons paprika

1 teaspoon Tabasco sauce

3 tablespoons unsalted butter, melted

1 pound crabmeat, picked over for shells and cartilage

2 cups Gruyère, shredded (about ½ pound)

1. Bring the Court Bouillon to a simmer in a large saucepan over high heat. Add one-third of the shrimp and cook until pink, about 3 minutes. Remove with a slotted spoon or a strainer and place in a large bowl. Bring the court bouillon back to a simmer and repeat with the remaining shrimp in two batches. Set the shrimp aside.

2. Place the bread in a large bowl. Bring the court bouillon back to a boil and boil for 15 minutes, or until reduced by half. Remove the pan from the heat and add the milk. Pour over the bread and let soak for 1 hour.

3. Preheat the oven to 350°F. Generously butter a 6-quart casserole or 9 × 13-inch baking pan.

4. Crack the eggs into a medium bowl. Add the paprika and Tabasco sauce; beat lightly, just until the eggs are foamy.

5. Add the beaten eggs to the bread mixture, along with the shrimp, melted butter, crabmeat, and half of the cheese. Mix until well blended.

6. Spread the shrimp mixture into the prepared casserole and sprinkle the top with the remaining cheese. Bake for 30 minutes, or until hot, bubbly, and golden brown.

COURT BOUILLON can be stored for up to 5 days, tightly covered, in the refrigerator or frozen for up to 2 months. **MAKES ABOUT 1 QUART**

2 cups dry white wine	3 sprigs dill
2 cups water	3 sprigs parsley
1 cup clam juice	5 whole peppercorns
3 small onions, peeled	1 tablespoon salt
3 bay leaves	1 teaspoon chopped oregano

1. Place all of the ingredients in a large pan. Bring to a boil over high heat, reduce the heat to low, and simmer for 10 minutes.

2. Strain the court bouillon through a fine sieve into a large bowl. Return it to the pan for the Shrimp Bread Pudding, or cool, cover, and refrigerate until ready to use.

CHEESY SHRIMP BREAD PUDDING Mix 2 cups grated firm sheep's milk cheese (such as Manchego, about ½ pound) with the Gruyère before adding to the dish.

CHILEAN CHUPE Increase the Tabasco sauce to 2 teaspoons. Add 2 teaspoons chopped oregano with the crabmeat. Spread half the shrimp mixture in the prepared baking dish. Top with a layer of 4 thinly sliced hard-boiled eggs, and then with the remaining shrimp mixture.

GREEK-INSPIRED SHRIMP BREAD PUDDING Omit the Gruyère and replace it with 2 cups diced feta (about ½ pound). Add 3 tablespoons capers, drained, and the grated zest of 1 lemon with the crabmeat.

HEARTY SEAFOOD BREAD PUDDING Add 1 pound of raw fish fillets (such as turbot or red snapper), cubed, with the crabmeat. Increase the cheese to 3 cups.

LOBSTER AND SHRIMP BREAD PUDDING Replace the crabmeat with 1 pound cooked lobster, chopped.

Shrimp Brunswick Stew

NAMED AFTER BRUNSWICK COUNTY, Virginia, this dish got its start as an antebellum stew of squirrel and onions. Traditionally, the roux was light, never cooked to a deep brown as it is in a New Orleans étouffée, because the richness of a dark roux would have overpowered the gamy meat. As tastes have changed, the meat has too—usually to chicken—and many other vegetables, such as okra and lima beans, have been added to the pot. In the South, Brunswick stew is often served over mashed potatoes; you might want to forgo the starch and simply let the hearty dish stand on its own. Leftovers will be terrific the next day—or freeze them, in individual servings, for up to a month. **MAKES 6 TO 8 LARGE SERVINGS**

¼ cup peanut oil

¼ cup all-purpose flour

1 large onion, finely chopped

2 celery stalks, finely chopped

2 garlic cloves, minced

2 teaspoons chopped thyme

1 teaspoon salt

2 cups canned or homemade chicken or vegetable broth

One 28-ounce can peeled tomatoes, chopped, with their juice

One 10-ounce package frozen sliced okra

One 10-ounce package frozen lima beans

2 pounds small shrimp (more than 55 per pound), peeled and deveined

1 teaspoon Tabasco sauce, or more to taste

Freshly ground black pepper to taste

1. Heat the peanut oil in a large heavy pot or a Dutch oven over medium-low heat. Add the flour and whisk until completely incorporated. Continue to cook, stirring or whisking often, until the mixture is lightly browned, about 4 minutes.

2. Add the onion, celery, and garlic and cook, stirring constantly, for 5 minutes, or until the vegetables soften and the flour mixture is golden. Stir in the thyme and salt; cook, stirring constantly, for 30 seconds.

3. Whisk in the broth, then continue to whisk until the sauce is smooth and thickens. Add the tomatoes, okra, and lima beans and bring to a simmer. Reduce the heat to low, cover the pot, and cook for 20 minutes, stirring occasionally.

4. Add the shrimp and stir until they are well incorporated, then cook, stirring once or twice, until firm and pink, about 3 minutes. Add the Tabasco sauce and pepper. Turn off the heat, cover the pot, and let the stew sit for 5 minutes before serving.

BUTTERY SHRIMP BRUNSWICK STEW Replace the peanut oil with 4 tablespoons (½ stick) unsalted butter.

HEARTY SHRIMP BRUNSWICK STEW Reduce the shrimp to 1 pound. Add ½ pound Italian sausage, cut into 1-inch slices and browned, with the shrimp.

ROCK SHRIMP BRUNSWICK STEW Replace the regular shrimp with 2 pounds peeled and cleaned rock shrimp.

SHRIMP AND CHICKEN BRUNSWICK STEW Reduce the shrimp to ¾ pound. Add ¾ pound boneless, skinless chicken breasts, cut into 1-inch cubes, with the tomatoes.

SHRIMP AND CLAM BRUNSWICK STEW Add 12 medium clams (such as cherrystone or Pacific littleneck), scrubbed, with the shrimp. Cover the stew and cook for 7 minutes, or until the clams open.

VEGETABLE SHRIMP BRUNSWICK STEW Substitute two 10-ounce packages of any frozen vegetable, either one type or any combination, such as baby carrots, corn, mixed vegetables, broccoli, Brussels sprouts, or English peas, for the okra and lima beans.

Shrimp Bruschetta

BRUSCHETTA, TOASTED BREAD REDOLENT of garlic and olive oil, is a Tuscan creation, a tasting vehicle for the new olive oil crop. (Olive oil should not be sampled alone, but in harmony with other ingredients.) Serve these little delights as quick appetizers, or with cocktails before dinner. Or take them on your next picnic. **MAKES 16 PIECES**

16 large shrimp (a little over a pound, at 12 to 15 shrimp per pound), peeled and deveined, or precooked cocktail shrimp, thawed and peeled

Twelve ¾-inch-thick slices Italian or French bread

2 large tomatoes, seeded and finely chopped

¼ cup finely chopped basil

1 tablespoon balsamic vinegar

Salt and freshly ground black pepper to taste

5 garlic cloves, peeled

¼ cup olive oil

1. If using raw shrimp, bring 2 quarts salted water to a boil in a large pot over high heat. Fill a large bowl halfway with ice water and set it aside. Add the shrimp to the boiling water and cook until pink and firm, about 4 minutes. Using a slotted spoon or a strainer, transfer the shrimp to the ice water and allow them to cool completely. Drain the shrimp and blot dry with paper towels. If you're using precooked cocktail shrimp, omit this step and skip to step 2.

2. Preheat the broiler.

3. Place the bread on a cookie sheet and set it under the broiler just until the toasts turn light brown, about 1 minute. Turn the slices over to brown the other side, about 1 minute. Set aside to cool.

4. Combine the tomatoes, basil, and vinegar in a food processor; pulse just until the tomatoes are finely chopped but not puréed. Add the salt and pepper and pulse once or twice more. Set aside.

5. Rub one side of each slice of bread with the garlic (each slice should take one-quarter to one-third of a clove). Using a pastry brush, generously brush the bread with the olive oil. Top each slice with 1 tablespoon of the tomato mixture.

6. Slice each shrimp lengthwise in half and place the halves cut side down on each slice of tomato-covered bread. Serve immediately.

ANCHOVY SHRIMP BRUSCHETTA Lay 1 anchovy fillet over the tomato mixture on each toast before topping with the shrimp.

CILANTRO SHRIMP BRUSCHETTA Replace the basil with chopped cilantro.

CURRIED SHRIMP BRUSCHETTA Omit the vinegar and substitute chopped cilantro for the basil. Add 1 tablespoon Indian curry paste to the food processor with the tomatoes.

GARLIC BREAD SHRIMP Omit the tomato-basil-vinegar mixture.

HUMMUS SHRIMP BRUSCHETTA Omit the tomato-basil-vinegar mixture. Spread 1 tablespoon purchased hummus on each garlic-rubbed toast before topping with the shrimp.

PESTO SHRIMP BRUSCHETTA Omit the tomatoes. Add ¼ cup pine nuts and 2 tablespoons olive oil to the food processor with the basil and vinegar. Process until a paste is formed.

PIMIENTO SHRIMP BRUSCHETTA Omit the tomato-basil-vinegar mixture. Mix ⅔ cup finely chopped pimientos with 1 tablespoon balsamic vinegar. Spread 2 teaspoons of the mixture on each slice of garlic-rubbed bread before topping with the shrimp.

SPICY SHRIMP BRUSCHETTA Omit the vinegar. Add 1 teaspoon Tabasco sauce, 1 teaspoon Worcestershire sauce, and 1 teaspoon bottled horseradish with the basil.

TANGY SHRIMP BRUSCHETTA Replace the vinegar with 1 tablespoon fresh lemon juice, and add 2 tablespoons drained capers to the food processor with the basil.

TAPENADE SHRIMP BRUSCHETTA Omit the tomato-basil-vinegar mixture. Spread each slice of garlic-rubbed bread with 1 tablespoon purchased olive tapenade before topping it with the shrimp.

Buffalo Shrimp

S INCE THE MID-1980S, Buffalo chicken wings have been a favorite in bars and restaurants across the United States and Canada. Hot and spicy, dipped into a tangy blue-cheese sauce—what could possibly be better? Nothing, except it's not shrimp. The spicy coating works well with shrimp's sweetness—a combination that practically screams for a cold beer or a glass of iced tea. Buffalo Shrimp are best served hot, right out of the pan. **MAKES 4 APPETIZER SERVINGS**

FOR THE BLUE CHEESE DIP

1 cup mayonnaise

½ cup sour cream (regular, low-fat, or fat-free)

⅓ cup crumbled blue cheese (such as Danish Blue or Gorgonzola; about 2 ounces)

Juice of 1 lemon

2 teaspoons onion salt

½ teaspoon garlic powder

¼ teaspoon freshly ground black pepper, or more to taste

FOR THE SHRIMP

1 tablespoon unsalted butter, melted

¼ cup hot sauce (such as Texas Pete or Tiger Sauce, not salsa)

8 cups peanut oil or vegetable oil

1 pound medium shrimp (35 to 40 per pound), peeled, leaving the final segment of the tail shell intact, and deveined

2 cups all-purpose flour

1. To prepare the blue cheese dip, combine the mayonnaise, sour cream, blue cheese, lemon juice, onion salt, garlic powder, and pepper in a small bowl and mix until well combined. (The dip can be prepared up to 24 hours in advance and kept covered in the refrigerator.)

2. To prepare the shrimp, combine the melted butter and hot sauce in a large mixing bowl and set aside.

3. Pour the oil into a large saucepan at least 4 inches deep and 10 inches in diameter; the oil should be 1½ inches deep but reach no more than halfway up the sides of the pan. Alternatively, fill an electric deep fryer with oil according to the manufacturer's instructions. If you're using a pan, clip a deep-frying thermometer to the inside and place the pan over medium heat. Heat the oil to 375°F. Adjust the heat to maintain that temperature while you prepare the shrimp. If you're using an electric deep fryer, set the temperature control to 375°F.

4. Dredge the shrimp in the flour and shake off the excess. Fry the shrimp, about 10 at a time, for 1 minute, or until lightly browned. Remove the shrimp from the pan with a slotted spoon or strainer, and place on paper towels to drain.

5. Toss the hot shrimp in the butter/hot sauce glaze, coating them completely. Serve warm with the blue cheese dipping sauce.

OTHER DIPPING SAUCES

Blue cheese sauce is the classic, but you can serve Buffalo Shrimp with any number of dipping sauces, including:

Barbecue Sauce (page 26) • Creamy Italian dressing • Ranch dressing • Thousand Island dressing • Sesame Dipping Sauce (page 203) • Szechwan Cold Garlic Sauce (page 194) • Tartar Sauce (page 51)

Butterfly Fried Shrimp

AN AMERICAN STANDARD. *Butterfly* refers to the technique that involves splitting the shrimp down the back and flattening the two halves so that they resemble the wings of a butterfly. Like most fried foods, the shrimp will taste best right out of the deep fryer. **MAKES 4 SERVINGS**

1 pound medium shrimp (35 to 40 per pound), peeled, leaving the final segment of the tail shell intact, and deveined

8 cups vegetable oil

1 large egg

¼ cup milk

1½ teaspoons salt

½ teaspoon sugar

¼ cup plain dry bread crumbs

Tartar Sauce (recipe follows)

1. To butterfly the shrimp, begin at the neck end of each and make a long cut with a paring knife down the back curve of the shrimp, about two-thirds of the way through, stopping just before the final tail segment. (You do not want to cut the shrimp in half.) Gently open the slit with your fingers, remove any remaining parts of the vein, and flatten the shrimp by pressing it cut side down gently onto the work surface. Set aside.

2. Pour the oil into a large saucepan at least 4 inches deep and 10 inches in diameter; the oil should be at least 1½ inches deep but reach no more than halfway up the sides of the pan. Alternatively, fill an electric deep fryer with oil according to the manufacturer's instructions. If you're using a pan, clip a deep-frying thermometer to the inside and place the pan over medium heat. Heat the oil to 375°F. Adjust the heat to maintain that temperature while you prepare the shrimp. If you're using an electric deep fryer, set the temperature control to 375°F.

3. Crack the egg into a large mixing bowl. Whisk in the milk, ½ teaspoon of the salt, and the sugar. Continue to whisk until the mixture is frothy, then whisk in the bread crumbs.

4. Dip a shrimp into the thin batter, then slip it into the hot oil. Repeat with the remaining shrimp, dipping and frying only as many shrimp at a time as will fit into the pan without crowding. Fry the shrimp until lightly golden, 1 to 2 minutes, turning occasionally with tongs. Remove each shrimp from the oil when it's done and drain on paper towels.

5. Sprinkle the shrimp with the remaining 1 teaspoon salt while they're hot. Serve immediately, with Tartar Sauce on the side.

Tartar Sauce

1 cup mayonnaise (regular, low-fat, or fat-free)

1 tablespoon finely chopped parsley

1 tablespoon finely chopped chives

1 tablespoon finely chopped dill

1 tablespoon capers, minced

4 cornichons, minced (or 2 gherkins, minced)

Combine the mayonnaise, parsley, chives, dill, capers, and cornichons in a small bowl. Mix until well blended. Cover and refrigerate until ready to use. (It will keep for up to 3 days, tightly covered in the refrigerator.)

CORNMEAL BUTTERFLY FRIED SHRIMP Replace the bread crumbs with ¼ cup cornmeal.

INDIAN BUTTERFLY FRIED SHRIMP Add 2 teaspoons curry powder with the bread crumbs.

ITALIAN BUTTERFLY FRIED SHRIMP Add 1 teaspoon chopped oregano, 1 teaspoon chopped thyme, and 1 teaspoon chopped parsley with the bread crumbs.

JAPANESE BUTTERFLY FRIED SHRIMP Replace the plain bread crumbs with ¼ cup Japanese-style bread crumbs (*panko*). After the shrimp are fried, dip them into a sauce made from ½ teaspoon wasabi paste and ¼ cup soy sauce, whisked together until well blended.

MEXICAN BUTTERFLY FRIED SHRIMP Add 1 teaspoon cumin, 1 teaspoon oregano, and 2 teaspoons pure chile powder with the bread crumbs.

Shrimp Cakes

WITH A VARIETY OF FILLERS, penurious Chesapeake Bay housewives once stretched shards and threads of crabmeat (i.e., the parts their husbands couldn't sell) into a full meal. But even crab scraps are hardly a bargain anymore. Made with shrimp, though, these luscious panfried patties can again be frugal delicacies. Serve them alongside a tossed green salad—or a bowl of strawberries macerated with a splash of balsamic vinegar. **MAKES 8 CAKES**

½ pound small shrimp (more than 55 per pound), peeled and deveined, or precooked cold-water (or baby) shrimp, thawed

¼ cup plus 2 tablespoons vegetable oil

2 celery stalks, minced

1 medium onion, minced

¼ cup mayonnaise (regular or low-fat, but not fat-free)

4 teaspoons Dijon mustard

¼ cup minced dill

4 dashes Tabasco sauce, or more to taste

2¼ cups plain dry bread crumbs

Salt and freshly ground black pepper to taste

1. If you're using raw shrimp, bring 1½ quarts salted water to a boil in a medium pot over high heat. Fill a medium bowl halfway with ice water and set it aside. Add the shrimp to the boiling water and cook until pink and firm, about 2 minutes. Using a slotted spoon or a strainer, transfer the shrimp to the ice water and let cool completely. Drain the shrimp and blot dry on paper towels. If you're using precooked shrimp, omit this step.

2. Heat 2 tablespoons of the vegetable oil in a large skillet set over medium heat. Add the celery and onion and cook, stirring often, until the onion is translucent and the celery softens, 2 to 3 minutes. Transfer to a large mixing bowl.

3. Add the mayonnaise, mustard, dill, Tabasco sauce, and ¼ cup of the bread crumbs to the cooked vegetables and mix until well blended. Add the salt and pepper.

4. Coarsely chop the shrimp and add to the mayonnaise mixture. Stir until well combined.

5. Place the remaining 2 cups bread crumbs on a plate. Using one-eighth of the shrimp mixture (about ⅓ cup), form a shrimp cake or patty with your hands. Lay the cake on the bread crumbs and press lightly so that the bread crumbs adhere to the bottom, then turn the cake over and repeat the process on the other side. Gently roll the patty's sides in the bread crumbs as well. The patty should be completely coated. Set the cake on a plate and repeat with the remaining shrimp mixture to make a total of 8 cakes.

6. Pour 2 tablespoons of the remaining oil into a skillet (preferably nonstick) large enough to hold 4 cakes in one layer without crowding, and set over medium heat. When the oil is hot, add 4 cakes. If you have a very large skillet, you can cook all 8 shrimp cakes at once, using all of the oil. Fry the cakes until they are golden on the bottom, about 2 minutes. Flip them and cook for 2 more minutes, or until they are golden all over. Repeat with the remaining 2 tablespoons oil and 4 shrimp cakes.

7. Serve the shrimp cakes hot, with Cocktail Sauce (page 62), Tartar Sauce (page 51), or purchased salsa on the side.

FLORIDA-STYLE SHRIMP CAKES Reduce the mustard to 2 teaspoons. Add the grated zest of 1 lemon and the juice of ½ lemon with the mayonnaise.

HERBED SHRIMP CAKES Omit the dill and Tabasco sauce. Toss 1 tablespoon minced parsley, 1 tablespoon minced thyme, and 1 tablespoon minced tarragon with the bread crumbs for coating the cakes.

LOUISIANA-STYLE SHRIMP CAKES Core, seed, and coarsely chop 1 green or red bell pepper. Sauté it with the celery and onion. Double the Tabasco sauce.

SOUTH-OF-THE-BORDER SHRIMP CAKES Omit the dill and Tabasco sauce. Seed and coarsely chop 1 jalapeño pepper. Add it with the mayonnaise, along with 1 teaspoon cumin and 1 teaspoon minced oregano.

TEXAS-STYLE SHRIMP CAKES Substitute coarsely ground saltine crackers for the bread crumbs. Add 1 teaspoon Worcestershire sauce with the mayonnaise.

Cashew Shrimp

A FAVORITE IN CHINESE-AMERICAN restaurants, this simple dish is a melting pot in and of itself. Cashews are indigenous to South America but are now cultivated mostly in eastern Africa. Celery made its first appearance in print in Homer's Greek epic, *The Odyssey*. Ginger is indigenous to China, but is now cultivated mostly in Jamaica. And rice wine vinegar, a staple of Chinese cooking, probably originated in Thailand. Stir-fries are always cooked quickly, so have all your ingredients ready before you begin. Served over steaming white rice, this dish makes a quick lunch or a satisfying midweek dinner. Follow it up with fresh mango slices for dessert. **MAKES 4 SERVINGS**

2 tablespoons peanut oil

1 pound medium shrimp (35 to 40 per pound), peeled and deveined, or precooked cocktail shrimp, thawed and peeled

2 celery stalks, diced

2 tablespoons minced ginger

2 garlic cloves, minced

1 teaspoon red pepper flakes

2 tablespoons soy sauce

2 tablespoons rice wine vinegar

1 cup unsalted cashews

1. Heat a large wok or saucepan (preferably nonstick) over medium-high heat. The moment it begins to smoke, add the peanut oil and swirl it in the wok for 30 seconds.

2. If using raw shrimp, add them and stir and toss constantly for 1 minute.

3. Add the celery and cook, stirring and tossing constantly for 1 minute, or until hot but still crisp. Add the ginger, garlic, and red pepper flakes. Stir and toss for another 30 seconds.

4. Add the soy sauce, vinegar, and the cocktail shrimp, if using. Raise the heat to high. When the sauce starts to boil, add the cashews. Stir and toss just until the nuts are well distributed and heated through. Serve immediately

BLACK BEAN CASHEW SHRIMP Reduce the soy sauce to 1 tablespoon. Add ¼ cup dried salted Chinese black beans, slightly crushed, with the soy sauce.

CASHEW SHRIMP AND BAMBOO SHOOTS Add 1 cup canned bamboo shoots, drained, with the ginger.

CASHEW SHRIMP AND BEAN THREAD NOODLES Pour boiling water over two 2-ounce packages dried bean thread noodles. Soak for 15 minutes. Drain and add them with the soy sauce. (Do not serve over rice.)

CASHEW SHRIMP AND CARROTS Add 1 cup peeled and thinly sliced carrots with the celery.

CASHEW SHRIMP AND STRAW MUSHROOMS Add 1 cup canned straw mushrooms, drained, with the ginger.

HEARTY CASHEW SHRIMP Add 1 onion, thinly sliced into rings, with the celery. Add 1 tablespoon hoi sin sauce with the soy sauce.

MILD CASHEW SHRIMP Omit the red pepper flakes. Add ½ cup sliced scallions with the celery.

SWEET AND SALTY CASHEW SHRIMP Use salted cashews, and add 1 teaspoon sugar with the soy sauce.

SZECHWAN CASHEW SHRIMP Omit the red pepper flakes. Add 1 teaspoon chili oil, or more, and ½ teaspoon sugar with the ginger, and ½ cup sliced bananas with the vinegar.

Shrimp Chiffon Ring

REMEMBER THE OLD-FASHIONED CHURCH SOCIAL? The food right off your grand-mother's recipe cards? This is one of those dishes. It's often made with crab, but it works even better with shrimp, partly because they contain plenty of natural gelatin and partly because the dish's resulting color is so . . . well, pink. Shrimp Chiffon Ring makes a great dish for a book group or a work potluck. Serve it with crackers and Cocktail Sauce (page 62). **MAKES 10 TO 12 SERVINGS**

1 pound small shrimp (more than 55 per pound), peeled and deveined

1 envelope unflavored gelatin

3 tablespoons cold water

1 can condensed tomato soup

4 ounces cream cheese (regular or low-fat, but not fat-free), softened

½ cup mayonnaise (regular or low-fat, but not fat-free)

1 celery stalk, minced

2 shallots, minced

Juice of ½ lemon

3 dashes Tabasco sauce, or more to taste

1 teaspoon salt

½ teaspoon freshly ground black pepper

Vegetable oil for the mold

1 pimiento, drained and cut into ¼-inch slices

1. Bring 2 quarts of salted water to a boil in a large pot set over high heat. Fill a large bowl halfway with ice water and set it aside. Add the shrimp to the boiling water and cook until pink and firm, about 2 minutes. With a slotted spoon or a strainer, transfer the shrimp to the ice water and allow them to cool completely. Drain the shrimp and blot dry with paper towels.

2. Place the gelatin in a large bowl and add the cold water. Set the gelatin aside to soften for 5 minutes.

3. Set aside 6 cooked shrimp. Place the remaining shrimp in a food processor and process until very finely chopped but not puréed—the shrimp should resemble crabmeat. Set aside.

4. Place the tomato soup in a small saucepan and bring to a boil over high heat. Immediately pour the soup over the softened gelatin and stir until the gelatin dissolves completely.

5. Add the cream cheese and mayonnaise to the bowl and beat with a whisk or a hand mixer until the mixture is smooth. Stir in the celery, shallots, lemon juice, Tabasco sauce, salt, pepper, and ground shrimp until well blended.

6. Lightly oil a 1-quart ring mold (or any 1-quart mold, even a fish mold). Arrange the reserved shrimp and pimiento strips in the bottom of the mold in a decorative pattern (this will be the top of the ring after it's unmolded). Without disturbing the pattern, carefully spoon the shrimp mixture into the mold, filling it as full as possible without overflowing (any extra shrimp mixture can be placed in a small oiled ramekin).

7. Set the mold in the refrigerator for 6 to 8 hours, or until it is set.

8. To unmold, dip the mold in a large bowl of hot water for 10 seconds. Dry the outside of the mold. Place a plate or platter larger than the mold over the top, turn them upside down together, and rap them gently on the counter to loosen the shrimp from the mold. (Repeat the dipping if necessary.) The shrimp ring should be unmolded as soon as it is set, but it can remain tightly covered in the refrigerator for up to 24 hours before serving.

BASIL SHRIMP CHIFFON RING Add ½ cup finely shredded basil with the celery.

CURRIED SHRIMP CHIFFON RING Add 1 teaspoon curry powder with the celery.

GREEK SHRIMP CHIFFON RING Omit the celery. Add ½ cup finely crumbled feta (about 2 ounces), ¼ cup finely chopped pitted olives, and 1 teaspoon grated lemon zest with the shallots.

ITALIAN SHRIMP CHIFFON RING Omit the celery. Add ¼ cup finely chopped pitted olives and 2 teaspoons minced oregano with the shallots.

MEXICAN SHRIMP CHIFFON RING Omit the celery. Add 2 teaspoons ground cumin, 2 teaspoons pure chile powder, and ½ teaspoon ground cinnamon with the shallots.

SPANISH SHRIMP CHIFFON RING Add ¾ cup frozen peas and ¼ teaspoon saffron threads crumbled to the tomato soup before it boils.

Shrimp Chowder

THERE ARE AS MANY types of chowder as there are regions of North America. The basic Shrimp Chowder offered here follows a long-standing tradition of cream and potatoes, popular in 1920s Boston society circles as the luncheon dish of choice. Serve with slices of crusty bread and perhaps a glass of a tangy German Riesling. **MAKES 4 TO 6 SERVINGS**

3 large waxy potatoes (such as Yukon Gold; about 1¼ pounds)

2 tablespoons unsalted butter

¾ pound medium shrimp (35 to 40 per pound), peeled and deveined, shells reserved

1½ cups water

1 cup fish stock or clam juice

1 cup milk (whole, 2%, or 1%, but not fat-free), or more as needed

6 strips bacon, finely chopped

1 large onion, finely chopped

1 garlic clove, minced

½ cup heavy cream

½ cup finely chopped parsley

Salt and freshly ground black pepper to taste

1. Peel the potatoes and cut them into ½-inch cubes. Place them in a bowl and cover them with water to prevent discoloring. Set aside.

2. Melt 1 tablespoon of the butter in a large pot or Dutch oven over medium heat. Add the shrimp shells and stir until they turn pink, about 1 minute. Add the water and fish stock and bring to a boil. Reduce the heat to low and simmer for 10 minutes.

3. Using a fine-mesh sieve, strain the liquid into a 1-quart measuring cup. Add enough milk to make 3½ cups liquid.

4. Rinse out the pot and return it to medium heat. Add the remaining 1 tablespoon butter, along with the bacon, onion, and garlic. Sauté, stirring often, until the onion softens and the bacon begins to brown, about 7 minutes.

5. Drain the potatoes and add them to the pot. Cook for 1 minute, stirring constantly. Add the milk–fish stock mixture, raise the heat to high, and bring to a boil. Reduce the heat to low, cover

the pot, and simmer for 20 minutes, or until the potatoes are tender. (The chowder can be made to this point up to 24 hours ahead of time. Keep covered in the refrigerator, then return to a simmer over medium heat before continuing.)

6. Uncover the soup and add the cream and shrimp. Return to a simmer and cook, stirring often, for 5 minutes.

7. Stir the parsley into the pot. Season with salt and pepper. Serve immediately.

CARROT SHRIMP CHOWDER Replace the potatoes with 5 large carrots, peeled and sliced into 1-inch pieces (there's no need to cover the sliced carrots with water).

ITALIAN SHRIMP CHOWDER Omit the cream and add ½ cup dry vermouth with the shrimp. Add 2 tablespoons minced oregano with the parsley.

MANHATTAN SHRIMP CHOWDER Replace the milk with additional fish stock or clam juice. Omit the cream, and add one 28-ounce can crushed tomatoes, with their juice, with the potatoes.

NEW ORLEANS SHRIMP CHOWDER Add 1 green or red bell pepper, cored, seeded, and chopped, with the bacon. Omit the cream. Add 1 teaspoon cayenne pepper, or more to taste, with the shrimp.

ROCK SHRIMP CHOWDER Substitute 1 pound peeled and cleaned rock shrimp for the regular shrimp.

SHRIMP AND CLAM CHOWDER Add 12 small clams (such as pismo), scrubbed, with the shrimp. Cook for an additional 3 minutes, or until the clams open.

SHRIMP AND MUSSEL CHOWDER Add 1 pound mussels, scrubbed and debearded, with the shrimp. Cook for an additional 2 minutes, or until the mussels open.

SPICY SHRIMP CHOWDER Add 1 teaspoon red pepper flakes, or more to taste, with the bacon.

Shrimp Cioppino

IT MAY SOUND AS if it comes from Sicily or Naples, but cioppino has American origins. Italian immigrants in San Francisco made this hearty stew to remember their homeland from afar. It's perfect for a cold winter evening or an elegant springtime dinner party. **MAKES 8 SERVINGS**

3 tablespoons olive oil

2 medium onions, finely chopped

3 garlic cloves, minced

2 teaspoons minced oregano

2 pounds medium shrimp (35 to 40 per pound), peeled and deveined, shells reserved

2 cups dry vermouth

½ cup minced parsley

2 bay leaves

4 cups fish stock or 2 cups clam juice plus 2 cups vegetable stock

Salt and freshly ground black pepper to taste

One 28-ounce can peeled tomatoes, drained and coarsely chopped

½ teaspoon red pepper flakes

1½ pounds mixed fish fillets (such as red snapper, sea bass, scrod, and/or turbot), skinned, picked over for bones, and cut into 3-inch pieces (about 16 pieces)

¼ cup packed shredded basil

1. Heat the oil in a large pot or Dutch oven over medium heat. Add the onions, garlic, and oregano and stir until the onions are soft and translucent, about 3 minutes. Turn the heat to high, add the reserved shrimp shells, and cook, stirring, until they turn pink, about 1 minute.

2. Add the vermouth and bring to a boil. Boil uncovered until the liquid is reduced by half.

3. Add the parsley, bay leaves, and stock. Bring back to a boil, then reduce the heat to low, cover, and simmer for 30 minutes.

4. Using a fine-mesh sieve, strain the stock into a large clean saucepan. Season with salt and pepper. Add the tomatoes and red pepper flakes, place the pan over medium heat, and bring to a simmer. Reduce the heat to low and simmer uncovered for 15 minutes.

5. Add the fish and simmer for 3 minutes, or until the fish turns opaque. Add the shrimp and gently stir to make sure it is completely submerged in the stock. Cook until the shrimp are pink and firm, about 3 minutes.

6. Discard the bay leaves. Gently stir in the basil; check for salt and pepper. Serve immediately.

CREAMY SHRIMP CIOPPINO Stir 1 cup heavy cream into the soup with the shrimp.

HEARTY SHRIMP CIOPPINO Add 1 cup peeled turnips cut into 1-inch cubes and 1 cup peeled carrots sliced into 1-inch rounds with the tomatoes.

LOBSTER AND SHRIMP CIOPPINO Omit the fish fillets. Add 1 pound cooked lobster meat, chopped, with the shrimp.

SHRIMP CIOPPINO PROVENÇAL Add ½ cup anise-flavored liqueur (such as pastis) with the shrimp.

SHRIMP CIOPPINO VELOUTÉ Before adding the fish, thicken the soup by whisking in a *beurre manié*, made by mashing 3 tablespoons softened salted butter into 3 tablespoons all-purpose flour until well combined. If desired, add 1 cup heavy cream with the shrimp.

Shrimp Cocktail

THE SPICY SHRIMP COCKTAIL is an American classic. Unfortunately, it's been stripped of some of its cachet by those little glass vials sold in the refrigerator section of supermarkets. Nothing beats the real thing for elegance, modern or retro. There's a debate about whether the shrimp should be boiled or broiled. We think broiling gives them a firmer texture—a better foil to the tomato sauce. **MAKES 6 TO 8 APPETIZER SERVINGS OR 4 MAIN-COURSE SERVINGS**

FOR THE SHRIMP

- 2 pounds medium shrimp (35 to 40 per pound), deveined but not peeled
- 1 teaspoon salt
- ½ teaspoon freshly ground black pepper
- 3 tablespoons olive oil

FOR THE COCKTAIL SAUCE

- 1 cup ketchup
- 2 tablespoons Worcestershire sauce
- 2 tablespoons bottled horseradish
- Juice of 2 lemons
- 4 dashes Tabasco sauce, or more to taste
- ½ teaspoon salt

1. To devein the shrimp without peeling them, gently hold a shrimp in one hand and pull the vein out of the neck with the other. If the vein doesn't come out whole, use a paring knife to cut down ¼ inch through the shell along the back curve of the shrimp (that is, the side opposite the legs). Gently pry the shell and meat open and remove the vein under running water. Repeat with the remaining shrimp. Preheat the broiler.

2. Combine the shrimp with the salt, pepper, and oil in a large bowl, tossing to coat. Arrange the shrimp in one layer on the broiler tray or a lipped baking sheet. Place under the broiler and broil for 1½ minutes per side, or until the shells start to turn a pinkish brown and the shrimp are firm. Remove from the broiler and allow to cool.

3. Shell the shrimp, leaving the tail segments intact. Cover and refrigerate until chilled.

4. Meanwhile, to prepare the cocktail sauce, combine the ketchup, Worcestershire, horseradish, lemon juice, Tabasco sauce, and salt in a medium bowl and stir until well combined. Cover and refrigerate until ready to serve. (The sauce can be made up to 4 days in advance.)

5. To serve, arrange the shrimp on a large platter, with a bowl of the cocktail sauce on the side for dipping or spooning. Or fill martini glasses or small bowls with the cocktail sauce and hang the shrimp over the edges.

BARBECUE SHRIMP COCKTAIL Replace the ketchup with barbecue sauce, purchased or homemade (page 26).

CHINESE SHRIMP COCKTAIL Replace the ketchup with hoi sin sauce. Omit the horseradish and add 1 tablespoon minced ginger to the sauce.

EASY SHRIMP COCKTAIL Substitute 2 pounds precooked cocktail shrimp, thawed, for the medium shrimp.

GAZPACHO SHRIMP COCKTAIL Replace the horseradish with 2 tablespoons diced onion, 2 tablespoons seeded and diced cucumber, and 3 tablespoons seeded and diced tomato.

MUSTARD SHRIMP COCKTAIL Replace the horseradish with 2 tablespoons Dijon mustard.

PICKLED SHRIMP COCKTAIL Replace the horseradish with 2 tablespoons pickle relish.

SWEET-AND-SOUR SHRIMP COCKTAIL Omit the horseradish. Add 1 tablespoon sweetened Chinese vinegar and 1 teaspoon oyster sauce to the sauce.

Coconut Shrimp

HANDS DOWN, THE MOST DECADENT dish in the book. The sweet coconut goes perfectly with the shrimp, creating a crispy yet succulent package that melts in your mouth. A cold glass of beer or iced tea only makes it better. Since these delights become soggy quickly, they don't travel well—so serve them hot and crispy, right out of the fryer. **MAKES 4 TO 6 SERVINGS**

8 cups vegetable oil

½ cup all-purpose flour

½ teaspoon salt, plus more to taste

½ teaspoon cayenne pepper

2 large egg whites

2 cups shredded sweetened coconut

1 pound medium shrimp (35 to 40 per pound), peeled and deveined

1. Pour the oil into a large saucepan at least 4 inches deep and 10 inches in diameter; the oil should be at least 1½ inches deep but reach no more than halfway up the sides of the pan. Alternatively, fill an electric deep fryer with oil according to the manufacturer's instructions. If you're using a pan, clip a deep-frying thermometer to the inside and place the pan over medium heat. Heat the oil to 375°F. Adjust the heat to maintain that temperature while you prepare the shrimp. If you're using an electric deep fryer, set the temperature control to 375°F.

2. Stir together the flour, ½ teaspoon salt, and cayenne pepper in a medium mixing bowl until well combined. Beat the egg whites with a fork or a small whisk in another medium bowl until frothy. Spread the coconut on a plate. Line up the bowls and plates on the counter as follows: dry ingredients, egg whites, and coconut.

3. Dip a shrimp first into the dry ingredients, then into egg whites, and finally into the coconut, rolling in the coconut until completely coated. Use the palm of your hand to press the coconut on firmly. Lay the shrimp on a cookie sheet or a cutting board; repeat with the remaining shrimp.

4. Gently slide only as many shrimp as will fit into the pan in one layer without crowding into the hot oil and fry until lightly golden, about 2 minutes, turning them occasionally with tongs. Remove the shrimp from the oil and drain them on paper towels. Repeat with the remaining shrimps. Sprinkle with salt to taste and serve immediately.

CURRIED COCONUT SHRIMP Omit the cayenne pepper. Add 1 teaspoon curry powder to the flour.

DOUBLE COCONUT SHRIMP Whisk ½ cup unsweetened coconut milk into the beaten egg whites.

ISLAND COCONUT SHRIMP Add 1 cup dried banana chips, pulverized in a food processor, to the coconut. Whisk ½ cup tamarind juice concentrate into the beaten egg whites.

MEXICAN COCONUT SHRIMP Add 1 teaspoon ground cumin and 1 teaspoon chopped oregano to the flour.

NUTTY COCONUT SHRIMP Add ½ cup chopped peanuts to the coconut.

PINEAPPLE COCONUT SHRIMP Whisk ½ cup pineapple juice concentrate into the beaten egg whites.

Shrimp Curry

DESPITE ITS NAME, this is American fare, part of a rich culinary heritage from all over the world. (For the traditional Indian dish, see Shrimp Vindaloo, page 230.) Shrimp Curry makes a satisfying, come-in-from-the-cold dish for a winter supper or a quick, easy summertime meal. It's a rich, full-bodied stew best served over aromatic rice. Serve a crisp green salad dressed with a light vinaigrette alongside.

MAKES 4 SERVINGS

2 tablespoons unsalted butter

1 large onion, finely chopped

1 celery stalk, minced

2 tablespoons curry powder

2 tablespoons all-purpose flour

2 cups milk, warmed

1 tart apple (such as Granny Smith), peeled, cored, and coarsely chopped

1 pound small shrimp (more than 55 per pound), peeled and deveined, or precooked cold-water (or baby) shrimp, thawed

¼ teaspoon grated nutmeg

2 teaspoons fresh lemon juice

1 teaspoon salt

¼ teaspoon ground white pepper or freshly ground black pepper

1. Melt the butter in a large heavy skillet set over medium heat. Add the onion and celery and cook, stirring often, until the onion is soft and translucent, about 3 minutes.

2. Reduce the heat to low and stir in the curry powder. Stir for 30 seconds, then whisk in the flour. Continue to whisk until the flour is completely incorporated, then cook and whisk for another 30 seconds, just until the flour loses its raw taste and stark-white color, not until it browns.

3. Raise the heat to medium and slowly whisk in the warm milk. Whisk constantly until the mixture comes to a simmer and thickens, about 2 minutes.

4. Add the apple and reduce the heat to low. Simmer until the apple is tender, stirring often, about 10 minutes.

5. Add the shrimp and cook, stirring often, until pink and firm, about 3 minutes. Stir in the nutmeg, lemon juice, salt, and white pepper. Serve immediately.

COCONUT SHRIMP CURRY Substitute coconut milk for 1 cup of the milk.

DOUBLE SHRIMP CURRY Add 2 tablespoons dried shrimp with the apple.

ENGLISH SHRIMP CURRY Add 1 cup frozen peas with the apple.

GINGER SHRIMP CURRY Add 2 tablespoons minced ginger with the onion.

NEW ENGLAND SHRIMP CURRY Add ½ cup dried cranberries, ½ cup chopped walnuts, and 1 teaspoon maple syrup with the apple.

NUTTY SHRIMP CURRY Add ½ cup raisins and ½ cup slivered almonds with the apple.

PEAR SHRIMP CURRY Substitute 1 ripe pear, peeled, cored, and coarsely chopped, for the apple.

TROPICAL SHRIMP CURRY Add 1 cup sliced bananas with the apple.

Deviled Shrimp

DEVILING ACTUALLY GOT ITS start in the eighteenth century. Fiery cayenne pepper, newly brought back from India, was added to meats, mostly to preserve them. Ministers railed against this food trend, saying it caused all sorts of immoral behaviors. You needn't worry about offending the neighbors with this dish. This blend of spices and shrimp is guaranteed to be a new favorite, for lunch or hors d'oeuvres. **MAKES ABOUT 2 CUPS**

1 pound small shrimp (more than 55 per pound), peeled and deveined, or 1 pound precooked cold-water (or baby) shrimp, thawed

1 anchovy fillet

3 tablespoons vegetable oil

2 tablespoons Dijon mustard

1 tablespoon cider vinegar

1 teaspoon minced thyme

½ teaspoon ground ginger

¼ teaspoon grated nutmeg

¼ teaspoon ground cloves

6 dashes Tabasco sauce, or more to taste

½ teaspoon salt, or more to taste

Freshly ground black pepper to taste

1. If you're using raw shrimp, bring 2 quarts salted water to a boil in a large pot over medium heat. Fill a large bowl halfway with ice water and set it aside. Add the shrimp to the boiling water and cook until pink and firm, about 2 minutes. Transfer the shrimp to the ice water with a strainer or a slotted spoon. Allow them to cool completely, then drain them and blot dry with paper towels. If you're using precooked shrimp, omit this step.

2. Combine the shrimp, anchovy, oil, mustard, vinegar, thyme, ginger, nutmeg, cloves, Tabasco sauce, and salt in a food processor. Pulse 2 or 3 times, until the shrimp are evenly chopped, scraping down the bowl as necessary. Process the mixture until smooth, about 1 minute longer. Check for salt and season with pepper. Serve immediately. (The deviled shrimp will keep for up to 2 days tightly covered in the refrigerator.)

SERVING SUGGESTIONS

Dissolved in tomato sauce for a rich pasta topping • Mounded in a sandwich with lettuce and tomato • Mounded in the hollows of hard-cooked egg whites • Spooned into celery stalks • Spooned into hollowed-out cherry tomatoes • Spread on garlic-rubbed bruschetta (see page 46) • Spread on saltines • Spread on table water crackers • Spread on Triscuits or other rough-grain crackers • Swirled into a can of condensed tomato soup with 1 cup milk for an easy lunch treat

BRITISH POTTED SHRIMP Omit the thyme, ginger, and Tabasco sauce. Spoon the shrimp mixture into small ramekins or bowls and smooth the tops. Top each with a layer of melted butter, poured on gently to form a thin coating. Refrigerate, covered, until the butter has hardened. Serve as a spread.

COUNTRY SHRIMP DIP Omit the ginger, and increase the oil to ¼ cup. Coarsely chop the ingredients in the processor—do not purée.

DEVILED SHRIMP AND EGGS Scoop out the yolks of a dozen hard-cooked eggs, halved. Reserve 6 of the yolks for another purpose. Increase the mustard to 3 tablespoons. Process the remaining 6 egg yolks with the shrimp and other ingredients in the food processor. Spoon this mixture into the hard-cooked egg whites.

DEVILED SHRIMP MELT Spread ¼ cup of the deviled shrimp onto each of 8 slices of bread. Cover each with 1 slice American or Swiss cheese. Place on a cookie sheet or a baking sheet and place under a preheated broiler until the cheese melts, about 20 seconds.

GREEK DEVILED SHRIMP Omit the nutmeg and cloves. Add 2 teaspoons minced oregano and 1 teaspoon grated lemon zest with the thyme.

HERBAL DEVILED SHRIMP Omit the ginger and cloves. Add 2 teaspoons minced parsley and 1 teaspoon minced basil with the thyme.

MOROCCAN DEVILED SHRIMP Omit the thyme and ginger. Add 1 teaspoon minced oregano and ½ teaspoon turmeric with the nutmeg.

Shrimp Diane

IN THE DAYS WHEN Bogart and Bacall were caught on camera dining at New York's "21," the dishes served at this formidable temple of chic became a nationwide craze—and Steak Diane led the way. Flambéed in a rich sauce of shallots, brandy, and cream, it set the tone for 1940s elegance. Shrimp Diane, a somewhat simplified version, good served over wide noodles or mashed root vegetables, or just with crusty bread. All you need is something to soak up the heavenly sauce. **MAKES 4 TO 6 SERVINGS**

3 tablespoons unsalted butter, or 1 tablespoon unsalted butter, if using precooked shirmp

1½ pounds medium shrimp (35 to 40 per pound), peeled and deveined, or precooked cocktail shrimp, thawed and peeled

2 shallots, minced

¼ cup dry vermouth or sherry

½ cup brandy

¾ cup fish stock or clam juice

¼ cup heavy cream

1 teaspoon Dijon mustard

1 teaspoon Worcestershire sauce

Salt and freshly ground black pepper to taste

1½ tablespoons minced chives

1. Melt 2 tablespoons of the butter in a large skillet over medium heat. Add the raw shrimp, if using, and cook, stirring often, until pink and firm, about 3 minutes. Transfer the shrimp to a bowl. Set aside.

2. Return the skillet to medium heat and add 1 tablespoon butter. Add the shallots and cook until soft and aromatic, about 2 minutes. Add the vermouth and allow it to come to a boil. Reduce the liquid until it is a glaze and the pan is nearly dry.

3. Remove the pan from the heat and quickly add the brandy, then return the skillet to medium heat—be careful, the brandy may ignite. If this happens, simply cover the pan for 1 minute to put out the flame. Add the stock and bring to a boil. Let the sauce boil, stirring often, until it is reduced to a thick glaze, about 10 minutes.

4. Add the cream and mustard and stir constantly until well combined. Reduce the heat to low and add the Worcestershire sauce and the shrimp, stirring to coat them well. Cook, stirring constantly, until the sauce is bubbling, about 2 minutes.

5. Season with salt and pepper. Serve immediately, sprinkling the dish or individual servings with chives.

ALCOHOL-FREE SHRIMP DIANE Omit the vermouth and brandy. Add 2 tablespoons water, 1 tablespoon cider vinegar, and ½ teaspoon sugar to the pan after the shallots have softened. Substitute beef broth for the fish stock, adding it after the vinegar has been reduced to a glaze.

ALMOND SHRIMP DIANE Finely grind 3 tablespoons blanched slivered almonds in a spice mill or a food processor. Add them with the cream, stirring constantly to prevent scorching.

HERBED SHRIMP DIANE Add 1 tablespoon minced thyme and 1½ tablespoons minced parsley with the cream.

ORANGE SHRIMP DIANE Substitute Grand Marnier for the brandy.

SHRIMP AND CRAB DIANE Reduce the shrimp to 1 pound. Add ½ pound lump crabmeat, picked over for shells and cartilage, with the cream.

SHRIMP AND SCALLOPS DIANE Reduce the shrimp to ¾ pound. Add ¾ pound sea scallops, cut in half, with the raw shrimp in step 1. If using precooked shrimp, cut the scallops into quarters and add them with the shrimp, cooking for 3 minutes.

Shrimp Dip

D IP IS THE ULTIMATE party food, great with beer, retro cocktails, or iced tea. This shrimp dip is excellent on crackers, with cut-up vegetables like carrots or broccoli, or on its own on buttered toast points. In the winter, you may want to warm it up just slightly: place in a microwave-safe bowl and heat on high for 2 minutes, stirring once. **MAKES ABOUT 3 CUPS**

1 pound small shrimp (more than 55 per pound), peeled and deveined, or precooked cold-water (or baby) shrimp, thawed

1 cup mayonnaise (regular, low-fat, or fat-free)

2 tablespoons yellow mustard

2 tablespoons minced pimientos

2 teaspoons curry powder

Juice of ½ lemon

Salt and freshly ground black pepper to taste

1. If using raw shrimp, bring 2 quarts salted water to a boil in a large pot over medium heat. Fill a large bowl halfway with ice water and set it aside. Add the shrimp to the boiling water and cook until pink and firm, about 2 minutes. Transfer the shrimp to the ice water with a strainer or slotted spoon. Allow the shrimp to cool completely, then drain and blot them dry with paper towels. If using precooked shrimp, omit this step.

2. Finely chop the cooked shrimp. Combine them with the mayonnaise, mustard, pimientos, curry powder, and lemon juice in a medium bowl. Stir until well blended. Season with salt and pepper. Serve immediately. (The dip can be made up to 24 hours in advance and kept tightly covered in the refrigerator.)

AFRICAN SHRIMP DIP Omit the curry powder. Add 1 tablespoon turmeric, 4 dashes Tabasco sauce, or more to taste, and ½ cup salted peanuts to the chopped shrimp.

ASIAN SHRIMP DIP Omit the pimientos and curry powder. Add 2 tablespoons five-spice powder and ½ cup minced water chestnuts to the chopped shrimp.

DRUNKEN SHRIMP DIP Omit the lemon juice. Add 2 tablespoons brandy to the chopped shrimp.

FRENCH SHRIMP DIP Omit the mustard and curry powder. Add 2 tablespoons minced basil and 2 tablespoons minced thyme to the chopped shrimp.

GREEK SHRIMP DIP Omit the curry powder. Add ½ cup chopped pitted black olives (such as Kalamata), 2 tablespoons minced oregano, and 1 teaspoon grated lemon zest to the chopped shrimp.

JAPANESE SHRIMP DIP Omit the mustard, pimientos, and curry powder, and increase the mayonnaise to 1¼ cups. Add 2 teaspoons wasabi paste to the chopped shrimp.

Shrimp Dressing

IT'S A SOUTHERN TRADITION at Thanksgiving and Christmas to serve baked oyster dressing with the turkey. This shrimp version honors an old favorite made with saltines. (And it's so much easier not to have to shuck all those oysters!) The casserole comes out of the oven bubbling and hot; but, unlike some dressings, it doesn't really hold its shape when cut, because there's no egg in it. The rich dressing's buttery, sweet flavor works with any number of roasted meats, from beef to chicken, and, of course, turkey. **MAKES 8 SIDE-DISH SERVINGS**

6 tablespoons (¾ stick) unsalted butter, plus additional for the pan

60 saltine crackers

1 pound small shrimp (more than 55 per pound), peeled and deveined

1½ teaspoons sweet paprika

1 teaspoon freshly ground black pepper

3½ cups milk (whole or 2%, but not 1% or fat-free)

1. Preheat the oven to 350°F. Generously butter a 9- or 10-inch square baking dish or casserole.

2. Crumble 20 of the crackers into the pan. Spread them evenly and top with half the shrimp. Dot the shrimp with 2 tablespoons butter and sprinkle with ½ teaspoon paprika and ½ teaspoon pepper. Create a second layer with 20 more crumbled crackers, the remaining shrimp, 2 more tablespoons butter, ½ teaspoon paprika, and ½ teaspoon pepper. Crumble the remaining 20 crackers over the top and dot with the remaining 2 tablespoons butter. Sprinkle the remaining ½ teaspoon paprika evenly over the top.

3. Gently pour the milk over the layers in a thin, steady stream, moistening the entire top of the dish.

4. Cover the dish with foil and bake for 40 minutes. Uncover and bake for 5 minutes longer to create a soft crust. Serve hot or at room temperature.

ASIAN SHRIMP DRESSING Substitute five-spice powder for the paprika.

FIERY SHRIMP DRESSING Add 1½ teaspoons red pepper flakes, dividing them equally among the layers.

FRENCH SHRIMP DRESSING Combine 1½ tablespoons chopped basil and 1½ teaspoons minced thyme with the paprika, dividing the mixture evenly among the layers.

ITALIAN SHRIMP DRESSING Omit the paprika. Combine 1½ tablespoons rosemary and 1½ teaspoons oregano and divide the mixture equally among the layers.

TEXAS SHRIMP DRESSING Seed and thinly slice 2 jalapeño peppers. Divide them equally among the layers.

Shrimp Dumplings

TRADITIONALLY, CHINESE SHRIMP DUMPLINGS are made with pork fat. But you won't miss this ingredient with our lighter version. Dumpling wrappers can be found in the produce section of most grocery stores. Best of all, these dumplings can absolutely be made ahead, frozen for up to 2 months, and taken out for a last-minute appetizer without even defrosting them before steaming. **MAKES ABOUT 20 DUMPLINGS**

Cornstarch for the cookie sheet

3 tablespoons rice wine vinegar

¼ cup soy sauce

½ pound small shrimp (more than 55 per pound), peeled and deveined

2 tablespoons minced chives

8 canned water chestnuts, drained and minced

1 teaspoon minced ginger

½ teaspoon toasted sesame oil

18 to 25 dumpling or wonton wrappers

Vegetable oil for the steamer

1. Lightly dust a cookie sheet or baking sheet with cornstarch.

2. In a small bowl, whisk together the rice wine vinegar and 3 tablespoons soy sauce. Set aside.

3. Place the shrimp in a food processor and pulse 2 or 3 times, until the shrimp are finely ground but not puréed. Transfer the shrimp to a medium mixing bowl.

4. Add the chives, water chestnuts, ginger, the remaining 1 tablespoon soy sauce, and the sesame oil to the shrimp. Stir until well blended.

5. Place 1 dumpling wrapper on the work surface. Put 1 heaping teaspoonful of the shrimp mixture in the middle of the wrapper. Dip your finger in water and moisten the edges of half of the wrapper. Fold the dry side of the wrapper over the filling until it reaches the moist edges, and press the edges together. Pick up the dumpling and use your fingers to pinch the edges closed—a tight seal is important so the filling will not leak while the dumpling cooks. Place the dumpling on the prepared cookie sheet and cover it with a clean dry kitchen towel. Repeat with the remaining wrappers and filling.

6. Lightly oil the bottom sections of a bamboo steamer or the bottom of a metal vegetable steamer basket. Set the dumplings in the steamer basket(s) about 1 inch apart. If you're using a bamboo steamer, choose a pot that is the same diameter as your bamboo steamer so that it fits snugly on top without allowing steam to escape. Fill the bottom of the steamer with 1 inch of water and bring it to a boil over high heat. Place the steamer basket on top of or in the pot; cover and steam the dumplings for 5 minutes, or until the dough is tender and the filling feels firm.

7. Serve the dumplings hot, with the soy sauce mixture for dipping.

OTHER DIPPING SAUCES

A light vinaigrette made with ¼ cup olive oil and 2 tablespoons balsamic vinegar • Barbecue Sauce (page 26) • Peanut Sauce (page 166) • Tartar Sauce (page 51) • Sesame Dipping Sauce (page 203) • Szechwan Cold Garlic Sauce (page 194)

ALMOND SHRIMP DUMPLINGS Add ½ cup ground almonds to the shrimp filling. You'll need about 30 dumpling wrappers.

BLACK BEAN SHRIMP DUMPLINGS Stir 3 tablespoons chopped dried salted Chinese black beans into the shrimp filling. You'll need about 30 dumpling wrappers.

HERB SHRIMP DUMPLINGS Stir ¼ cup minced parsley, ¼ cup minced tarragon, and 2 tablespoons grated lemon zest into the shrimp filling until well combined. You'll need about 35 dumpling wrappers.

MUSHROOM SHRIMP DUMPLINGS Stir ½ cup finely chopped shiitakes, into the shrimp filling until well combined. You'll need about 35 dumpling wrappers.

SPICY SHRIMP DUMPLINGS Add 1 teaspoon chili oil, or more, to the food processor with the shrimp.

Shrimp Enchiladas

THE EASY RED SAUCE for these enchiladas is Texas through and through, and its sweet-hot flavor marries perfectly with the shrimp. Serve with purchased guacamole or refried beans.   **MAKES 4 SERVINGS**

FOR THE SAUCE

3 tablespoons vegetable oil

1 large onion, coarsely chopped

3 garlic cloves, coarsely chopped

4 cups canned or homemade chicken stock

1 tablespoon minced oregano

1 teaspoon salt

12 dried mild red chiles (such as New Mexican), stems and seeds removed, torn into 2-inch pieces

FOR THE ENCHILADAS

1 tablespoon vegetable oil, plus more for the baking dish

2 medium onions, sliced into ¼-inch rings

1 garlic clove, finely chopped

Eight 8-inch flour tortillas

2 pounds large shrimp (12 to 15 per pound), peeled and deveined

4 cups shredded Monterey Jack (about 1 pound)

1. To prepare the sauce, heat the oil in a large skillet over medium heat. Add the onion and garlic; cook, stirring often, until the onion is soft and translucent, about 3 minutes.

2. Stir in the stock, oregano, salt, and chiles. Bring to a simmer, reduce the heat to low, and simmer for 20 minutes. Adjust the heat so that the stock barely bubbles.

3. Purée the hot mixture in a blender; you may have do this in batches. Set the sauce aside. (Prepare the sauce ahead of time and store it in the refrigerator, covered, for up to 3 days.)

4. To prepare the enchiladas, preheat the oven to 350°F. Oil a 9 × 13-inch baking dish and set aside.

5. Heat the vegetable oil in a medium skillet over medium heat. Add the onions and garlic and cook, stirring often until the onions are soft and fragrant, about 5 minutes. Remove the skillet from the heat.

6. Place 1 tortilla on the work surface. Lay 3 shrimp neck to tail in the middle of the tortilla. Top with ⅓ cup of the shredded cheese and one-eighth of the onion and garlic mixture (about 2 tablespoons). Fold the bottom of the tortilla up over the filling, then roll up to create a sealed roll. Using both hands or a large spatula, carefully transfer the tortilla to the baking dish, placing it seam side down across one of the short ends.

7. Continue making the enchiladas and placing them in the pan one next to the other. They should fit snugly in the pan. (The dish can be made to this point up to 12 hours in advance. Store the dish and the sauce, separate and covered, in the refrigerator. Allow both to come to room temperature before proceeding.)

8. Pour the sauce over the top of the enchiladas and scatter the remaining 1⅓ cups shredded cheese evenly over the sauce.

9. Bake for 25 minutes, or until the cheese is melted and shrimp are cooked through. Let stand for 10 minutes, then serve.

GOAT CHEESE SHRIMP ENCHILADAS Substitute 3 cups soft goat cheese (about 10 ounces) for the Monterey Jack; reduce the amount of cheese in each enchilada to ¼ cup.

HOT SHRIMP ENCHILADAS Substitute 3 seeded and coarsely chopped ancho chiles for 3 of the red chiles.

SHRIMP AND BEAN ENCHILADAS Drain, rinse, and purée one 14-ounce can black beans in a food processor. Spoon about 2 tablespoons of the purée into each enchilada before rolling it.

SHRIMP AND CORN ENCHILADAS Sprinkle 2 tablespoons frozen corn, thawed (1 cup total), inside each enchilada before adding the filling.

TEXAS SHRIMP ENCHILADAS Sprinkle 1 teaspoon chopped pickled jalapeño pepper (about 2 peppers total) inside each enchilada before rolling.

Shrimp Étouffée

C AJUN CUISINE, typified by spicy dishes like this one, is part of the New Orleans heritage. Modern-day Cajuns are descended from the French Acadians forced off Nova Scotia by the British in 1758. The word *étouffée* comes from the French *étouffer* ("to smother") and refers to the slow cooking of the meat in the sauce. Fiery Cajun cooking is often defined by a trio of vegetables—onion, celery, and bell pepper—cooked in a deep brown roux (a classic flour and fat mixture, cooked to just this side of burned). Serve Shrimp Étouffée over fluffy white rice, although there are Cajuns who insist on mashed potatoes, mashed turnips, or even braised turnip greens.   **MAKES 4 TO 6 SERVINGS**

¼ cup peanut oil

¼ cup all-purpose flour

1 large onion, coarsely chopped

2 celery stalks, coarsely chopped

1 green bell pepper, cored, seeded, and coarsely chopped

3 garlic cloves, finely chopped

1 tablespoon minced thyme

2 teaspoons salt

2 cups fish stock or vegetable stock

1½ pounds medium shrimp (35 to 40 per pound), peeled and deveined

5 dashes Tabasco sauce, or more to taste

Freshly ground black pepper to taste

1. Heat the peanut oil in a large heavy saucepan over medium heat until it is hot and rippling. Add the flour and whisk until it's completely incorporated. Reduce the heat to medium-low and cook, stirring or whisking often, until the mixture is golden brown, about 10 minutes.

2. Add the onion, celery, bell pepper, and garlic and cook, stirring constantly, for 5 minutes, or until the vegetables soften and the flour mixture is deeply browned. Stir in the thyme and salt. Cook, stirring constantly, for 30 seconds more.

3. Whisk in the stock and continue to whisk until the sauce is smooth and comes to a simmer. Reduce the heat to the merest flame to keep the mixture at a simmer, cover the pan, and simmer for 15 minutes, stirring occasionally.

4. Add the shrimp and stir until they are well coated with sauce. Cook, stirring once or twice, until the shrimp are just beginning to turn pink, about 1 minute. Add the Tabasco sauce and black pepper. Turn off the heat, cover the pan, and let sit for 5 minutes before serving. The heat of the sauce will continue to cook the shrimp.

HEARTY SHRIMP ÉTOUFFÉE Add 1 cup diced turnips and 1 cup diced carrots with the other vegetables.

SHRIMP AND CRAB ÉTOUFFÉE Reduce the shrimp to 1 pound. Add ½ pound lump crabmeat, picked over for shells and cartilage, with the shrimp.

SHRIMP AND CRAWFISH ÉTOUFFÉE Reduce the shrimp to ¾ pound. Add ¾ pound purchased cooked crawfish meat with the shrimp.

SHRIMP AND RED BEAN ÉTOUFFÉE Add one 14-ounce can red beans, drained and rinsed, after whisking in the stock.

SHRIMP AND SCALLOPS ÉTOUFFÉE Reduce the shrimp to 1 pound. Add ½ pound large sea scallops, cut in half, with the shrimp. Let the pan sit covered for 10 minutes after you remove it from the heat.

Shrimp Fajitas

FAJITAS ARE THE QUINTESSENCE of Tex-Mex cuisine. The marinated meat is grilled or sautéed, then served with tortillas and a variety of sides. For steak or chicken fajitas, the meat is usually marinated overnight, but shrimp need only 10 minutes or so in the lime juice and chile blend. There are more ideas for combinations and flavorings following the recipe. **MAKES 4 TO 6 SERVINGS**

1¼ pounds medium shrimp (35 to 40 per pound), peeled and deveined

½ teaspoon salt

½ teaspoon ground cumin

½ teaspoon pure chile powder

½ teaspoon chopped oregano

¼ teaspoon garlic powder

Juice of 1 lime

8 to 12 flour or soft corn tortillas

2 tablespoons vegetable oil

6 scallions, cut into thirds

2 green bell peppers, cored, seeded, and sliced into ⅓-inch strips

ON THE SIDE

½ cup sour cream (regular, low-fat, or fat-free)

¼ cup finely chopped cilantro

¼ cup minced red onion

1. Preheat the oven to 350°F.

2. Combine the shrimp, salt, cumin, chile powder, oregano, garlic, and lime juice in a large bowl. Toss until the spices are evenly distributed and the shrimp are well coated. Set aside to marinate for 10 minutes.

3. Wrap the tortillas tightly in a large piece of aluminum foil. Place the tortillas in the preheated oven.

4. Heat the vegetable oil in a large heavy skillet or oil a stove-top grill over high heat. Add the scallions and peppers and cook, stirring occasionally, until they soften slightly, 2 minutes.

5. Add the shrimp with their marinade and cook, stirring constantly, until they are pink and firm, about 3 minutes.

6. Transfer the shrimp and vegetables to a serving platter and serve with the warmed tortillas, sour cream, cilantro, and red onion on the side.

BARBECUE SHRIMP FAJITAS Serve the fajitas with Barbecue Sauce (page 26) on the side.

CALIFORNIA SHRIMP FAJITAS Omit the sour cream, cilantro, and red onion, and serve 2 Hass avocados, peeled, pitted, and sliced, 1 cup crumbled soft goat cheese (about 4 ounces), and 1 cup yogurt as sides with the tortillas.

LOUISIANA SHRIMP FAJITAS Reduce the shrimp to ¾ pound. Add ½ pound Spanish or Portuguese andouille sausage, sliced into ½-inch pieces, to the marinade. (Do not use Mexican andouille, which includes raw pork.)

OTHER SIDES

2 cups chopped tomatoes • 1 cup crumbled feta (about 4 ounces) • 1 jícama, peeled and sliced • 2 cups salsa • 4 cups shredded lettuce • 2 cups shredded Monterey Jack or Cheddar (about 8 ounces) • 6 fresh or pickled jalapeños, sliced

Shrimp Fra Diavolo

THE CULINARY DEBATE RAGES ON: Is Fra Diavolo an American dish or an Italian? One side claims the dish originated in the early 1900s among Italian immigrants in New York; this camp claims the heavy sauce is strictly an Italian-American invention, not representative of the way people eat in Italy. The other side argues that Fra Diavolo was once a specialty of the Amalfi Coast. In the end, it doesn't really matter, for spicy *pasta fra diavolo* is on every Italian-American menu across the U.S. This recipe offers the simplest version, long a favorite in New York's Little Italy; roasting the tomatoes concentrates their flavor, balancing the garlic and red pepper. Serve hot right out of the pan, accompanied by a crisp salad and sliced fruit for dessert. **MAKES 4 TO 6 SERVINGS**

2 pounds plum tomatoes (about 12), halved

¼ cup olive oil

6 garlic cloves, minced

1 pound spaghetti, linguine, or fettuccine

1½ teaspoons red pepper flakes

1 pound medium shrimp (35 to 40 per pound), peeled and deveined, or precooked cocktail shrimp, thawed and peeled

Salt and freshly ground black pepper to taste

1. Preheat the oven to 450°F.

2. Place the tomatoes cut side down in a roasting pan or a lipped baking sheet just large enough to hold them in one layer. Drizzle them evenly with the olive oil and sprinkle with the minced garlic.

3. Bake the tomatoes for 1 hour, or until they are lightly browned and very soft. Remove the tomatoes from the oven and allow them to cool for 10 minutes.

4. Transfer the tomatoes, garlic, and all the juices from the roasting pan to a food processor. Process until the tomatoes are puréed.

5. Cook the pasta according to the package directions in a large pot of boiling water. Drain thoroughly.

6. Meanwhile, place a large saucepan over medium heat and heat until it's hot but not smoking. Add the red pepper flakes and stir them around for 10 seconds to release their flavor. Add the tomato purée and the raw shrimp, if using. Bring the sauce to a simmer and cook, stirring constantly, until the shrimp are pink and firm, about 3 minutes. Or, if using cocktail shrimp, add them when the sauce is simmering and cook until heated through, about 1 minute. Season with salt and pepper.

7. Add the cooked pasta to the sauce and toss until well combined and heated through.

HERBED SHRIMP FRA DIAVOLO Add 3 tablespoons minced parsley and 2 tablespoons chopped rosemary with the shrimp.

SHRIMP AND CRAB FRA DIAVOLO Reduce the shrimp to ½ pound. Add ½ pound lump crabmeat, picked over for shells and cartilage, with the shrimp.

SHRIMP AND LOBSTER FRA DIAVOLO Reduce the shrimp to ½ pound. Add ½ pound cooked lobster meat, chopped, with the cooked pasta.

SHRIMP AND SCALLOP FRA DIAVOLO Reduce the shrimp to ½ pound. Add ½ pound large sea scallops, cut in half, with the shrimp. If using precooked shrimp, cut the scallops into quarters. Add them with the shrimp and simmer an additional 2 minutes.

SHRIMP FRA DIAVOLO À LA VODKA Add 3 tablespoons vodka with the shrimp. When the shrimp are cooked, stir 1 cup heavy cream into the sauce.

Shrimp Fried Rice

THERE ARE TWO TRICKS to perfect fried rice: the cooked rice must be cooled completely (so its moisture content is low and it doesn't steam the dish) and the oil must be very hot (so that the rice doesn't turn gummy). Standard white or brown rice works well, but fragrant rices such as jasmine, basmati, or Texmati are equally delicious. Never use instant rice, Arborio, or Thai sticky rice. **MAKES 4 TO 6 SERVINGS**

2 teaspoons plus 2 tablespoons peanut oil

2 large eggs, lightly beaten

3 scallions, thinly sliced

1 garlic clove, minced

1 teaspoon minced ginger

1 celery stalk, cut into ⅛-inch dice

1 carrot, cut into ⅛-inch dice

½ cup fresh or defrosted frozen peas

¾ pound small shrimp (more than 55 per pound), peeled and deveined, or precooked cold-water (or baby) shrimp, thawed

3 cups cooked white rice, cooled thoroughly

1 tablespoon soy sauce

1. Place a large wok or skillet (preferably nonstick) over medium heat until it is hot but not smoking. Add 2 teaspoons of the peanut oil and swirl it around to coat the wok. Add the eggs and scramble them very quickly. When the eggs are just set, transfer to a plate and set aside.

2. Wipe out any bits of egg sticking to the wok, turn the heat up to high, and place the wok over the heat. Allow it to get very hot again. Add the remaining 2 tablespoons peanut oil, then add the scallions, garlic, and ginger. Stir and toss them for 20 seconds.

3. Add the celery and carrot; cook, stirring and tossing, for another 30 seconds. Add the peas and the raw shrimp, if using, and toss and stir until the shrimp are pink and firm, about 2 minutes. Lower the heat to medium if the vegetables begin to burn.

4. Raise the heat to high and add the rice and the precooked shrimp, if using. Stir and toss for 2 minutes, or until the rice is hot and the grains are separate and well distributed among the other ingredients.

5. Toss the eggs back into the wok, along with the soy sauce, and cook, stirring and tossing, for 30 seconds more. Serve immediately or at room temperature.

BLACK BEAN SHRIMP FRIED RICE Add 2 tablespoons dried salted Chinese black beans, slightly crushed, with the peas.

DOUBLE SHRIMP FRIED RICE Add 2 tablespoons dried shrimp, soaked in water for 10 minutes and drained, with the peas.

MUSHROOM SHRIMP FRIED RICE Add 1 cup sliced button mushrooms with the celery.

SPICY SHRIMP FRIED RICE Add 1 tablespoon chili oil, or more to taste, with the peas.

SWEET-AND-SAVORY SHRIMP FRIED RICE Omit the soy sauce. Add 2 tablespoons hoi sin sauce and 1 tablespoon oyster sauce with the rice.

SZECHWAN SHRIMP FRIED RICE Add 2 tablespoons crushed Szechwan peppercorns with the celery.

THAI SHRIMP FRIED RICE Omit the carrots and soy sauce. Add 2 teaspoons fish sauce, ½ cup unsalted peanuts, and ¼ cup chopped basil with the cooked eggs. Top the dish with ½ cup finely diced cucumber.

VEGETABLE SHRIMP FRIED RICE Add ½ cup finely minced canned water chestnuts and ½ cup thinly sliced canned bamboo shoots with the celery. Increase the soy sauce to 2 tablespoons.

Shrimp Frittata

UNLIKE A FRENCH OMELET, an Italian frittata is cooked at a low heat and left flat. The frittata first entered the American consciousness in 1952 when Ruth Casa-Emellos, writing for the *New York Times,* tried to re-create the dishes served on the fashionable Italian cruise line, the *Saturnia*. Shrimp Frittata makes a spectacular brunch dish, a nice addition to a casual buffet, or a quick summer supper, served with a glass of good Italian wine, such as a hearty Montepulciano. **MAKES 2 SERVINGS**

6 large eggs

3 tablespoons milk (whole or 2%, but not 1% or fat-free)

2 tablespoons olive oil

2 scallions, thinly sliced

¾ pound small shrimp (more than 55 per pound), peeled and deveined

½ teaspoon salt

Freshly ground black pepper to taste

1. In a medium bowl, beat the eggs and milk with a small whisk or a fork until lightly frothy.

2. Heat the oil in a 10- to 12-inch skillet (preferably nonstick) over medium heat. Add the scallions and cook, stirring constantly, just until they are soft, about 1 minute. Do not let them brown.

3. Add the shrimp and salt; cook, stirring often, until the shrimp are pink and firm, about 2 minutes.

4. Reduce the heat to low. Pour the eggs into the skillet and shake the pan lightly to distribute the shrimp and scallions evenly in the egg mixture. Cover the skillet and cook undisturbed until the eggs are set, about 8 minutes.

5. Carefully run a long thin flexible spatula around the sides and under the frittata to release it from the pan, and slide it onto a serving platter. Cut the frittata in half or into wedges. Serve hot or at room temperature.

EXTRA-RICH SHRIMP FRITTATA Substitute heavy cream or half-and-half for the milk.

FIERY SHRIMP FRITTATA Whisk 4 dashes Tabasco sauce, or more to taste, with the eggs and milk.

HERBED SHRIMP FRITTATA Add 1 tablespoon minced thyme, 1 tablespoon minced parsley, and 2 teaspoons minced oregano with the shrimp.

INDIAN SHRIMP FRITTATA Add 1 tablespoon minced ginger and 2 teaspoons curry powder with the shrimp.

MUSHROOM SHRIMP FRITTATA Add 1 cup thinly sliced button or cremini mushrooms with the shrimp.

NEW ENGLAND SHRIMP FRITTATA Add 1 cup cubed boiled potatoes and ½ pound cooked lobster, chopped, with the shrimp.

PROVENÇAL SHRIMP FRITTATA Add ½ cup diced tomatoes, ¼ cup chopped pitted black olives, and 1 tablespoon chopped rosemary with the shrimp.

ROCK SHRIMP FRITTATA Use ¾ pound peeled and cleaned rock shrimp instead of the raw shrimp.

SPANISH SHRIMP FRITTATA Add ¼ teaspoon saffron threads, crumbled, to the eggs and milk. Add 1 cup frozen peas, thawed, with the shrimp.

Shrimp Fritters

LET'S FACE IT: Fritters are just too good to pass up. Your doctor won't advocate eating these shrimp-stuffed bundles of crispy, salty batter, deep-fried to a golden brown. In fact, throughout history, health-care officials have agreed: Roman doctors thought they caused cholera; medieval apothecaries, heresy. Defy all authorities once in a while and serve these crunchy wonders, the ultimate indulgence, hot, right out of the fryer. **MAKES ABOUT 30 FRITTERS**

1½ pounds small shrimp (more than 55 per pound), peeled and deveined, or precooked cold-water (or baby) shrimp, thawed

8 cups vegetable oil

2 large eggs, well beaten

1¼ cups milk

2 tablespoons unsalted butter, melted

2 teaspoons baking powder

2 cups all-purpose flour

2 teaspoons salt

½ teaspoon freshly ground black pepper

1. If you're using raw shrimp, bring 3 quarts salted water to a boil in a large pot set over high heat. Fill a large bowl halfway with ice water and set it aside. Add the shrimp to the boiling water and cook until pink and firm, about 2 minutes. Using a slotted spoon or strainer, transfer the shrimp to the ice water and allow them to cool completely. Drain the shrimp and pat with paper towels. If using precooked shrimp, omit this step.

2. Coarsely chop the cooked shrimp; set aside.

3. Pour the oil into a large saucepan at least 4 inches deep and 10 inches in diameter; the oil should be at least 1½ inches deep but reach no more than halfway up the sides of the pan. Alternatively, fill an electric deep fryer with oil according to the manufacturer's instructions. If you're using a pan, clip a deep-frying thermometer to the inside and place the pan over medium heat. Heat the oil to 375°F. Adjust the heat to maintain this temperature while you prepare the fritters. If you're using an electric deep fryer, set the temperature control to 375°F.

4. Combine the eggs, milk, and melted butter in a large bowl. Whisk until light and frothy. Add the baking powder, flour, 1 teaspoon of the salt, and the pepper; mix until the dry ingredients are well incorporated and the batter is smooth. Add the shrimp and mix until they are well incorporated into the batter.

5. Drop heaping tablespoonfuls of the batter into the hot oil, adding only as many at a time as will fit in one layer without crowding the pan. Fry for 1 minute, or until golden brown on the bottom. Turn the fritters and fry for another minute, or until golden brown all over.

6. Remove the fritters from the oil and drain them on paper towels. Serve the fritters hot, sprinkled with the remaining 1 teaspoon salt.

CAJUN SHRIMP FRITTERS Sauté 1 cup minced onion, ½ cup finely diced celery, and ½ cup finely chopped green bell pepper in 2 teaspoons vegetable oil over medium heat until softened, about 5 minutes. Cool completely. Increase the milk to 1¾ cups and add a third egg. Add the vegetable mixture to the batter with the flour, adding 4 dashes Tabasco sauce, or more to taste, as well.

CORNMEAL SHRIMP FRITTERS Substitute 1 cup yellow or white cornmeal for 1 cup of the flour.

OKRA AND SHRIMP FRITTERS Add 1½ cups thinly sliced okra with the flour.

ROCK SHRIMP FRITTERS Substitute 1½ pounds peeled and cleaned rock shrimp for the regular shrimp.

SHRIMP AND CRAB FRITTERS Reduce the shrimp to ¾ pound. Add ¾ pound crabmeat, picked over for shells and cartilage, to the batter.

SPICY SHRIMP FRITTERS Add 1 teaspoon red pepper flakes with the flour.

Garlic Sauce Shrimp

A HONG KONG SPECIALTY, Garlic Sauce Shrimp has become standard Chinese-American fare. Following tradition, this recipe makes just enough sauce to coat the shrimp without masking their taste. The garlic sauce is fiery, so beware. You can always cut down on the number of dried red chiles—but eat them at your own risk. Serve this dish over white or brown rice. It will also make great cold leftovers the next day, the sauce mellowing somewhat. **MAKES 4 TO 6 SERVINGS**

3 tablespoons peanut oil, or 1 tablespoon peanut oil, if using precooked shrimp

1½ pounds medium shrimp (35 to 40 per pound), peeled and deveined, or precooked cocktail shrimp, thawed and peeled

4 small dried red Asian chiles

2 tablespoons minced ginger

8 garlic cloves, finely chopped

1 shallot, minced

5 scallions, cut into 1-inch pieces

1½ tablespoons dry sherry

3 tablespoons soy sauce

2 teaspoons sugar

¼ cup plus 2 tablespoons canned or homemade chicken stock

1 tablespoon toasted sesame oil

1. Set a large wok or a skillet (preferably nonstick) over high heat. When the wok is hot but not smoking, add 2 tablespoons of the peanut oil. Swirl it around to coat the wok, then add the raw shrimp, if using. Cook, stirring and tossing constantly, until pink and firm, about 3 minutes. Remove the shrimp from the wok and set them aside.

2. Lower the heat to medium and add 1 tablespoon peanut oil to the wok. Immediately add the dried chiles and stir them for 30 seconds. Add the ginger, garlic, shallot, and scallions. Cook, stirring constantly, for 30 seconds.

3. Add the sherry, soy sauce, sugar, stock, and sesame oil and stir until the sauce is bubbling and slightly thickened, about 2 minutes.

4. Add the shrimp to the wok and toss until well coated and heated through. Serve immediately.

DOUBLE SHRIMP IN GARLIC SAUCE Add 2 tablespoons dried shrimp, soaked in water for 10 minutes and drained, with the ginger.

GARLIC SAUCE SHRIMP AND ASPARAGUS Add 1 cup sliced asparagus with the ginger.

GARLIC SAUCE SHRIMP AND BROCCOLI Add 1 cup broccoli florets with the ginger.

GARLIC SAUCE SHRIMP AND CHINESE VEGETABLES Add ½ cup canned sliced water chestnuts, drained, and ½ cup canned sliced bamboo shoots, drained, with the ginger.

GARLIC SAUCE SHRIMP AND MUSHROOMS Add 1 cup canned straw mushrooms, drained, with the ginger.

GARLIC SAUCE SHRIMP AND NOODLES Pour boiling water over two 2-ounce packages dried bean thread noodles. Soak them for 15 minutes. Add the noodles to the wok with the cooked shrimp. (Do not serve this variation over rice.)

GARLIC SAUCE SHRIMP AND SNOW PEAS Add 1 cup snow peas with the cooked shrimp.

General Tsao's Shrimp

IT IS SAID THAT this "hot-headed" dish was created for a Chinese general with impeccable culinary and military skills. But because his name slips from Tsao to Tang to Shek, the story is probably the stuff of legend. But so's the dish—crispy shrimp in a sweet and hot sauce. This Szechwan dish will make a nice contribution to a potluck or buffet, or a satisfying dinner on a cold winter evening. Just be sure to have lots of fluffy white rice ready. **MAKES 4 SERVINGS**

FOR THE SAUCE

1 tablespoon peanut oil

8 dried red Asian chiles

6 garlic cloves, minced

2 tablespoons minced ginger

1 teaspoon salt

3 tablespoons sugar

3 tablespoons black vinegar

1 cup canned or homemade chicken stock

FOR THE SHRIMP

8 cups peanut oil

½ cup all-purpose flour

2 tablespoons cornstarch

1 teaspoon baking powder

1 teaspoon salt

⅔ cup water

1 teaspoon toasted sesame oil

1 pound medium shrimp (35 to 40 per pound), peeled and deveined

2 teaspoons cornstarch, dissolved in 1 teaspoon water

1. To prepare the sauce, heat a large wok or skillet (preferably nonstick) over medium-high heat until it is hot but not smoking. Add the peanut oil and heat until hot, about 15 seconds. Add the chiles and cook, stirring and tossing constantly, for 10 seconds. Add the garlic and ginger; cook, stirring and tossing constantly, for 30 seconds.

2. Add the salt, sugar, and vinegar. Cook, stirring constantly, for 20 seconds, or until the sugar dissolves. Add the chicken stock and bring to a boil. Reduce the heat to low and simmer for 5 minutes. Remove from the heat and set aside while you prepare the shrimp.

3. To prepare the shrimp, pour the oil into a large saucepan at least 4 inches deep and 10 inches in diameter; the oil should be at least 1½ inches deep but reach no more than halfway up the

sides of the pan. Alternatively, fill a deep fryer with oil according to the manufacturer's instructions. If you're using a pan, clip a deep-frying thermometer to the inside and place the pan over medium heat. Heat the oil to 375°F. Adjust the heat to maintain that temperature while you prepare the shrimp. If you're using an electric deep fryer, set the temperature control to 375°F.

4. Combine the flour, cornstarch, baking powder, and salt in a large mixing bowl. Whisk gently until well combined. Add the water and sesame oil; whisk until the batter is completely smooth.

5. Dip a shrimp into the batter until it is completely coated and let the excess batter drip off. Gently slide the coated shrimp into the hot oil. Repeat with the remaining shrimp, dipping and frying only as many shrimp at a time as will fit in the pan in one layer without crowding. Fry the shrimp until they are lightly golden, 1 to 2 minutes, turning once or twice with tongs. Remove the shrimp from the oil and drain them on paper towels.

6. To finish the dish, place the sauce over high heat and bring it to a boil. Add the cornstarch mixture, stirring constantly until the sauce thickens, about 1 minute.

7. Immediately remove the pan from the heat and add the shrimp. Toss until all the shrimp are well coated in the sauce. Serve with white or brown rice.

GENERAL TSAO'S SHRIMP AND BROCCOLI Reduce the shrimp to ¾ pound. Dip 2 cups broccoli florets into the batter to coat and deep-fry after the shrimp. Add the broccoli to the sauce as well.

GENERAL TSAO'S SHRIMP AND CHICKEN Reduce the shrimp to ½ pound. Dip ½ pound boneless, skinless chicken breasts, cut into 1-inch cubes, into the batter to coat, and deep-fry, cooking the chicken pieces for 3 to 4 minutes. Add them to the sauce as well.

GENERAL TSAO'S SHRIMP AND SCALLOPS Reduce the shrimp to ½ pound. Dip ½ pound medium sea scallops into batter to coat and deep-fry with the shrimp. Add them to the sauce as well.

GENERAL TSAO'S SHRIMP AND TOFU Reduce the shrimp to ½ pound. Slice ½ pound firm tofu into 1-inch cubes. Stir the pieces into the heated sauce and simmer for 1 minute before adding the deep-fried shrimp.

Shrimp Gumbo

ONE OF LOUISIANA'S MOST famous dishes, gumbo is Creole rather than Cajun, a dish from the descendents of African slaves, Native Americans, and French traders. The word *gumbo* is derived from an African word for okra, the dish's main vegetable and one of its three thickening agents, along with a dark roux (a browned fat and flour mixture) and filé powder (dried sassafras, available in gourmet markets, or from outlets in the Source Guide, page 239). The filé must be added off the flame, because it turns stringy when cooked. Shrimp Gumbo is a one-pot meal, perfect for a crowd—and can easily be doubled or tripled. Serve it over rice or noodles. One of the variations below allows you to fix the traditional Gumbo z'Herbes, a dish served on Good Friday for good luck. **MAKES 6 TO 8 SERVINGS**

FOR THE ROUX

3 tablespoons peanut oil

3 tablespoons all-purpose flour

FOR THE GUMBO

2 tablespoons peanut oil

1 large onion, coarsely chopped

3 celery stalks, cut into ½-inch pieces

2 garlic cloves, minced

2 cups chopped okra or one 12-ounce package frozen okra, thawed

2 teaspoons minced thyme

½ teaspoon cayenne pepper

2 bay leaves

4 cups fish stock or 2 cups vegetable stock plus 2 cups clam juice

2 pounds medium shrimp (35 to 40 per pound), peeled and deveined

2 teaspoons filé powder

3 dashes Tabasco sauce, or more to taste

Salt and freshly ground black pepper to taste

1. To prepare the roux, heat a small saucepan or skillet over medium heat until it is hot but not smoking. Add the peanut oil and swirl it around the pan. Whisk the flour into the oil until it is completely incorporated. Reduce the heat to medium-low and cook, whisking constantly, until the mixture turns a deep brown and smells nutty but is not burnt, about 10 minutes. Remove the pan from the heat and set aside.

2. To prepare the gumbo, heat a large heavy saucepan or Dutch oven over medium heat until it is hot but not smoking. Add the peanut oil and swirl it around the pan. Add the onion and celery and cook, stirring often, until the vegetables soften, about 3 minutes.

3. Add the garlic, okra, thyme, cayenne, bay leaves, and stock. Bring to a boil and boil for 1 minute. Stir in the roux. Cook, stirring constantly, until the stock thickens, about 1 minute. Reduce the heat to low, cover, and simmer for 5 minutes.

4. Add the shrimp and stir until they are well coated. Cover and cook slowly until the shrimp are pink and firm, about 5 minutes. Remove the pan from the heat, stir in the filé and Tabasco sauce, and season with salt and black pepper. Discard the bay leaves.

5. Serve immediately, alone, over rice, or over noodles.

BAYOU SHRIMP GUMBO Do not peel the shrimp: cook them in their shells. Or, better yet, buy head-on shrimp, about 3 pounds, and cook them. Add 1 cup chopped cooked ham and one 12-ounce package frozen corn, thawed, with the shrimp.

ROCK SHRIMP GUMBO Substitute 2 pounds peeled and cleaned rock shrimp for the regular shrimp.

SHRIMP AND CRAB GUMBO Reduce the shrimp to 1 pound. Add 1 pound lump crabmeat, picked over for shells and cartilage, or 2 pounds stone crab claws, with the shrimp.

SHRIMP AND CRAWFISH GUMBO Reduce the shrimp to 1 pound. Add 2 pounds live crawfish with the shrimp, and cook for an additional 5 minutes. Chopped cooked crawfish meat can also be used; add it with the shrimp but do not increase the cooking time.

SHRIMP GUMBO Z'HERBES Increase the stock to 6 cups. Add ½ cup *each* of shredded greens to the pot with the shrimp, choosing a total of seven kinds: mustard greens, turnip greens, collard greens, fennel fronds, dandelion greens, watercress, broccoli rabe, romaine lettuce, escarole, and/or chicory.

TOMATO SHRIMP GUMBO Reduce the stock to 2 cups. Add one 28-ounce can tomatoes, chopped, with their juices, along with the stock.

Honey Grilled Shrimp

THIS IS SUMMER GRILL FARE AT ITS FINEST: sweet, salty, hot shrimp right off the barbecue. You'll want to have plenty of cold beer or iced tea on hand. You can dip these shrimp in Barbecue Sauce (page 26) or Szechwan Cold Garlic Sauce (page 194), but they're quite good on their own. Make sure you have enough, because everyone will want another round. **MAKES 6 TO 8 APPETIZER SERVINGS OR 4 MAIN-COURSE SERVINGS**

⅔ cup fresh lemon juice

⅔ cup soy sauce

⅔ cup dark honey (such as chestnut or pine) or clover honey

2 pounds large shrimp (12 to 15 per pound), peeled, leaving the final segment of the tail shell intact, and deveined

1. Combine the lemon juice, soy sauce, and honey in a medium bowl. Whisk until well blended.

2. Place the shrimp in a large bowl and pour the honey mixture over them. Toss until they are well coated. Cover and set aside in a cool place for 30 minutes to marinate.

3. Meanwhile, light the coals in a barbecue at least 20 minutes before you're ready to cook the shrimp. Or, if you're using a gas grill or the broiler, preheat it 5 minutes before you're ready to cook.

4. When the coals are glowing red with a thin covering of ash, place the rack on the barbecue. One or two at a time, hold the shrimp by the tails and shake off any excess marinade, then lay the shrimp on the barbecue rack, directly over the coals. Cook for 2 minutes per side, or until the shrimp are firm and the sauce turns golden. Or, if you're using a broiler, lay the shrimp on a baking sheet and place them 4 inches from the flame. Cook for 2 minutes, turn them with tongs, and cook for 2 more minutes, or until they are firm and the sauce turns golden.

5. Serve the shrimp hot or at room temperature.

CHINESE HONEY GRILLED SHRIMP Use hoi sin sauce instead of soy sauce.

KEY WEST HONEY GRILLED SHRIMP Substitute Key lime juice, fresh or bottled, for the lemon juice.

SESAME HONEY GRILLED SHRIMP Add 2 tablespoons toasted sesame oil to the marinade.

SPICY HONEY GRILLED SHRIMP Add 4 dashes Tabasco sauce, or more to taste, to the marinade.

THAI HONEY GRILLED SHRIMP Use fish sauce instead of soy sauce, and add 1 teaspoon chili oil.

Iberian Stewed Shrimp

THIS IS A SIMPLIFIED take on a classic Spanish stew, flavored with hazelnuts and thickened with bread. Rich and satisfying, it's a popular late-night dish in neighborhood restaurants around Madrid. Some of the variations even let you try regional versions of the dish. This stew thickens considerably as it sits, so you may need to thin it out with fish or vegetable stock if you're making it early in the day or serving leftovers. **MAKES 4 TO 6 SERVINGS**

½ cup hazelnuts

3 slices day-old bread, crumbled

½ cup tightly packed parsley leaves

3 tablespoons olive oil, plus additional for garnishing

3 leeks, cut lengthwise in half, washed of any sand, and sliced into ¼-inch half-moons

1 medium onion, coarsely chopped

3 garlic cloves, minced

1 to 2 teaspoons red pepper flakes

One 28-ounce can peeled tomatoes

¼ teaspoon saffron threads

1 cup frozen peas

½ pound green beans, cut into 1-inch pieces

1 cup dry sherry or dry vermouth

1½ cups water

1½ pounds medium shrimp (35 to 40 per pound), peeled and deveined, or precooked cocktail shrimp, thawed and peeled

Salt and freshly ground black pepper to taste

1. Preheat the oven to 350°F.

2. Place the hazelnuts in a small baking dish and bake for 10 minutes, or until they give off a light nutty aroma. Shake the pan once or twice to keep the nuts from burning. Remove them from the oven and let cool completely.

3. Combine the nuts, bread, and parsley in a food processor and pulse 2 or 3 times, until the nuts are finely chopped and the mixture is well blended. Set it aside.

4. Place the oil in a large pot or Dutch oven over medium heat. Add the leeks and onion; sauté, stirring often, until the leeks and onions are softened and fragrant, about 3 minutes. Add the garlic and red pepper flakes. Cook, stirring constantly, for 1 minute.

5. Add the tomatoes to the pot, along with their juice, and break them up with the back of a wooden spoon. Crumble the saffron threads into the pot, then add the peas, green beans, sherry, and water. Bring to a simmer. Cover the pot, reduce the heat to medium-low, and simmer for 20 minutes, stirring occasionally.

6. Add the shrimp and cook, stirring often, until pink and firm, about 3 minutes.

7. Stir in the hazelnut mixture and cook, stirring often, until the stew thickens, about 2 minutes. Season with salt and pepper. As a garnish, you can drizzle to 1 teaspoon of olive oil over the stew in each dish as you serve it.

BARCELONA STEWED SHRIMP Omit the saffron. Add ¼ cup Pernod or pastis with the tomatoes.

BILBAO STEWED SHRIMP Use walnuts instead of the hazelnuts. Add ½ cup raisins with the shrimp.

CATALAN STEWED SHRIMP Omit the saffron. Add 1 teaspoon ground cinnamon and ½ teaspoon ground allspice with the peas.

FLAVORED IBERIAN STEWED SHRIMP Use a flavored oil, such as basil, sun-dried tomato, or black pepper oil, for garnishing the dish.

IBERIAN STEWED SHRIMP WITH CLAMS AND MUSSELS Add 10 medium clams (such as cherrystone or Pacific littleneck), scrubbed, and 1 pound mussels, scrubbed and debearded, with the shrimp. Cover the pot and cook for an additional 5 minutes, or until the clams and mussels open.

MADEIRA STEWED SHRIMP Use ½ cup pine nuts instead of the hazelnuts. Substitute dry Madeira for the sherry.

SEVILLE STEWED SHRIMP Omit the green beans. Add 1½ cups potatoes, peeled and cut into 1-inch cubes, with the peas.

Kung Pao Shrimp

THE SAUCE FOR THIS fiery farrago from China's Szechwan province is made from chiles, peanuts, and ginger. Although the dish is usually prepared with chicken, shrimp gives the stir-fry a delicate sweetness that counterbalances its spiciness. Don't eat the red chiles, just let them flavor the dish. Serve with bowls of fluffy white rice. **MAKES 4 SERVINGS**

¼ cup dry sherry

1 tablespoon soy sauce

1 tablespoon hoi sin sauce

2 teaspoons rice wine vinegar

3 tablespoons peanut oil

1 pound medium shrimp (35 to 40 per pound), peeled and deveined

16 dried red Asian chiles

1 tablespoon minced ginger

3 garlic cloves, minced

¼ teaspoon Szechwan peppercorns, crushed

2 scallions, cut into 1-inch pieces

1 green bell pepper, cored, seeded, and cut into ¼-inch strips

1 cup unsalted peanuts

2 teaspoons cornstarch, dissolved in 1 tablespoon water

2 teaspoons toasted sesame oil

1. In a small bowl, whisk together the sherry, soy sauce, hoi sin sauce, and vinegar. Set aside.

2. Set a large wok or skillet over medium-high heat until it is hot but not smoking. Add the oil and swirl it around the wok. Add the shrimp and stir and toss until pink and firm, about 3 minutes.

3. Add the chiles, ginger, garlic, Szechwan peppercorns, scallions, green pepper, and peanuts. Stir and toss for 1 minute. Turn the heat to high and add the sherry mixture. Cook, stirring constantly, until the sauce comes to a boil. Add the cornstarch mixture and stir and toss until the mixture thickens, almost instantly. Remove the pan from the heat.

4. Sprinkle the dish with the sesame oil. Serve hot.

KUNG PAO SHRIMP AND BROCCOLI Omit the green pepper. Add 1 cup broccoli florets with the chiles.

KUNG PAO SHRIMP AND CHICKEN Reduce the shrimp to ½ pound. Stir-fry ½ pound chicken tenders or ½ pound boneless, skinless chicken breasts, cut into 1-inch cubes, with the shrimp.

KUNG PAO SHRIMP AND MUSHROOMS Add one 15-ounce can straw mushrooms, drained, with the chiles.

KUNG PAO SHRIMP AND SNOW PEAS Omit the green bell pepper. Add 1 cup snow peas with the sherry mixture.

MILD KUNG PAO SHRIMP Omit the chiles.

TRADITIONAL KUNG PAO SHRIMP Increase the Szechwan peppercorns to 1 teaspoon. Add 1 cup sliced bananas and ¼ cup shredded basil with the chiles.

Shrimp Lasagne

LONG BEFORE GARFIELD BEGGED for lasagne, this casserole of tomatoes, flat noodles, and cheese was an American favorite. And long before that, lasagne was a Roman favorite: the poet Horace eulogized his lasagne of leeks and noodles (no tomatoes, of course, because the Americas hadn't been colonized). Shrimp Lasagne makes a great dinner party or buffet dish. But if you're not having company, leftovers freeze well, cut into squares for individual meals. It can keep for up to 2 months and can be reheated, covered, in a 350°F oven for 30 minutes, or until hot. **MAKES 6 TO 8 SERVINGS**

FOR THE TOMATO SAUCE

- ¼ cup olive oil
- 1 large onion, finely chopped
- 2 celery stalks, finely chopped
- 1 carrot, finely chopped
- 3 garlic cloves, minced
- 2 tablespoons minced parsley
- 1 tablespoon minced oregano
- 1 teaspoon minced thyme
- ¼ teaspoon red pepper flakes
- ½ cup dry vermouth
- 1 bay leaf
- One 28-ounce can crushed tomatoes
- Salt and freshly ground black pepper to taste

FOR THE CHEESE MIXTURE

- One 15-ounce container ricotta (regular, low-fat, or fat-free)
- 2 cups mozzarella, shredded (about 8 ounces)
- 1 large egg
- ½ teaspoon grated nutmeg
- ½ teaspoon salt
- ¼ teaspoon freshly ground black pepper

- 1 tablespoon olive oil
- 1 pound dried lasagne noodles
- 1½ pounds small shrimp (more than 55 per pound), peeled and deveined
- ¾ cup freshly grated Parmigiano-Reggiano (about 3 ounces)

1. To prepare the tomato sauce, heat the oil in a large saucepan over medium heat. Add the onion, celery, and carrot; sauté, stirring often, until they soften and are fragrant, about 5 minutes. Add the garlic and cook for 30 seconds.

2. Add the parsley, oregano, thyme, and red pepper flakes. Stir for 10 seconds, then add the vermouth. Bring to a boil and cook until the liquid is reduced by half, about 2 minutes.

3. Add the bay leaf and tomatoes, with their juices, and stir until well combined. Bring the sauce to a simmer, then reduce the heat to low, cover, and cook for 10 minutes, stirring once or twice. Uncover the pan and cook for another 15 minutes or so, stirring often. The sauce should have the consistency of a fairly thick spaghetti sauce.

4. Season with salt and pepper, remove the pan from the heat, and allow the sauce to cool. Remove and discard the bay leaf.

5. To prepare the cheese mixture, combine the ricotta, mozzarella, egg, nutmeg, salt, and pepper in a large mixing bowl. Stir until well blended. Set aside.

6. To cook the noodles, bring 6 quarts salted water to a boil in a large pot. Add the oil, then add the noodles one at a time. Cook, stirring occasionally to prevent sticking, until the noodles are tender and pliable but not soft, 6 to 8 minutes.

7. Drain the noodles in a colander and rinse them with cold water to prevent sticking. Set aside.

8. To assemble the lasagne, preheat the oven to 375°F. Lightly oil a 9 × 13-inch baking dish.

9. Spread one-quarter (about 1 cup) of the tomato sauce over the bottom of the baking dish. Place a single layer of noodles over the sauce, using one-third of them and overlapping the edges slightly. (If they have stuck together in the colander, rinse them with cold water to release them from each other.) Spread half the cheese sauce (about 1½ cups) in an even layer over the noodles. Evenly space half the shrimp in a single layer on top of the cheese mixture. Top the shrimp with another quarter of the tomato sauce. Repeat the layering: noodles, cheese, shrimp, and tomato sauce.

10. Top with the remaining noodles, overlapping them by at least ½ inch and sealing the dish. Spread the remaining tomato sauce evenly over the top, reaching all the way to the edges and corners. Sprinkle evenly with the Parmigiano-Reggiano.

11. Bake for 50 minutes, or until the lasagne is bubbling and the Parmigiano-Reggiano is golden brown. If the cheese begins to brown too fast, cover the pan loosely with aluminum foil. Remove the pan from the oven and let the lasagne cool for at least 15 minutes before serving.

Lemon Shrimp

THIS IS A SWEET, sour, and salty Chinese dish, perfect as a foil to hotter fare such as Kung Pao Shrimp (page 102) or General Tsao's Shrimp (page 94), or delicious on its own. The shrimp are deep-fried, then coated with a thick lemon sauce. Serve with white or brown rice. **MAKES 4 SERVINGS**

FOR THE LEMON SAUCE

Grated zest of 1 lemon

⅔ cup fresh lemon juice, strained

¼ cup plus 2 tablespoons sugar

¼ cup canned or homemade chicken stock

2 tablespoons soy sauce

1 tablespoon cornstarch, dissolved in 1 tablespoon water

FOR THE SHRIMP

8 cups peanut oil

½ cup all-purpose flour

2 tablespoons cornstarch

1 teaspoon baking powder

1 teaspoon salt

⅔ cup water

1 teaspoon toasted sesame oil

1 pound medium shrimp (35 to 40 per pound), peeled and deveined

1. To prepare the Lemon Sauce, combine the lemon zest, lemon juice, sugar, stock, and soy sauce in a medium saucepan. Stir over medium heat, until the sugar is completely dissolved and the sauce comes to a boil, about 3 minutes. Remove from the heat, cover the pan, and set it aside.

2. To prepare the shrimp, pour the oil into a large saucepan at least 4 inches deep and 10 inches in diameter; the oil should be at least 1½ inches deep but reach no more than halfway up the sides of the pan. Alternatively, fill an electric deep fryer with oil according to the manufacturer's instructions. If you are using a pan, clip a deep-frying thermometer to the inside and place the pan over medium heat. Heat the oil to 375°F. Adjust the heat to maintain that temperature while you prepare the shrimp. If you're using an electric deep fryer, set the temperature control to 375°F.

3. Combine the flour, cornstarch, baking powder, and salt in a large mixing bowl. Whisk gently until well combined. Add the water and sesame oil and whisk until the batter is completely smooth.

4. Dip a shrimp into the batter until it is completely coated, and let any excess batter drip off. Gently slide the shrimp into the hot oil. Repeat with the remaining shrimp, dipping and frying only as many shrimp at a time as will fit in the pan in one layer without crowding. Fry the shrimp until lightly golden, 1 to 2 minutes, turning occasionally with tongs. Remove the shrimp from the oil, and drain on paper towels.

5. To finish the dish, place the lemon sauce over medium-high heat and bring it back to a boil. Add the cornstarch mixture, stirring constantly until the sauce thickens, about 30 seconds.

6. Place the shrimp on a large platter and pour the sauce over the top. Serve immediately.

HERBED LEMON SHRIMP Add 1 tablespoon chopped parsley and 2 teaspoons chopped tarragon with the lemon juice.

LEMON SHRIMP AND MUSHROOMS Reduce the shrimp to ½ pound. Dip ½ pound whole button mushrooms, cleaned, in the batter and fry them as you do the shrimp.

LEMON SHRIMP AND SCALLOPS Reduce the shrimp to ½ pound. Dip ½ pound sea scallops in the batter and fry them as you do the shrimp.

SAVORY LEMON SHRIMP Add 1 tablespoon hoi sin sauce and 1 teaspoon oyster sauce with the lemon juice.

SPICY LEMON SHRIMP Add 8 dried red Asian chiles with the lemon juice.

SZECHWAN LEMON SHRIMP Add 6 dried red Asian chiles and 2 tablespoons Szechwan peppercorns with the lemon juice.

Shrimp Lo Mein

A FAVORITE IN SHANGHAI, Lo Mein is a savory stir-fried dish with round thin noodles, sometimes called *Shanghai noodles*. You can find them in the Asian section of some supermarkets, in Chinese markets, and through outlets listed in the Source Guide, page 239. In a pinch, substitute spaghetti or Japanese udon noodles. Serve lo mein hot or at room temperature. **MAKES 4 TO 6 SERVINGS**

8 ounces dried Shanghai noodles or spaghetti

1 cup canned or homemade chicken stock

¼ cup soy sauce

3 tablespoons black vinegar or Worcestershire sauce

2 tablespoons dry sherry

1 teaspoon toasted sesame oil

1 tablespoon sugar

2 teaspoons cornstarch

3 tablespoons peanut oil, or 1 tablespoon peanut oil if using precooked shrimp

¾ pound small shrimp (more than 55 per pound), peeled and deveined, or precooked coldwater (or baby) shrimp, thawed

2 tablespoons minced ginger

2 garlic cloves, minced

6 scallions, cut into 1-inch pieces

One 8-ounce can sliced water chestnuts, drained

One 15-ounce can straw mushrooms, drained

1. Bring 2 quarts salted water to a boil in a large pot over high heat. Add the noodles and cook according to the package instructions, usually 5 to 7 minutes. Drain the noodles in a colander and rinse them with cold water to prevent sticking. Set aside.

2. Combine the chicken stock, soy sauce, vinegar, sherry, sesame oil, sugar, and cornstarch in a medium bowl, stirring until the cornstarch is completely dissolved. Set aside.

3. Heat a large wok or skillet (preferably nonstick) over high heat until hot but not smoking. Add 2 tablespoons of the peanut oil and swirl it around to coat the wok. Add the raw shrimp, if using, and stir and toss them until pink and firm, about 2 minutes. Remove from the wok and set them aside.

4. Add 1 tablespoon peanut oil to the wok and place it back over high heat. Add the ginger, garlic, and scallions and toss and stir for 20 seconds. Add the water chestnuts and mushrooms and toss and stir for another 10 seconds. Add the noodles and toss until all is well incorporated.

5. Stir the chicken stock mixture to reincorporate the cornstarch, and pour it into the wok. Stir until the mixture comes to a boil and thickens, about 30 seconds. Add the shrimp. Toss and stir until all the ingredients are well coated with the bubbling sauce.

6. Serve hot or at room temperature.

SESAME SHRIMP LO MEIN Add ¼ cup white sesame seeds with the ginger. Add 2 teaspoons toasted sesame oil with the cooked shrimp.

SHRIMP LO MEIN WITH BLACK BEANS Reduce the soy sauce to 3 tablespoons. Add ¼ cup dried salted Chinese black beans, slightly crushed with the side of a chef's knife or the bottom of a pot, with the cooked shrimp.

SPICY SHRIMP LO MEIN Add 1 teaspoon chili oil, or more to taste, with the cooked shrimp.

Shrimp Maki

IN NORTH AMERICA, sushi comes as a piece of fish either on seasoned rice (*nigiri* in Japanese— see Shrimp Sushi, page 190) or in a roll (*hosomaki*, thin rolls, and *futomaki*, thick rolls). To make maki, or rolls, you'll need a sushi mat (see page 17), sushi rice, nori, and a large wide shallow dish for cooling the rice. Once you get the hang of it, invite your family and friends to roll their own shrimp maki, with individual sushi mats. **MAKES 30 PIECES**

FOR THE MAKI

1 pound medium shrimp (35 to 40 per pound), peeled and deveined, or precooked cocktail shrimp, thawed and peeled

½ cup water

¾ cup rice wine vinegar

5 cups just-cooked short-grain sushi rice (about 2½ cups raw rice, cooked according to the package directions), still hot

1½ teaspoons sugar

½ teaspoon salt

5 nori sheets

ON THE SIDE

¼ cup wasabi paste

½ cup soy sauce

½ cup pickled sliced ginger

Thirty 6-inch bamboo skewers (if starting with raw shrimp)

1. To prepare the shrimp, if you're using raw shrimp, thread 1 shrimp onto each skewer, starting at the thick end of the shrimp, pushing the skewer through the shrimp the long way until it comes out of the tail. (This will keep the shrimp from curling up while it cooks.) If you're using precooked shrimp, omit this step and skip to step 4.

2. Bring 3 quarts salted water to a boil in large saucepan set over high heat. Fill a large bowl halfway with ice water and set it aside. Add as many shrimp skewers to the saucepan as will fit at a time while allowing the shrimp to be submerged. Cook until the shrimp are pink and firm, about 2 minutes. Using tongs, transfer the shrimp to the ice water. Allow all to cool.

3. Drain the shrimp and remove from the skewers. Set aside.

4. To prepare the maki, combine the water and ½ cup of the vinegar in a small bowl. Set aside.

5. In a small bowl or jar, mix together the remaining ¼ cup vinegar, the sugar, and salt, stirring or shaking the jar until the sugar and salt are completely dissolved. Set it aside.

6. Spread the hot rice in a wide shallow pan (such as an 11 × 17-inch lipped baking sheet or a 12- to 15-inch shallow round casserole).

7. Sprinkle the sugared vinegar evenly over the rice. Using a rubber spatula, gently toss the rice, flattening it out after each toss. This will evenly distribute the flavored vinegar while cooling the rice. Be sure to reach the corners and include all the rice in your tossing and spreading. If possible, use your other hand to fan the rice with a magazine or hand-held fan at the same time. The rice should be tossed and spread until it is just cool to the touch and slightly sticky.

8. Place a bamboo rolling mat on your work surface with one of the short ends nearest you. Lay a nori sheet on the rolling mat, facing in the same direction. Moisten your fingers in the prepared water and vinegar mixture, and use your fingers to spread 1 cup of the rice evenly over the nori. Use your index finger to spread about 1½ teaspoons of the wasabi paste evenly across the center of the rice, from right to left. Place 6 cooked shrimp in a row, covering the line of wasabi. Switch the direction of each shrimp so that the thinner tails overlap the thicker ends, and overlap them as necessary to keep all 6 shrimp on the rice.

9. Place your fingers on the shrimp to hold them down as you start to roll up the maki roll, and use your thumbs to lift the edge of the bamboo mat closest to you. Gently but firmly fold the entire roll over, sealing it. Gently squeeze the mat to create a compact cylinder. Remove the maki from the mat and set aside. Repeat with the remaining nori sheets, rice, and shrimp.

10. Using a wet knife, slice each maki into 6 pieces. Serve immediately, with wasabi paste, the soy sauce, and pickled ginger on the side. (You can also make a soy sauce paste by mixing 5 parts soy sauce to 1 part wasabi paste, or more to taste.)

Taking care not to make the maki too big, place other ingredients alongside the shrimp before you roll the maki.

Bean sprouts • Minced ginger • Paper-thin carrot slices (use a vegetable peeler) • Paper-thin cucumber slices • Picked jalapeño rings • Radish sprouts • Thinly sliced peeled Hass avocado • Thinly sliced preserved daikon radish

Shrimp Mole

MOLE (FROM A NAHUATL WORD MEANING *"JUMBLED"*) is a stewed sauce of chiles, a favorite of the Aztecs, still served as an accompaniment to grilled or roasted meats. This mole recipe uses chocolate, probably not the most authentic version of the dish, but now surely the most famous. Chocolate gives the sauce a sweetened bitterness that's impossible to match. Mole takes quite a long time to prepare, but this recipe makes about 6 cups more than you need, so you can freeze the extra in small containers to use as a sauce, thinned out with chicken stock, for grilled steaks, chicken, or fish—or for more Shrimp Mole at a later date. There really are no variations here, but plenty of different suggestions for serving. **MAKES 4 SERVINGS**

1½ cups Mole (recipe follows)

¼ cup canned or homemade chicken stock, plus additional for thinning the mole if desired

1½ pounds large shrimp (12 to 15 per pound), peeled and deveined

2 tablespoons vegetable oil

2 teaspoons pure chile powder

1 teaspoon ground cumin

1 teaspoon minced oregano

½ teaspoon salt

Tortillas and chopped lettuce as garnish

1. Combine the mole and chicken stock in a small saucepan, place it over low heat, and stir until the mole is smooth and the mixture comes to a slow simmer. The mole should be the consistency of a thick spaghetti sauce. If it is too thick, thin it out with more stock, 1 tablespoon at a time, until the desired consistency is reached. Remove the pan from the heat and cover it to keep warm while you prepare the shrimp.

2. Preheat the broiler.

3. In a large bowl, combine the shrimp, oil, chile powder, cumin, oregano, and salt. Toss until the spices are evenly distributed and the shrimp are well coated.

4. Place the shrimp in a single layer on the broiler pan or a lipped cookie sheet. Broil for 2 minutes, then turn the shrimp with tongs or a spatula and broil for 2 more minutes, or until pink and firm.

5. Divide the shrimp among four plates, and spoon about ⅓ cup mole over the shrimp on each plate. Serve immediately with tortillas and chopped lettuce as a garnish.

Mole

MAKES ABOUT 2 QUARTS

8 ancho chiles

8 mulato chiles

8 pasilla chiles

8 dried figs

5 medium plum tomatoes

6 medium tomatillos, husks removed and rinsed

¼ cup white sesame seeds

⅓ cup unsalted, shelled raw pepitas (also called pumpkin seeds)

⅓ cup sliced almonds

2 teaspoons peanut oil

1 ripe plantain, peeled and cut into ½-inch rounds

6 garlic cloves

4 cups canned or homemade chicken stock

3 tablespoons vegetable shortening or lard

5 teaspoons ground cinnamon

2 teaspoons salt

½ teaspoon freshly ground black pepper

½ teaspoon ground allspice

½ teaspoon ground cloves

2 ounces semisweet chocolate, finely chopped

2 ounces unsweetened chocolate, finely chopped

2 teaspoons honey

1. Preheat the oven to 400°F.

2. Split the anchos, mulatos, and pasillas open and remove the stems and seeds. Tear or break the chiles into large pieces and place them on a baking sheet in one layer. Bake them for 3 to 5 minutes, or until they give off a sweet, peppery aroma.

3. Transfer the chile pieces to a large bowl and cover them with boiling water. You may need to place a small plate on top to ensure that the chiles stay fully submerged. Set aside.

4. Place the figs in a small bowl and cover with boiling water. Set aside.

5. Preheat the broiler.

6. Place the plum tomatoes and tomatillos on the broiler pan or a baking sheet and place them under the broiler to char them, about 5 minutes. Turn them as necessary to ensure that they are blackened all over. Transfer to a large bowl and set aside.

7. Place the sesame seeds in a medium skillet over medium heat and toast, stirring and tossing constantly, until they give off a slightly nutty aroma and begin to turn light brown, about 3 minutes. Add the sesame seeds to the tomatoes.

8. Place the skillet back over medium heat and add the pepitas. Stir and toss until the seeds pop and begin to brown lightly, about 2 minutes. Add the pepitas to the tomatoes.

9. Place the skillet back on the heat and add the almonds. Stir and toss until the almonds give off a nutty aroma and begin to brown lightly, about 2 minutes. Transfer to the bowl of tomatoes.

10. Heat the peanut oil in the same skillet over medium heat. When the oil is hot, add the plantain slices in one layer and cook until they are lightly browned on the bottom, about 2 minutes. Turn the plantain slices over, add the garlic, and cook until the plantains are tender and lightly browned on the second side, about 2 minutes more. Transfer the plantains and garlic to the bowl of tomatoes.

11. Drain the chiles and figs and add them to the bowl. Stir all the ingredients until they are well combined. Purée the ingredients in a food processor or blender, adding just enough stock so the mixture blends easily. You may need to purée the ingredients in batches, using only as much stock as necessary for each batch.

12. Melt the shortening in a deep pot or a large Dutch oven over medium heat. Add the purée, along with any remaining stock, the cinnamon, salt, black pepper, allspice, and cloves. Stir until the stock and spices are incorporated and the mixture comes to a simmer. Reduce the heat to low. Add the chocolate and honey and cook, stirring constantly, for 15 minutes.

13. The mole will be thick and slightly grainy from bits of nuts and sesame seed hulls that did not completely purée. If desired, strain the sauce through a sieve, rubbing and pushing it through with the back of a wooden spoon or heavy-duty rubber spatula. (The mole will keep for up to 2 weeks tightly covered in the refrigerator, or up to 6 months in the freezer. It's best to freeze the mole in 1-cup containers, so that you don't need to defrost more than you need. Before serving, thin the mole with additional stock until it is the consistency of a thick spaghetti sauce.)

SERVING SUGGESTIONS

Shrimp Mole is great eaten with or inside warmed flour or corn tortillas. You can accompany it with:

Black beans or refried beans • Purchased guacamole • Rice • Shredded Monterey Jack • Sliced Hass avocados • Sliced mango • Sliced pickled jalapeños • Sliced plums • Sliced red onions • Sliced tomatoes

Shrimp Mousse with Hollandaise

A HOT, CREAMY SHRIMP MOUSSE is an elegant addition to any buffet, especially when there's hollandaise sauce on the side. Serve the mousse with toast points, crackers, or crusty bread. You can also make it ahead and serve it cold or at room temperature, with a green salad or steamed vegetables. **MAKES 8 TO 10 SERVINGS**

1½ pounds small shrimp (more than 55 per pound), peeled and deveined

1 teaspoon salt

½ teaspoon ground white pepper

½ teaspoon grated nutmeg

2 cups heavy cream

Unsalted butter for the baking dish and foil

Easy Blender Hollandaise Sauce (recipe follows)

1. Preheat the oven to 350°F. Butter a 9 × 5-inch loaf pan and set it aside. Butter a piece of aluminum foil long enough to cover the pan and set the foil aside.

2. Combine the shrimp, salt, pepper, and nutmeg in the food processor and process until the shrimp are very finely chopped but not puréed, about 20 seconds. Scrape down the bowl.

3. With the motor running, slowly pour the cream through the feed tube, processing until the shrimp has absorbed all the cream and the mixture is smooth.

4. Spoon the shrimp mixture into the prepared pan. Pack it down tightly so that there are no air spaces. Cover the loaf pan with the foil, buttered side down.

5. Place the loaf pan in a deep 9 × 13-inch baking pan and fill the baking pan with hot water to reach halfway up the sides of the loaf pan. Bake for 35 minutes, or until the mousse is pink and the edges have started to pull away from the sides of the loaf pan.

6. Remove the loaf pan from the larger pan and drain off any liquid that has accumulated around the mousse. Unmold the mousse onto a serving platter. Serve hot, warm, or cold, with the hollandaise sauce on the side.

Easy Blender Hollandaise Sauce

3 large egg yolks, at room
   temperature

2 tablespoons boiling water

½ pound unsalted butter (2
   sticks), melted

1 tablespoon Dijon mustard

2 tablespoons fresh lemon juice

½ teaspoon salt, or more to taste

½ teaspoon freshly ground black
   pepper, or more to taste

Place the egg yolks in a blender. Cover the blender, turn it on low, and pour the boiling water through the hole in the lid. With the blender still running, drizzle in the melted butter in a thin stream. Blend until the sauce is thickened and pale yellow. Add the mustard, lemon juice, salt, and pepper; blend until smooth. Check for seasoning, and add more salt and pepper, if desired. Serve immediately.

HERBED SHRIMP MOUSSE Add 1 tablespoon minced parsley and 2 teaspoons minced tarragon to the shrimp in the food processor.

SHRIMP TERRINE Pour half the shrimp mixture into the prepared loaf pan. Arrange a layer of vegetables such as asparagus, baby carrots, or thinly sliced zucchini over the mousse. Top with the remaining mousse. Bake as directed.

Shrimp Mussel and Clam Stew

THIS HEARTY STEW GETS its depth from beer. Use a premium-quality dark or light beer, preferably one with plenty of barley and hops. (Don't use a fruit-flavored beer.) Since mussels and clams don't keep well, make this stew the day you buy them. For storage tips for mussels and clams, see page 9. Have plenty of crunchy bread on hand to sop up every drop of the broth. **MAKES 4 TO 6 SERVINGS**

2 tablespoons olive oil

½-pound piece pancetta, diced, or Canadian bacon, diced

1 large onion, cut into ¼-inch rings

3 celery stalks, cut into 1-inch pieces

4 medium tomatoes, seeded and finely chopped

½ cup packed shredded basil

2 teaspoons minced thyme

½ teaspoon red pepper flakes

One 12-ounce bottle beer

2 cups fish stock or clam juice

1 pound large shrimp (12 to 15 per pound), peeled and deveined

1 pound mussels, scrubbed and debearded

12 medium clams (such as cherrystone or Pacific littleneck), scrubbed

1½ teaspoons salt

½ teaspoon freshly ground black pepper, or more to taste

¼ cup finely chopped parsley

1. Heat the oil in a large soup pot over medium heat. Add the pancetta and cook, stirring often, until lightly browned, about 3 minutes. Add the onion and celery and cook, stirring often, until the onion is softened and translucent, about 4 minutes.

2. Add the tomatoes, basil, thyme, and red pepper flakes. Raise the heat to high and cook for 1 minute. Pour the beer and stock into the pot and bring to a boil. Lower the heat to medium and add the shrimp, mussels, and clams. Toss the shellfish gently until they and the vegetables are well combined. Cover and cook for 6 minutes, or until the shrimp are pink and firm and the clams and mussels have opened.

3. Add the salt, pepper, and parsley. Serve immediately.

BELGIAN SHRIMP AND MUSSEL STEW Omit the basil and clams, and use 2 pounds mussels, scrubbed and debearded. Add 1 tablespoon caraway seeds with the tomatoes.

FRENCH SHRIMP, MUSSEL, AND CLAM STEW Omit the beer. Substitute 1 tablespoon minced tarragon for the basil, and add 2 cups red wine with the stock.

JAPANESE SHRIMP, MUSSEL, AND CLAM STEW Omit the basil and beer. Add 2 cups sake and 1 tablespoon minced ginger with the stock.

SHRIMP AND COCKLES STEW Omit the clams and mussels. Add 2 pounds New Zealand cockles, scrubbed, with the shrimp.

SPANISH SHRIMP, MUSSEL, AND CLAM STEW Omit the basil. Add ¼ teaspoon crumbled saffron threads and 2 garlic cloves, minced, with the tomatoes. Add 1 cup fresh or frozen peas with the shellfish. Drizzle 1 teaspoon olive oil, or more to taste, over each serving of stew.

Shrimp Newburg

IN 1876, when the United States was reeling from the economic aftershocks of the Civil War, Delmonico's, that Manhattan institution of the good life, wanted to make a dish that could take away the nation's woes. *Voilà*, Lobster Newburg: an opulent seafood concoction in a rich cream sauce. Traditionally, Newburgs are served over buttered toast points. You might want to try this one over wide egg noodles, alongside white rice, or in hollowed-out bread bowls. **MAKES 4 SERVINGS**

4 tablespoons (½ stick) unsalted butter, or 2 tablespoons unsalted butter, if using precooked shrimp

1 pound medium shrimp (35 to 40 per pound), peeled and deveined, or precooked cocktail shrimp, thawed and peeled

2 tablespoons all-purpose flour

2 cups half-and-half

2 large egg yolks

3 tablespoons dry sherry

¼ teaspoon grated nutmeg

1 teaspoon salt

Freshly ground black pepper to taste

1. If using raw shrimp, melt 2 tablespoons of the butter in a medium skillet over medium heat. Add the shrimp and cook, stirring often, until pink and firm, about 3 minutes. Cover the skillet to keep the shrimp warm and set it aside while you prepare the sauce. If using precooked shrimp, omit this step.

2. Melt 2 tablespoons butter in a large heavy saucepan over medium heat. Add the flour and whisk until it is completely incorporated. Continue to cook and whisk for 2 minutes, instantly lowering the heat to low if the mixture starts to brown, or simply removing the pan from the heat.

3. Reduce the heat to low and slowly whisk in the half-and-half. Cook, whisking constantly, until the sauce is thickened and smooth, about 3 minutes. Reduce the heat so that the sauce barely bubbles.

4. Place the egg yolks in a medium bowl and beat them lightly with a fork or a small whisk. Slowly beat 2 tablespoons of the hot cream sauce into the eggs. (This will raise the temperature of the egg yolks without scrambling them.) Whisking constantly, add the warmed egg yolks back into the pan of sauce, making sure the sauce does not come back to a boil. Quickly whisk in the sherry, nutmeg, salt, and pepper.

5. Add the shrimp to the sauce and heat, without boiling, until they are warmed through. Serve immediately.

PORTUGUESE SHRIMP NEWBURG Substitute dry Madeira for the sherry, and add 3 dashes Tabasco sauce, or more to taste, with it.

SHRIMP AND CRAB NEWBURG Reduce the shrimp to ½ pound. Add ½ pound lump crabmeat, picked over for shells and cartilage, with the sherry.

SHRIMP AND LOBSTER NEWBURG Reduce the shrimp to ½ pound. Stir ½ pound cooked lobster, chopped, into the sauce when you add the cooked shrimp.

SHRIMP AND OYSTER NEWBURG Add ½ cup shucked oysters (about 6) after you add the egg yolk mixture to the sauce.

SHRIMP AND PEA NEWBURG Add one 10-ounce package frozen peas, thawed, after you add the egg yolk mixture to the sauce.

SHRIMP AND SCALLOP NEWBURG Reduce the shrimp to ½ pound. Cook ½ pound sea scallops, cut in half, with the raw shrimp.

Shrimp Noodle Soup

IN TOKYO'S NOODLE SHOPS, businessmen and construction workers sit side by side, slurping thick noodles out of bowls of savory steaming broth. This recipe simplifies the soup, making it an easy lunch or dinner for you and yours, but the variations allow you to experiment with more exotic tastes, deeper flavors, more extraordinary textures. **MAKES 6 SERVINGS**

2 teaspoons vegetable oil

1 garlic clove, minced

1 tablespoon minced ginger

12 shiitake mushrooms, stems removed and discarded, caps cleaned and thinly sliced

1 cup snow peas

1 small Napa cabbage, shredded

¼ cup dry sake

1 tablespoon soy sauce

6 cups fish stock or 4 cups vegetable stock plus 2 cups clam juice

1 pound small shrimp (more than 55 per pound), peeled and deveined, or precooked cold-water (or baby) shrimp, thawed

½ pound udon noodles or flat egg noodles, cooked according to the package directions, drained and rinsed

2 scallions, cut into 1-inch pieces

Salt and freshly ground black pepper to taste

1. Heat the oil in a large soup pot over medium heat. Add the garlic, ginger, and mushrooms; cook, stirring constantly, for 30 seconds. Add the snow peas and cabbage and toss them in the oil for 10 seconds.

2. Add the sake and cook for 2 minutes, stirring often. The cabbage will wilt, giving off much of its liquid as the steam from the sake rises. Add the soy sauce and stock; bring to a simmer. Reduce the heat to medium-low, cover the pot, and cook for 10 minutes.

3. Raise the heat to medium. Add the shrimp and cook until pink and firm, about 3 minutes. If using precooked shrimp, warm only 1 minute.

4. Add the noodles and scallions and cook for 2 minutes, or until the soup returns to a simmer and the noodles are heated through. Season with salt and pepper. Serve immediately.

CHINESE SHRIMP NOODLE SOUP Omit the soy sauce. Add 1 tablespoon hoi sin sauce, 2 teaspoons black vinegar, and 1 teaspoon oyster sauce with the stock.

EGG DROP SHRIMP NOODLE SOUP Once the soup is cooked and simmering, slowly drizzle in 1 large beaten egg, stirring constantly until the egg cooks in ribbons.

HOT AND SAVORY SHRIMP NOODLE SOUP Omit the soy sauce. Add 2 teaspoons fish sauce and 1 teaspoon chili oil with the stock.

HOT-AND-SOUR SHRIMP NOODLE SOUP Add 2 tablespoons rice wine vinegar and 1 teaspoon red pepper flakes with the soy sauce.

SHRIMP AND FISH NOODLE SOUP Reduce the shrimp to ½ pound. Add ½ pound fish fillets, cut into 1-inch cubes and picked over for bones, with the shrimp.

SHRIMP AND SCALLOP NOODLE SOUP Reduce the shrimp to ½ pound. Add ½ pound sea scallops, cut in half, with the shrimp.

WAKAME SHRIMP NOODLE SOUP Add ¼ cup dried wakame (edible seaweed, available in Japanese markets and health food stores) with the soy sauce. Increase the stock to 8 cups.

Shrimp Pad Thai

P AD THAI IS A sweet, salty, and spicy mix of noodles, bean sprouts, scrambled eggs, and shrimp. It's the most familiar Thai dish in North America. Milky white rice noodles (sometimes called *rice stick noodles*) are sold in Asian markets or in the Asian section of some supermarkets. Prepare the rest of the ingredients while the noodles are soaking because the dish comes together quickly. Serve Pad Thai hot, right out of the wok, with lime wedges and a bottle of chili oil on the side, so your friends and family can spice the dish to their tastes. **MAKES 4 SERVINGS**

7 ounces dried rice (or rice stick) noodles, about ¼ inch thick

¼ cup packed brown sugar

6 tablespoons fish sauce

¼ cup hoi sin sauce

¼ cup canned or homemade chicken stock

2 tablespoons plus 2 teaspoons peanut oil

2 large eggs, beaten until frothy

4 scallions, cut into 1-inch pieces

3 garlic cloves, minced

¾ pound medium shrimp (35 to 40 per pound), peeled and deveined

1 cup bean sprouts

¼ cup unsalted peanuts

¼ cup finely chopped cilantro

½ teaspoon chili oil

Juice of 1 lime

1. Soak the rice noodles in warm water for 10 minutes.

2. Bring 2 quarts salted water to a boil in a large pan set over high heat. Lift the noodles from the warm water and drop them into the boiling water. Cook for 2 minutes. Drain the noodles in a colander and rinse them under cold water to keep them from sticking. Set aside.

3. Combine the brown sugar, fish sauce, hoi sin sauce, and stock in a small bowl. Stir until the sugar is completely dissolved. Set aside.

4. Heat a large wok or skillet (preferably nonstick) over medium heat until it is hot but not smoking. Add 2 teaspoons of the peanut oil and swirl it around to coat the pan. Add the beaten eggs and cook, stirring occasionally, to scramble them just until they are set, about 1 minute. Transfer the eggs to a plate and set aside.

5. Add the remaining 2 tablespoons oil to the wok and raise the heat to high. When the oil is hot, add the scallions and garlic and cook, stirring constantly, for 15 seconds. Add the shrimp and stir and toss until pink and firm, about 3 minutes.

6. Lower the heat to medium-high and add the bean sprouts, noodles, scrambled eggs, and sauce mixture. Toss and stir for 10 seconds, then raise the heat to high. When the sauce comes to a boil, add the nuts, cilantro, and chili oil. Toss and stir until well combined.

7. Transfer the pad Thai to a serving bowl and sprinkle with lime juice. Serve immediately.

BANGKOK-STYLE SHRIMP PAD THAI Omit the brown sugar, and reduce the fish sauce to ¼ cup. Add 2 tablespoons rice wine vinegar and 3 tablespoons tamarind paste (available in Indian and some Asian markets) to the fish sauce.

CARROT AND SHRIMP PAD THAI Omit the bean sprouts. Add 1 cup shredded carrots with the cooked noodles.

SHRIMP AND SCALLOP PAD THAI Reduce the shrimp to ½ pound. Add ½ pound sea scallops, cut in half, with the shrimp.

SHRIMP AND TOFU PAD THAI Reduce the shrimp to ½ pound. Add ½ pound firm tofu, diced into 1-inch cubes, with the bean sprouts.

Shrimp Paella

THE WORD *PAELLA* ACTUALLY refers to the flat, wide two-handled pan you'll need to create this saffron-scented Spanish delicacy of seafood, vegetables, and seasoned short-grained rice. Spanish Bajia rice is preferred (available in some Latin American and specialty markets), but you can substitute Arborio, which is widely available in supermarkets. Although some of the cooking is last minute, Shrimp Paella will make your next dinner party an elegant affair. **MAKES ABOUT 6 SERVINGS**

2 pounds large shrimp (12 to 15 per pound), peeled and deveined, shells reserved

6 cups fish stock or 3 cups vegetable stock plus 3 cups clam juice

¼ teaspoon saffron threads

3 tablespoons olive oil

1 medium onion, minced

3 garlic cloves, minced

1 bay leaf

1 tablespoon minced thyme

1 tablespoon chopped rosemary

1 teaspoon sweet paprika

2 medium tomatoes, chopped

2 cups Spanish Bajia rice or Italian Arborio rice

1 teaspoon salt, or more to taste

1 cup fresh or thawed frozen peas

Freshly ground black pepper to taste

1. Combine the shrimp shells and stock in a large pot. Crumble in the saffron. Place the pot over high heat and bring to a boil. Cover and simmer for 15 minutes. Using a fine-mesh strainer, strain the stock into a large saucepan. Place the pan over medium heat and bring the stock back to simmer. Adjust the heat so the stock barely bubbles.

2. Preheat the oven to 400°F.

3. Place the oil in a 14- or 16-inch paella pan and heat over low heat for 1 minute. Add the onion, garlic, bay leaf, thyme, and rosemary. Cook, stirring often, until the onion is lightly browned and very soft, about 15 minutes.

4. Add the paprika and tomatoes, raise the heat to medium, and cook until the tomatoes give off their liquid and the juices are reduced to a thin glaze, about 5 minutes.

5. Add the rice and stir until it is well mixed with the tomatoes and onions. Add the hot stock and the salt and reduce the heat to low. Simmer the rice slowly—just one or two bubbles at a time—uncovered, stirring frequently, for 15 minutes. Should the pan become too dry, lower the heat and add water 1 tablespoon at a time until the rice is again moistened. (You do not want to make a soup.)

6. Stir the peas into the rice. Push the shrimp into the rice, distributing it evenly in one layer. Again, if the rice is dry or sticking to the pan, add 1 to 2 tablespoons water.

7. Place the pan in the oven and bake for 10 minutes. Remove the pan from the oven and cover loosely with foil. Set aside for 10 minutes.

8. Discard the bay leaf and serve the paella hot or at room temperature.

SHRIMP AND CLAM PAELLA Before the paella goes in the oven, top it with 16 medium clams (such as cherrystone or Pacific littleneck), scrubbed. If the clams have not opened after 10 minutes, bake for an additional 5 minutes.

SHRIMP AND DUCK CONFIT PAELLA Pull the meat off 2 legs of duck confit; you should have about ⅔ cup meat. Shred it and push the meat into the rice mixture with the shrimp. Duck confit is available at many gourmet markets.

SHRIMP AND LOBSTER PAELLA Before the paella goes in the oven, lay 4 frozen lobster tails, thawed and split lengthwise in half, or 4 fresh tails, split lengthwise in half, over the dish. Increase the baking time to 15 minutes.

SHRIMP AND MUSSELS PAELLA Before the paella goes in the oven, top it with 2 pounds mussels, scrubbed and debearded. If the mussels have not opened after 10 minutes, bake for an additional 5 minutes. Discard any unopened mussels.

SHRIMP AND SAUSAGE PAELLA Reduce the shrimp to 1¼ pounds. Add 1 pound cooked spicy sausage (such as andouille, chorizo, or Italian pork sausage), cut into 1-inch pieces, with the shrimp.

SHRIMP AND VEGETABLE PAELLA Skip making the stock, and use 1½ quarts Court Bouillon (page 43). Add 1 cup sliced carrots, 1 cup sliced parsnips, and 1 bell pepper, cored, seeded, and coarsely chopped, with the tomatoes.

Shrimp Paprikash

A HEARTY HUNGARIAN STEW traditionally prepared with chicken, this dish was first popularized in the 1906 *Boston Cooking-School Cook Book*. Depending on the version, the dish, which is thickened with paprika and sour cream, can be quite spicy. Our basic recipe here, however, is mild and sweet, more in keeping with the dish's current interpretation. **MAKES 4 TO 6 SERVINGS**

3 tablespoons unsalted butter, or 1 tablespoon unsalted butter, if using precooled shrimp

1½ pounds medium shrimp (35 to 40 per pound), peeled and deveined, or precooked cocktail shrimp, thawed and peeled

1 large onion, finely chopped

1½ tablespoons sweet paprika

¾ cup beef stock or vegetable stock

1 cup sour cream (regular or low-fat, but not fat-free)

Salt and freshly ground black pepper to taste

12 ounces egg noodles, cooked according to the package directions, drained, rinsed, covered, and kept warm

2 tablespoon finely chopped parsley

1. If using raw shrimp, melt 2 tablespoons of the butter in a large skillet set over medium heat. Add the shrimp and cook, stirring often, until firm and pink, 3 to 5 minutes. Transfer the shrimp to a bowl and set aside. If you're using precooked shrimp, skip this step.

2. Add 1 tablespoon butter to the skillet and set it over low heat. Add the onion and cook, stirring often, until it is browned, softened, and fragrant, about 15 minutes.

3. Stir in the paprika and cook for 10 seconds. Add the stock, raise the heat to medium, and bring to a slow simmer.

4. Add the shrimp to the skillet, along with the sour cream, and stir until well combined with the paprika mixture. Heat just until the first bubble appears in the sauce, then remove the pan from the heat. Do not let the sauce boil, or the sour cream will curdle. Season with salt and pepper.

5. Place the noodles on a large platter and spoon the paprikash over them. Sprinkle with the parsley and serve immediately.

GARLIC SHRIMP PAPRIKASH Add 3 garlic cloves, minced, with the onion.

HEARTY SHRIMP PAPRIKASH Reduce the butter to 1 tablespoon. Fry 5 slices bacon in the butter in a large skillet over medium heat. Remove the bacon and cook the paprikash in the drippings. Coarsely chop the cooked bacon and sprinkle it over the finished dish.

HOT HUNGARIAN SHRIMP PAPRIKASH Use 1 teaspoon hot Hungarian paprika, or more to taste, instead of the sweet paprika.

SHRIMP AND EGG PAPRIKASH Reduce the shrimp to 1 pound. Add 3 hard-boiled eggs, coarsely chopped, with the sour cream.

SHRIMP AND MUSHROOM PAPRIKASH Add 1 pound button or cremini mushrooms, cleaned and thinly sliced, to the onions after 10 minutes. Cook until the mushrooms have given off their juices and the pan is nearly dry.

Shrimp Parmesan

SHRIMP PARMESAN, like most Italian-American "classics," is a heavier dish than its counterparts in Italy; fried shrimp are baked in a thick tomato sauce, topped with cheese—hardly frugal peasant fare. Shrimp Parmesan is best when hot, while the coating on the shrimp is still crisp. **MAKES 4 SERVINGS**

FOR THE TOMATO SAUCE

2 tablespoons olive oil

1 medium onion, minced

4 garlic cloves, minced

1 tablespoon minced oregano

2 teaspoons chopped basil

1 teaspoon minced thyme

¼ teaspoon red pepper flakes

½ cup sweet vermouth

1 bay leaf

One 28-ounce can crushed tomatoes

1 teaspoon salt

Freshly ground black pepper to taste

1½ pounds large shrimp (12 to 15 per pound), peeled, leaving the final segment of the tail shell intact, and deveined

2 cups shredded mozzarella, (about 8 ounces)

½ cup freshly grated Parmigiano-Reggiano (about 2 ounces)

2 large egg whites, lightly beaten with a fork until frothy

3 cups plain dry bread crumbs

3 tablespoons olive oil, or more as needed

1. To prepare the tomato sauce, heat the oil in a large saucepan over medium heat. Add the onion and garlic; cook, stirring often, until softened and fragrant, about 5 minutes.

2. Add the oregano, basil, thyme, and red pepper flakes and stir for 10 seconds, then add the vermouth. Cook until the liquid is almost evaporated.

3. Add the bay leaf and tomatoes, with their juices, and stir until well combined. Bring the sauce to a simmer, then reduce the heat to low, cover the pan, and cook, stirring once or twice, for 10 minutes. Uncover the pan and cook for another 10 minutes, stirring often. The sauce should have the consistency of a fairly thick spaghetti sauce. Stir in the salt and pepper. Discard the bay leaf. Remove the pan from the heat and set it aside while you prepare the shrimp. (The sauce can be prepared up to to 2 days in advance and kept tightly covered in the refrigerator. Bring to room temperature before proceeding.)

4. To butterfly the shrimp, begin at the neck end of each and make a long slice with a paring knife down the back of the shrimp (opposite where the little legs were), about two-thirds of the way through, stopping just before the tail segment. (You do not want to cut the shrimp in half.) Gently open the slit with your fingers, remove any remaining parts of the vein, and flatten the shrimp by pressing it cut side down onto the work surface. Set the shrimp aside.

5. Preheat the oven to 500°F.

6. Combine the mozzarella and Parmigiano-Reggiano in a medium bowl, tossing well to mix. Set aside.

7. One at a time, open the shrimp flat and dip them into the beaten egg whites until well coated, then dip in the bread crumbs, covering them on all sides.

8. Pour the olive oil into a large skillet (preferably nonstick) and set it over medium heat. When the oil is hot and rippling, add as many shrimp as will fit in one layer without crowding and cook until they are lightly browned on the bottom, about 1 minute. Turn them over and cook for 1 more minute, or until they are lightly browned on both sides. Remove the shrimp from the skillet and fry the remaining shrimp, adding more olive oil to the skillet if necessary.

9. Spoon ½ cup of the tomato sauce into a 9 × 13-inch baking dish and spread it evenly over the bottom. Place the shrimp on top of the sauce, overlapping them slightly as necessary. Spoon the remaining sauce over the shrimp. Sprinkle the cheese mixture over the top.

10. Bake for 10 minutes, or until the cheese is melted and the sauce is hot and bubbling. Let the dish stand for 5 minutes, then serve.

GOAT CHEESE SHRIMP PARMESAN Omit the mozzarella, and stir 8 ounces soft goat cheese with the Parmigiano-Reggiano. This mixture will need to be dropped by teaspoonfuls onto the shrimp and tomato sauce.

SHRIMP AND EGGPLANT PARMESAN Cut 1 eggplant into ½-inch slices. After spooning the ½ cup tomato sauce into the pan, cover it with a layer of the eggplant slices. Top with the fried shrimp, the remaining tomato sauce, and the cheese mixture.

Peel and Eat Shrimp

IT DOESN'T GET ANY easier than this—shrimp in their shells, first simmered in a robust sauce, then marinated and chilled. You can make this well ahead of time, because the longer the shrimp sit in the marinade, the better they taste. When you serve the shrimp, make sure you have plenty of napkins and a bowl for the shells. **MAKES 4 TO 6 SERVINGS**

One 12-ounce bottle dark beer (such as Dos Equis, Negra Modelo, or Bass)

¼ cup cider vinegar

1 tablespoon celery seeds

1 tablespoon mustard seeds

1 teaspoon salt

1 teaspoon freshly ground black pepper

2 dashes Tabasco sauce, or more to taste

1 bay leaf

1½ pounds medium shrimp (35 to 40 per pound), deveined but not peeled

1. Combine the beer, vinegar, celery seeds, mustard seeds, salt, pepper, Tabasco sauce, and bay leaf in a large pot. Stir to combine, and bring to a boil over high heat.

2. To devein the shrimp without peeling them, gently hold a shrimp in one hand and pull the vein out of the neck with the other. If the vein doesn't come out whole, use a paring knife to cut down ¼ inch through the shell along the back curve of the shrimp (that is, the side opposite the legs). Gently pry the shell and meat open and remove the vein under running water. Repeat with the remaining shrimp. Add the shrimp to the pot and bring back to a boil, then reduce the heat to low, cover, and simmer for 5 minutes.

3. Turn off the heat. Transfer the shrimp to a large bowl, using a slotted spoon—do this a few shrimp at a time, bringing as few spices along with the shrimp as possible.

4. Place the cooking liquid back over high heat and bring it to a boil. Boil for 15 minutes or until it is reduced by half and thickened slightly. Remove from the heat and allow to cool.

5. Strain the liquid through a fine sieve over the shrimp. Cover and refrigerate for at least 4 hours before serving.

CHINESE PEEL AND EAT SHRIMP Omit all the spices and the vinegar. Add 2 tablespoons hoi sin sauce, 1½ teaspoons oyster sauce, 1½ teaspoons sweetened Chinese vinegar, and ½ teaspoon red pepper flakes to the beer.

COCA-COLA PEEL AND EAT SHRIMP Omit the beer. Add one 12-ounce can Coca-Cola with the shrimp.

GINGER BEER PEEL AND EAT SHRIMP Substitute ginger beer for the dark beer.

HARD CIDER PEEL AND EAT SHRIMP Substitute hard cider for the beer.

PEEL AND EAT SHRIMP IN A BREAD BOWL Hollow out one 12-inch round of crusty bread by cutting off the top and scooping out the insides, leaving the crust intact. Fill the bowl with the chilled shrimp and their marinade. Serve immediately.

PEEL AND EAT SHRIMP IN COURT BOUILLON Omit the beer marinade. Cook the shrimp in 3 cups strained Court Bouillon (page 43). Reduce the Court Bouillon by half after the shrimp are removed, then cool the liquid and marinate the shrimp as directed.

RED WINE PEEL AND EAT SHRIMP Substitute 2 cups red wine for the beer.

WHITE WINE PEEL AND EAT SHRIMP Substitute 2 cups white wine for the beer.

Shrimp Penne à la Vodka

THIS DISH IS A staple in Italian restaurants from Boston to Baltimore. The vodka works well with both the cream and the shrimp's natural sweetness. In the final dish, the alcohol cooks away, so you're left with a delightful, aromatic dish, perfect for a midweek supper, a weekend bridge game, or a church potluck (although you might need to explain how you happened to have vodka lying around the house). **MAKES 4 TO 6 SERVINGS**

2 tablespoons olive oil

1 large onion, thinly sliced

2 garlic cloves, minced

1 tablespoon minced oregano

1 tablespoon minced thyme

2 tablespoons chopped basil

4 large tomatoes, finely chopped

½ cup vodka

1 cup heavy cream

1 pound medium shrimp (35 to 40 per pound), peeled and deveined, or precooked cocktail shrimp, thawed and peeled

Salt and freshly ground black pepper to taste

1 pound dried penne, cooked according to the package instructions, drained, rinsed, covered, and kept warm

1. Heat the olive oil in a large pot over medium heat. Add the onion and cook, stirring often, until soft and translucent, about 3 minutes.

2. Add the garlic, oregano, thyme, and basil; stir for 30 seconds. Add the tomatoes, stir well, and cook for 10 minutes, or until the tomatoes have broken down and most of the liquid has evaporated.

3. Remove the pan from the heat and add the vodka. (By removing the pan from the heat, you reduce the chance that the alcohol will flame. If the vodka does flame, simply place the lid over the pan to put out the flame.) Stir until the vodka is well incorporated with the tomato mixture.

4. Place the pan back over medium heat and add the cream. When the sauce comes to a simmer, add the raw shrimp, if using, and cook, stirring constantly, until pink and firm, about 2 minutes. If using precooked shrimp, simply allow them to heat through. Season with salt and pepper.

5. Add the penne to the sauce and toss until the pasta is well coated and heated through. Serve immediately.

NUTTY SHRIMP PENNE À LA VODKA Add ½ cup toasted pine nuts with the shrimp.

SHRIMP AND CARROT PENNE À LA VODKA Add 4 carrots, sliced into thin rounds, after you have sautéed the herbs.

SHRIMP AND PEA PENNE À LA VODKA Add one 10-ounce package frozen peas or 2½ cups fresh peas after you've sautéed the herbs.

SHRIMP FLORENTINE À LA VODKA Add one 10-ounce package spinach, thawed and squeezed of excess liquid, with the shrimp.

SHRIMP PENNE À LA BEER Substitute amber beer or pale ale for the vodka.

SHRIMP PENNE À LA GIN Substitute gin for the vodka and add 2 tablespoons juniper berries with it.

SPICY SHRIMP PENNE À LA VODKA Add ½ teaspoon red pepper flakes, or more to taste, with the garlic and herbs.

Shrimp Pesto

PESTO—THAT LUSCIOUS MIXTURE of olive oil, pine nuts, basil, garlic, and Parmesan—hails from the Italian seaport of Genoa. Traditionally, it's made with a mortar and pestle; fortunately, the food processor takes most of the hassle out of this classic sauce. Shrimp Pesto calls for fresh pasta: its delicate taste simply works better with the sweet shrimp, and you can cook the pasta and shrimp together. If you want to use dried pasta, cook it separately according to the package instructions. The pesto will keep covered in the refrigerator for up to a week—simply pour a thin coating of olive oil on top to prevent discoloration. You might want to make a larger batch: it's delicious over grilled vegetables or simply on toasted bread. **MAKES 4 MAIN-DISH SERVINGS OR 6 TO 8 APPETIZER SERVINGS**

4 cups tightly packed basil leaves

2 large garlic cloves, quartered

⅔ cup extra virgin olive oil

½ cup pine nuts

½ cup freshly grated Parmigiano-Reggiano (about 2 ounces)

1 teaspoon salt

Freshly ground black pepper to taste

1 pound fresh spaghetti, linguine, or fettuccine

1 pound medium shrimp (35 to 40 per pound), peeled and deveined

1. Combine the basil, garlic, and olive oil in a food processor and pulse 4 or 5 times, or until the basil is puréed, stopping the machine to scrape down the sides as necessary. Add the pine nuts, cheese, and salt. Process until the pesto is smooth, about 30 seconds. Season with pepper. Transfer the pesto to a medium bowl. (The pesto can be made ahead and kept covered in the refrigerator for up to 7 days, provided you pour a thin coating of olive oil over the top to forestall discoloration.)

2. Bring 6 quarts salted water to a boil in a large pot over high heat. Add the pasta and shrimp and cook until the pasta is al dente and the shrimp are pink and firm, about 4 minutes.

3. Drain the pasta and shrimp, reserving ½ cup of the liquid. Return the pasta and shrimp to the pot, add the pesto and the reserved cooking liquid, and toss until the pasta is well coated. Serve immediately.

CHOPPED SHRIMP PESTO SALAD Omit the pasta. Increase the shrimp to 1½ pounds, and cook it in the boiling water as directed. Drain well. Coarsely chop the shrimp. Toss it in the pesto until it is well coated. Serve the salad in endive spears or radicchio cups, warm or at room temperature.

CILANTRO SHRIMP PESTO Substitute chopped cilantro for the basil.

MINT SHRIMP PESTO Substitute 2 cups tightly packed mint leaves and 2 cups chopped parsley for the basil.

SHRIMP PESTO IN LETTUCE CUPS Omit the pasta. Increase the shrimp to 1½ pounds, and cook it in boiling water as directed. Drain well. Serve the cooked shrimp in small lettuce cups or boats (washed leaves of iceberg or romaine lettuce), with the pesto poured on top.

SHRIMP PESTO TOMATO SOUP Omit the pasta. Increase the shrimp to 1½ pounds, and cook it in boiling water as directed. Combine the cooked shrimp and half the pesto with two 14-ounce cans tomato soup and 3 cups milk in a large saucepan and heat over medium heat until the mixture simmers.

SUN-DRIED TOMATO SHRIMP PESTO Add ½ cup drained sun-dried tomatoes packed in oil to the food processor with the basil.

Shrimp Phyllo Pillows

THESE BUNDLES ARE ELEGANT party food, and the recipe doubles or triples easily. You can find phyllo dough in the freezer section of your supermarket; thaw it according to the package instructions. While these phyllo pillows are juicy and tender on their own, you might want to serve them with of dipping sauce, such as Lemon Sauce (page 106) or Peanut Sauce (page 166). **MAKES 12 PIECES**

12 large shrimp (about 1 pound at 12 to 15 per pound), peeled and deveined, or precooked cocktail shrimp, thawed and peeled

One 16-ounce package frozen phyllo dough, thawed

8 tablespoons (1 stick) unsalted butter, melted

12 paper-thin slices prosciutto, (about ⅓ pound)

12 thin slices Swiss cheese (such as Emmenthaler or Gruyère; about 4 ounces)

¼ cup purchased fruit chutney (such as Patek's Mango Chutney or Stonewall Kitchen's Farmhouse Chutney)

1. If you're using raw shrimp, bring 2 quarts salted water to a boil in a large pot over high heat. Fill a large bowl halfway with ice water and set it aside. Add the shrimp to the boiling water and cook until pink and firm, about 4 minutes. Transfer the shrimp to the ice water using a slotted spoon. When they're cool, blot the shrimp dry with paper towels and set aside. If you're using precooked shrimp, omit this step.

2. Preheat the oven to 450°F.

3. Unroll the phyllo dough and place 1 sheet of dough horizontally on your work surface. Cover the remaining sheets with paper towels dampened with a few drops of water.

4. Imagine a vertical line running down the middle of the sheet, dividing it. Brush one half of the sheet with melted butter, just up to that line. Fold the dry half over, like a page in a book, covering the buttered half. Place 1 slice of prosciutto on the bottom half of the dough, close to the edge nearest you. (If the prosciutto slice is large, fold it so that it fits on the bottom half of the sheet of phyllo, leaving at least ½ inch uncovered dough on both the right and left sides.) Place 1 slice of cheese, 1 whole shrimp, and 1 teaspoon chutney on top of the prosciutto. Carefully roll the phyllo up away from you, stopping halfway, when the filling is fully encased. Brush the exposed dough with butter and fold the long sides of the dough over toward the middle, about ½ inch on each side. Finish rolling up the phyllo, creating what looks like a small egg roll. Brush the phyllo pillow with more butter and place it on an ungreased cookie sheet seam side down.

5. Repeat with 11 more sheets of dough and the remaining prosciutto, cheese, shrimp, and chutney. If a phyllo sheet tears while using it, simply discard it and use a new sheet. Tightly wrap any remaining phyllo dough in plastic and refrigerate for another use.

6. Bake the phyllo pillows for 15 minutes, or until lightly browned. Serve hot or at room temperature.

BASIL AND SHRIMP PHYLLO PILLOWS Omit the prosciutto. Place 2 basil leaves in each phyllo packet before rolling.

BLUE CHEESE AND SHRIMP PHYLLO PILLOWS Omit the Swiss cheese and prosciutto. Spread 2 teaspoons blue cheese (such as Gorgonzola) in each phyllo pillow before rolling.

CHINESE SHRIMP PHYLLO PILLOWS Omit the cheese and chutney. Place 1 teaspoon minced ginger and 1 tablespoon hoi sin sauce on top of the prosciutto in each pillow.

CURRIED SHRIMP PHYLLO PILLOWS Omit the prosciutto. Sprinkle ¼ teaspoon curry powder on top of the cheese in each phyllo pillow. Use mango chutney, spicy or mild.

GREEK SHRIMP PHYLLO PILLOWS Omit the Swiss cheese. Place 2 teaspoons feta and ½ teaspoon capers, drained, on top of the prosciutto in each phyllo pillow.

Pickled Shrimp

THIS OLD-FASHIONED DISH, once a favorite in bars across the Upper Midwest, is overdue for a comeback. The shrimp pickle in a tangy brine, giving them a piquant taste and a firm texture. They are great with beer, martinis, or iced tea. You'll need to make it at least one day before serving. Have plenty of crackers and grainy mustard on hand. (Pickling spices are available in most supermarkets, usually with the other spices or home canning ingredients.) **MAKES 4 TO 6 APPETIZER SERVINGS**

2 cups cider vinegar

½ cup sugar

¼ cup pickling spices, without salt

1 teaspoon salt

1 pound medium shrimp (35 to 40 per pound), peeled and deveined

2 large red onions, thinly sliced, (about 3 cups)

1. Combine the vinegar and sugar in a medium nonreactive saucepan (ceramic or stainless steel) set over high heat and stir until the sugar dissolves, then add the pickling spices and salt. Bring to a boil, then reduce the heat to low to keep the liquid barely at a simmer. Cover the pan.

2. Meanwhile bring 2 quarts salted water to a boil in a large pot over high heat. Add the shrimp and cook just until they've lost their raw translucence, about 1 minute. Drain the shrimp and carefully blot them dry with paper towels.

3. Place one-third of the onions in the bottom of a nonreactive bowl. Place half the shrimp on top of the onions. Add another layer of onions. Top with the remaining shrimp, then top them with the last of the onions.

4. Pour the simmering vinegar mixture over the onions and shrimp. Set aside to cool thoroughly.

5. Cover the bowl tightly and refrigerate for at least 24 hours before serving. (The shrimp can be made up to a week in advance. Keep them tightly covered in the refrigerator.)

CHINESE PICKLED SHRIMP Omit the pickling spices. Substitute rice wine vinegar for the cider vinegar, and add ½ cup chopped cilantro, ½ teaspoon red pepper flakes, and one 2-inch piece of ginger, peeled and sliced, to the pickling mixture.

CINNAMON PICKLED SHRIMP Omit the pickling spices. Substitute cranberry vinegar for the cider vinegar, and add 1 teaspoon whole cloves and 4 cinnamon sticks to the pickling mixture.

DILL PICKLED SHRIMP Substitute white wine vinegar for the cider vinegar. Layer ½ cup dill fronds on each shrimp layer before adding the simmering marinade.

PEPPER PICKLED SHRIMP Substitute white wine vinegar for the cider vinegar and add 5 pepperoncini (Italian hot peppers) to the pickling mixture.

SZECHWAN PICKLED SHRIMP Use 2 cups sweetened Chinese vinegar, 1 tablespoon Szechwan peppercorns, 2 teaspoons oyster sauce, 1 teaspoon chili oil, 6 cloves, and 3 dried red Asian peppers to make the pickling mixture, and proceed as directed.

TARRAGON PICKLED SHRIMP Omit the pickling spices. Substitute white wine vinegar for the cider vinegar, and add ½ cup chopped tarragon to the pickling mixture.

Shrimp Pizza

THE NEXT TIME YOUR kids have a sleepover or the next time unexpected guests drop by, put together this easy pizza and earn all the kudos you could want. You can make it really simple by purchasing an unbaked pizza crust from your local pizzeria or by buying a prepared pizza shell at the supermarket. And make a double batch of the sauce and freeze half of it, if you like, so you can have pizza again whenever you want it. **MAKES TWO 12-INCH PIZZAS**

FOR THE DOUGH

1 package active dry yeast

¾ cup lukewarm water (105° to 115°F)

¼ cup sweet vermouth

¼ cup olive oil, plus additional for the bowl and baking sheet

½ teaspoon salt

3 to 3½ cups all-purpose flour

FOR THE SAUCE

¼ cup olive oil

1 small onion, finely chopped

1 garlic clove, minced

½ teaspoon red pepper flakes

One 28-ounce can peeled tomatoes, drained and chopped

2 teaspoons tomato paste

2 teaspoons chopped basil

2 teaspoons minced oregano

Salt and freshly ground black pepper to taste

FOR THE TOPPING

1 pound small shrimp (more than 55 per pound), peeled and deveined

2 cups mozzarella, shredded (about 8 ounces)

1. To prepare the dough, combine the yeast, water, and vermouth in a large bowl and stir until the yeast is dissolved. Set aside to proof. After 5 minutes, there should be small bubbles and foam on the surface of the liquid.

2. Add the olive oil, salt, and half the flour to the bowl and mix thoroughly, adding more flour as necessary to create a soft dough. (The amount of flour needed will vary with your kitchen's temperature and the day's humidity.)

3. Lightly flour your work surface. Place the dough on the work surface and knead for 10 minutes, adding more flour as necessary to keep it from sticking. Knead the dough by pressing into it with the heel of one hand, pulling the bottom lip of the dough back with the other. When the dough is smooth and elastic (that is, it stretches a bit before breaking and has the look of very smooth skin), place it in a clean bowl and rub the top lightly with a little olive oil. Turn the dough over once or twice to coat both the bowl and the entire surface of the dough with oil. Cover the bowl and set it in a warm place to allow the dough to rise for 1 hour, or until doubled in bulk.

4. Meanwhile, prepare the sauce. Heat the olive oil in a large saucepan over medium heat. Add the onion, garlic, and red pepper flakes and cook, stirring often, until the onion is softened and fragrant, about 5 minutes.

5. Add the tomatoes, tomato paste, basil, and oregano and bring to a simmer; then reduce the heat to low. Slowly simmer the sauce, uncovered, for 30 minutes, stirring often.

6. Remove the pan from the heat and let the sauce cool. Season with salt and pepper.

7. To assemble the pizza, adjust the racks in the oven so that one is on the lowest level and the other is in the upper third of the oven, and preheat the oven to 450°F. Lightly oil two large baking sheets.

8. Punch down the dough with your fist to deflate it. Remove the dough from the bowl and divide it into 2 equal pieces.

9. Stretch and pull half of the dough into a rough 12-inch circle. You can use a rolling pin, if desired. Place the dough circle in the middle of one of the prepared baking sheets. Place half of the sauce in the middle of the dough and spread it evenly, leaving a ¼-inch border of dough all the way around. Place half the shrimp on top of the sauce in one layer, then sprinkle the entire pizza with half of the cheese. Repeat with the remaining ingredients to make a second pizza on the second baking sheet.

10. Bake the pizzas for 7 minutes. Reverse the baking sheets, top to bottom, and front to back. Bake for 8 more minutes, or until the cheese is melted and bubbling and the crust is beginning to brown.

Popcorn Shrimp

LONG BEFORE RED LOBSTER made it an American favorite, Popcorn Shrimp was popular fare in diners along the Gulf Coast. To replicate the texture of popcorn, you'll want to chop the shrimp up, so you get an equal amount of crust and shrimp in every bite. Peanut oil gives the dish a nuttier, crunchier texture and taste, but you can use vegetable oil if allergies are a problem. Serve Popcorn Shrimp the moment they're done. Have lots of cold drinks handy—and a second batch of ingredients on hand, since the crowd will probably soon clamor for more. **MAKES 6 TO 8 SERVINGS**

8 cups peanut oil or vegetable oil

1 large egg

⅓ cup milk

⅓ cup cornmeal

½ teaspoon salt, plus more to taste

½ teaspoon cayenne pepper

1½ pounds small shrimp (more than 55 per pound), peeled, deveined, and cut into thirds

1. Pour the oil into a large saucepan at least 4 inches deep and 10 inches in diameter; the oil should be at least 1½ inches deep but reach no more than halfway up the sides of the pan. Alternatively, fill an electric deep fryer with oil according to the manufacturer's instructions. If you're using a pan, clip a deep-frying thermometer to the inside and place the pan over medium heat. Heat the oil to 375°F. Adjust the heat to maintain that temperature while you prepare the shrimp. If you're using an electric deep fryer, set the temperature control to 375°F.

2. Whisk the egg and milk in a large mixing bowl until well combined and lightly frothy. Whisk in the cornmeal, salt, and cayenne pepper, then continue to whisk until the batter is light and very smooth, about 3 minutes.

3. Add all the shrimp to the bowl and toss to coat them completely. With a wooden spoon, scoop up a handful of batter-covered shrimp—only as many shrimp as will fit the pan without crowding—and carefully but quickly slide them into the hot oil. Fry the shrimp until they are golden brown all over, turning them once or twice with tongs, about 2 minutes. Break up any clumps of shrimp. Remove the shrimp from the oil, drain them on paper towels, and sprinkle lightly with salt. Repeat with the remaining batter-dipped shrimp.

Note: You can keep the first batches of fried shrimp warm, spread out on a cookie sheet in a 250°F oven, while you prepare the remaining shrimp. Or you can serve the hot shrimp in batches as soon as they are fried and drained.

BARBECUED POPCORN SHRIMP Pour Barbecue Sauce (page 26) over the shrimp once they are done. Or use the sauce as a dip.

CHINESE POPCORN SHRIMP Whisk together ¼ cup oyster sauce and 2 tablespoons water and pour it over the shrimp once they're done. Or use the sauce as a dip.

EXTRA-CRUNCHY POPCORN SHRIMP Substitute Japanese bread crumbs (*panko*) for the cornmeal.

GARLIC SAUCE POPCORN SHRIMP Pour Szechwan Cold Garlic Sauce (page 194) over the shrimp once they are done. Or use the sauce as a dip.

HERBED POPCORN SHRIMP Omit the cayenne pepper. Whisk 2 tablespoons chopped parsley, thyme, rosemary, or oregano into the batter.

LEMON POPCORN SHRIMP Pour Lemon Sauce (page 106) over the shrimp once they are done. Or use the sauce as a dip.

SMOOTH BATTER POPCORN SHRIMP Substitute all-purpose flour for the cornmeal. You may need to add a small amount more, depending on your kitchen's temperature and the day's humidity, but the point is to make a thin batter.

VINEGARY POPCORN SHRIMP Sprinkle the hot shrimp with malt vinegar as they drain on the paper towels.

Portuguese Shrimp

S AUSAGE AND CLAMS ARE a common Portuguese combination: a little bit of the earth, a little bit of the sea. When you add shrimp, this spicy dish becomes a full meal. Chorizo sausage is popular in both Iberian and Mexican cooking—the Spanish and Portuguese varieties often use smoked pork; the Mexican, fresh. Either will work here, and both are available at the butcher counter of larger supermarkets or in Latin American markets. For an all-shrimp meal, try Shrimp Phyllo Pillows (page 138) on toast points as a starter. **MAKES 4 TO 6 SERVINGS**

2 tablespoons olive oil

¼ pound chorizo sausage, cut into ¼-inch cubes

1 medium red onion, thinly sliced

1 garlic clove, minced

1 teaspoon red pepper flakes

1 large tomato, coarsely chopped

2 cups dry white wine or dry sherry

1 pound medium shrimp (35 to 40 per pound), peeled and deveined, or precooked cocktail shrimp, thawed and peeled

18 medium clams (such as cherrystone or Pacific littleneck), scrubbed

12 ounces fresh or dried linguine, cooked, drained, rinsed, covered, and kept warm

Salt and freshly ground black pepper to taste

¼ cup finely chopped parsley

2 tablespoons finely chopped mint

1. Heat a large skillet over medium heat until it is hot but not smoking. Add the olive oil, then the sausage, and cook, stirring constantly, until the sausage is browned, about 4 minutes. Remove the sausage with a slotted spoon and drain it on paper towels.

2. Reduce the heat to low and add the onion to the pan. Cook, stirring often, until soft and golden, about 10 minutes. If the onion begins to brown, lower the heat further.

3. Add the garlic and red pepper flakes and toss for 1 minute. Add the chopped tomato and cook, stirring constantly, for 30 seconds more. Add the wine and scrape up any browned bits stuck to the bottom of the pan; then raise the heat to high and bring the sauce to a boil. Boil the sauce for 1 minute.

4. Add the cooked sausage to the sauce, along with the raw shrimp, if using, and the clams. Cook just until the shrimp are pink and firm and the clams have opened, about 6 minutes.

5. Add the pasta and the precooked shrimp, if using, and toss until everything is well coated and the pasta is heated through, about 1 minute. Season with salt and pepper and serve, sprinkled with the parsley and mint.

COCKLES AND PORTUGUESE SHRIMP Omit the clams. Add 2 pounds New Zealand cockles, scrubbed, with the cooked sausage.

FIERY PORTUGUESE SHRIMP Add 4 dashes Tabasco sauce, or more to taste, with the cooked pasta.

FISH AND PORTUGUESE SHRIMP Omit the clams. Add 1½ pounds fish fillets (such as red snapper), cut into 1-inch pieces and picked over for bones, with the cooked sausage.

HAM AND PORTUGUESE SHRIMP Reduce the shrimp to ½ pound. Stir in ½ pound cooked smoked ham, cut into ½-inch cubes, with the cooked pasta.

MADEIRAN SHRIMP Substitute dry Madeira for the white wine.

MUSSELS AND PORTUGUESE SHRIMP Omit the clams. Add 2 pounds mussels, scrubbed and debearded, with the cooked sausage.

OLIVES AND PORTUGUESE SHRIMP Add 1 cup sliced pitted black olives with the cooked pasta.

PORTUGUESE SHRIMP WITH HAZELNUTS Add ½ cup toasted hazelnuts with the cooked pasta.

Shrimp Pot Stickers

POT STICKERS ARE TRADITIONAL Chinese dumplings, both chewy and crisp, so named because of their propensity to stick to the pan. They have plenty of opportunity, since the cooking involves a three-step process: frying, steaming, and then frying again. These little shrimp and pork bundles are best hot right out of the pan. Serve them with the dipping sauce suggested in the recipe, or with purchased hoi sin sauce or homemade Barbecue Sauce (page 26). **MAKES ABOUT 20 POT STICKERS**

Cornstarch for the cookie sheet

3 tablespoons plus 2 teaspoons soy sauce

3 tablespoons rice wine vinegar

½ pound small shrimp (more than 55 per pound), peeled and deveined

2 ounces pork fat, minced, or 2 tablespoons lard

1 scallion, minced

8 canned water chestnuts, drained and minced

1 teaspoon minced ginger

18 to 25 wonton or dumpling wrappers

1 tablespoon toasted sesame oil or more as needed

1. Dust a large cookie sheet or baking sheet with cornstarch. Set it aside.

2. Whisk together 3 tablespoons of the soy sauce and the rice wine vinegar until well combined. Set this dipping sauce aside.

3. Place the shrimp and pork fat in a food processor and pulse until the shrimp are finely ground but not puréed. Transfer the mixture to a medium mixing bowl.

4. Stir the scallion, water chestnuts, ginger, and the remaining 2 teaspoons soy sauce into the ground shrimp mixture until well combined.

5. Place 1 dumpling wrapper on your work surface. Put 1 heaping teaspoonful of the shrimp mixture in the middle of the wrapper. Dip your finger in water and moisten the edges around one half of the wrapper. Fold the dry side of the wrapper over the filling until it reaches the moist edges, completely encasing the filling. Press the edges of the dough together. Pick up the pot sticker and use your fingers to pinch the edges tightly closed. A tight seal is important so the filling will not leak out while the pot sticker cooks. Set the pot sticker on the prepared cookie sheet and cover it with a kitchen towel or paper towels. Repeat with the remaining filling and wrappers.

6. Pour the sesame oil into a lidded skillet (preferably nonstick) large enough to hold all the dumplings comfortably in a single layer (if necessary, use two skillets with 1 tablespoon sesame oil in each, or cook the dumplings in batches). Place the pan over high heat; when the oil is hot, add the dumplings. Cook for 1 minute, shaking the pan occasionally to prevent sticking, or until the bottoms of the pot stickers turn golden brown.

7. Add ½ cup water to the skillet. There will be much sizzling—be careful. Immediately cover the skillet with a tight-fitting lid or with aluminum foil pressed around the skillet's lip to seal in the steam. Reduce the heat to medium-low and cook for 7 to 10 minutes, or until all of the water has been absorbed by the dumplings.

8. Shake the pan vigorously to release the pot stickers if they've stuck. Remove the lid. Continue to cook, shaking the pan often, until the tops of the pot stickers are dry and the bottoms are brown and crisp.

9. Slide the pot stickers onto a platter. If necessary, use a flat wooden spatula or heatproof rubber spatula to release any that are stuck. Serve immediately with the dipping sauce.

COUNTRY CHINESE SHRIMP POT STICKERS Stir 1 teaspoon five-spice powder into the filling mixture.

CRAB AND SHRIMP POT STICKERS Add ¼ cup limp crabmeat, picked over for shells and cartilage, and 1 tablespoon vegetable oil to the food processor with the shrimp. You will need about 25 dumpling wrappers.

DOUBLE SHRIMP POT STICKERS Add 1 tablespoon dried shrimp to the filling mixture.

SCALLOP AND SHRIMP POT STICKERS Add 3 medium sea scallops, cut in half, to the food processor with the shrimp. You will need about 25 dumpling wrappers.

SPICY SHRIMP POT STICKERS Add 1 teaspoon chili oil, or more to taste, to the filling mixture.

VIETNAMESE SHRIMP POT STICKERS Omit the water chestnuts. Add ½ cup chopped basil, 1 tablespoon fish sauce, 1 teaspoon freshly ground black pepper, and 1 teaspoon sugar to the filling mixture. You will need about 25 dumpling wrappers.

Provençal Stewed Shrimp

PROVENCE, THAT LOOSE COLLECTION of coastal bays and valleys that worm up south-western France, is the northernmost outpost of the Saharan ecosystem. The flavors of Provence, there-fore, are typical of desert environments—both refreshing and filling. This thick stew is spiked with Pernod or pastis, the "national" aperitif of the region. You can serve the stew on its own, on top of wilted greens, or in large bowls with white rice. The best wine to go with it would be one from Provence itself: Châteauneuf-du-Pape, Gigondas, or Vacqueryas. **MAKES 4 TO 6 SERVINGS**

¼ cup olive oil

1 large onion, chopped

2 garlic cloves, minced

1 teaspoon chopped thyme

½ teaspoon saffron threads, crumbled

1 cup dry vermouth

One 28-ounce can peeled tomatoes

2 bay leaves

1 large baking potato, peeled and cut into 1-inch dice

1½ pounds cod fillets, cut into 2-inch cubes and picked over for bones

2 pounds large shrimp (12 to 15 per pound), peeled and deveined

1 tablespoon anise liqueur (such as Pernod or pastis)

Grated zest of 1 lemon

1 tablespoon minced basil

2 teaspoons salt

Freshly ground black pepper to taste

1. Heat the olive oil in a large heavy soup pot or Dutch oven set over medium heat. Add the onion, garlic, and thyme; cook, stirring often, until the onion is softened, about 3 minutes.

2. Add the saffron and vermouth and bring to a boil. Cook until the liquid is reduced by half, about 4 minutes.

3. Add the tomatoes with their juice, breaking them up with the back of a wooden spoon. Add the bay leaves. Bring to a boil, reduce the heat to low, and simmer uncovered for 5 minutes, stirring often.

4. Stir the potato and cod into the pot, cover it, and simmer for 35 to 40 minutes, until the potatoes are tender and the cod is falling apart. The fish will help thicken the stew.

5. Add the shrimp and simmer until they are pink and firm, about 5 minutes.

6. Add the liqueur, lemon zest, basil, salt and, black pepper. Discard the bay leaves. Serve immediately.

ALCOHOL-FREE PROVENÇAL STEWED SHRIMP Omit the potato and liqueur. Add 1¼ cups diced fennel bulb (white part only) after the tomatoes have cooked.

PROVENÇAL SHRIMP AND SCALLOP STEW Omit the cod. Add 1 pound sea scallops, cut in half, with the shrimp.

PROVENÇAL SHRIMP AND VEGETABLE STEW Omit the cod. Add 1 cup sliced carrots, ¾ cup sliced celery, and ½ cup fresh or frozen peas with the potato cubes.

PROVENÇAL STEWED SHRIMP AND CHICKEN STEW Omit the cod. Add 1½ pounds boneless, skinless chicken breasts, cut into 2-inch cubes, with the shrimp. Cook for an additional 8 minutes.

THICKENED PROVENÇAL SHRIMP STEW Add ½ cup ground almonds with the shrimp. Stir constantly while the shrimp cooks.

Shrimp Puffs

SHRIMP PUFFS BEGIN WITH a classic French dough: *pâte à choux,* or choux paste. Here, the traditional fat—butter—is replaced with olive oil, making a more savory dough to encase the shrimp. The choux paste will be quite sticky, but don't be tempted to dip your spoon in water to make it stick less. The excess moisture could cause the puffs to steam, making them soggy. Make sure your hands are clean and gently push the dough off the spoon onto the baking sheet. **MAKES ABOUT 3 DOZEN PUFFS**

¾ pound small shrimp (more than 55 per pound), completely peeled and deveined, or precooked cold-water (or baby) shrimp, thawed

1 cup water

3 tablespoons olive oil

½ teaspoon salt

¼ teaspoon freshly ground black pepper

1 cup all-purpose flour, plus additional for the baking sheet

2 large eggs

3 large egg whites

Shortening or unsalted butter for the baking sheet

½ cup freshly grated Parmigiano-Reggiano (about 2 ounces)

3 dashes Tabasco sauce, or more to taste

1 teaspoon minced thyme

1. If you're using raw shrimp, bring 2 quarts salted water to a boil in a large saucepan over high heat. Fill a large bowl halfway with ice water and set it aside. Add the shrimp to the boiling water and cook until pink and firm, about 2 minutes. With a slotted spoon, transfer the shrimp to the ice water and cool completely. Drain the shrimp and pat them dry with paper towels. If you're using precooked shrimp, skip this step.

2. Preheat the oven to 400°F. Grease and flour a large baking sheet and set it aside.

3. Combine the water, olive oil, salt, and pepper in a medium saucepan over high heat and bring to a boil. Reduce the heat to medium-low and add the flour all at once. Using a wooden spoon, stir constantly until a soft dough forms. Continue to cook and stir until the dough dries out a bit, leaving a film around the inside of the pan. Remove the pan from the heat and transfer the dough to a large mixing bowl.

4. Using a wooden spoon or an electric mixer, beat the eggs into the dough one at a time, making sure the first one is well incorporated before adding the next. Do the same with the 3 egg whites.

5. Add the grated Parmigiano-Reggiano, Tabasco sauce, and thyme to the dough, stirring until well incorporated.

6. Finely chop the cooked shrimp and add to the dough, mixing until well incorporated.

7. Drop the dough by tablespoonfuls 2 inches apart onto the prepared baking sheet. Bake for 30 minutes, or until the puffs are lightly browned. Serve hot.

BLUE CHEESE SHRIMP PUFFS Reduce the Parmigiano-Reggiano to ¼ cup. Add ¼ cup finely crumbled blue cheese (such as Roquefort or Gorgonzola; about 1 ounce) with the Parmigiano-Reggiano.

CHINESE SHRIMP PUFFS Omit the Tabasco sauce and thyme. Add 2 teaspoons minced ginger, 1 teaspoon chopped cilantro, and ½ teaspoon chili oil to the dough with the cheese.

CURRIED SHRIMP PUFFS Omit the Tabasco sauce and thyme. Add 1½ teaspoons curry powder to the dough with the cheese.

JAPANESE SHRIMP PUFFS Omit the Tabasco sauce and thyme. Add 1 teaspoon wasabi paste and 2 teaspoons soy sauce to the dough with the cheese.

ROSEMARY SHRIMP PUFFS Substitute 1½ teaspoons chopped rosemary for the thyme.

TARRAGON SHRIMP PUFFS Substitute 2 teaspoons chopped tarragon for the thyme.

THAI SHRIMP PUFFS Substitute chopped basil for the thyme, and add 2 teaspoons fish sauce to the dough with the cheese.

Shrimp Quiche

MADE WITH EGGS AND CHEESE, a quiche is good almost anytime. All it needs is a tossed green salad or a simple steamed vegetable (such as baby beets or carrots) to make it a complete meal. You can even bake it ahead of time to take on a picnic or to a potluck. And it makes great leftovers rewarmed in foil in a 300°F oven for 10 minutes. **MAKES 6 SERVINGS**

⅓ pound small shrimp (more than 55 per pound), peeled and deveined, or precooked cold-water (or baby) shrimp, thawed

One 9- or 10-inch frozen piecrust, thawed (but still in its aluminum baking dish)

1¼ cups half-and-half

4 large eggs

¼ teaspoon grated nutmeg

½ teaspoon salt

¼ teaspoon freshly ground black pepper

2 cups shredded Gruyère or Swiss cheese (about 8 ounces)

1. If you're using raw shrimp, bring 1 quart salted water to a boil in a medium pot over high heat. Fill a large bowl halfway with ice water and set it aside. Add the shrimp to the boiling water and cook until pink and firm, about 2 minutes. With a slotted spoon or strainer, transfer the shrimp to the ice water and allow them to cool completely. Drain the shrimp and blot dry with paper towels. If you're using precooked shrimp, skip this step.

2. Preheat the oven to 425°F.

3. Press aluminum foil over the piecrust and fill with pie weights, rice, or dried beans. Bake the pie crust for 10 minutes. Remove the crust from the oven, remove the foil, and reduce the oven temperature to 400°F.

4. Meanwhile, beat the half-and-half, eggs, nutmeg, salt, and pepper in a medium bowl until well blended. Set aside.

5. Place half the shrimp in the bottom of the pie shell. Sprinkle half the cheese over them. Repeat with a second layer of shrimp and cheese. Pour the half-and-half mixture over the top.

6. Bake the quiche until a knife inserted into the center comes out clean, about 45 minutes.

7. Remove the quiche from the oven and let it rest for at least 5 minutes before serving. Serve it hot, warm, or at room temperature. (The quiche can be made up to 1 day in advance. Keep it covered in the refrigerator. If desired, reheat, wrapped in foil, in a preheated 300°F oven for 10 to 15 minutes.)

The easiest way to vary this recipe is to add a thin layer of any of the following between the first shrimp-and-cheese layer and the second.

6 paper-thin slices cored sweet baking apple (such as Macoun) • 6 thin strips of roasted and seeded poblano chiles • 2 radishes, sliced paper-thin • 2 pimientos, thinly sliced • 2 tablespoons mango chutney • 2 tablespoons honey mustard • ¼ cup sliced almonds • ¼ cup chopped parsley • 12 to 16 basil leaves • 3 tablespoons chopped tarragon • 3 tablespoons chopped dill • 2 tablespoons toasted pine nuts

Shrimp Rémoulade

SHRIMP RÉMOULADE IS A time-honored New Orleans dish. A classic French *rémoulade* is mayonnaise flavored with mustard and capers. The Cajuns created their own spicy version, adding hot sauce and often horseradish. This version's a little different: it's made with cooked egg yolks, to avoid the health hazards sometimes associated with raw eggs. Serve Shrimp Rémoulade in lettuce-leaf cups or on a bed of steamed watercress. **MAKES 6 TO 8 APPETIZER SERVINGS OR 4 TO 6 MAIN-COURSE SERVINGS**

4 cups Court Bouillon (page 43)
(omit if using precooked shrimp)

2 pounds medium shrimp (35 to 40 per pound), peeled, leaving the final segment of the tail shell intact, and deveined, or precooked cocktail shrimp, thawed and peeled

FOR THE SAUCE

3 hard-boiled large egg yolks

2 tablespoons bottled horseradish

2 tablespoons fresh lemon juice

1 tablespoon Dijon mustard

1 teaspoon salt

½ teaspoon freshly ground black pepper

½ teaspoon celery seeds

¼ teaspoon onion powder

½ cup olive oil

2 tablespoons mayonnaise, if necessary

¼ teaspoon Tabasco sauce, or more to taste

1. If you're using raw shrimp, bring the court bouillon to a boil in a large pot over high heat. Fill a large bowl halfway with ice water and set it aside. Add half the shrimp to the boiling court bouillon and cook until pink and firm, about 4 minutes. Use a slotted spoon or strainer to transfer the shrimp to the ice water. Repeat with the remaining shrimp. When all the shrimp are cool, drain and blot dry with paper towels. (The shrimp can be prepared ahead and kept covered in the refrigerator for up to 2 days.) If you're using precooked shrimp, skip this step.

2. To prepare the sauce, using the back of a wooden spoon, mash the egg yolks, horseradish, lemon juice, mustard, salt, pepper, celery seeds, and onion powder together in a medium bowl. Slowly whisk in the olive oil, then keep whisking until the sauce is emulsified into a semi-thick may-

onnaise. If necessary, add the prepared mayonnaise to help thicken the sauce. Whisk in the Tabasco sauce.

3. Cover the sauce and refrigerate until ready to serve. (The sauce can be made up to 2 days ahead. Allow it to come back to room temperature before you use it.)

4. To serve, arrange the shrimp in lettuce cups or on an attractive platter, surrounded by sliced tomatoes and sliced red onions. Top with the remoulade sauce.

BASIL SHRIMP RÉMOULADE Omit the celery seeds in the sauce, and add 2 tablespoons chopped basil and 1 garlic clove, minced.

CAESAR SALAD SHRIMP RÉMOULADE Add 1 teaspoon garlic powder to the sauce. Mound the shrimp onto a bed of torn romaine lettuce leaves. Pour on the remoulade. Garnish with anchovy fillets and ¼ cup shaved Parmigiano-Reggiano.

CURRIED SHRIMP RÉMOULADE Omit the celery seeds and Tabasco sauce in the sauce, and add 1½ teaspoons curry powder.

DILL SHRIMP RÉMOULADE Omit the lemon juice and celery seeds in the sauce, and add 1 tablespoon chopped dill and 2 teaspoons cider vinegar.

TARRAGON SHRIMP RÉMOULADE Omit the lemon juice in the sauce, and add 1 tablespoon minced tarragon and 2 teaspoons red wine vinegar.

Shrimp Risotto

SURPASSING EVEN PASTA, risotto may be the mainstay of Lombardy, the Italian region around Lake Como. For this deep, delicious dish, Arborio, a short-grained rice, is cooked very slowly, with stock gradually added by the ladleful over a period of twenty minutes or so. The creamy result is pure magic. (If you want a faster version, check out the pressure-cooker variation.) Shrimp Risotto is a luxurious dinner on its own, or it can be an elegant first course before a standing rib roast or a roast chicken. **MAKES 4 MAIN-COURSE OR 8 FIRST-COURSE SERVINGS**

6 cups fish stock or 4 cups vegetable stock plus 2 cups clam juice

2 tablespoons olive oil

1 garlic clove, minced

1 pound medium shrimp (35 to 40 per pound), peeled and deveined

4 tablespoons (½ stick) unsalted butter

1 large yellow onion, finely chopped

2 cups Arborio rice

1 cup dry white wine or dry vermouth

Salt and freshly ground black pepper to taste

¼ cup freshly grated Parmigiano-Reggiano (about 1 ounce)

1. Place the stock in a large saucepan and bring to a simmer over medium heat. Adjust the heat to keep the stock hot but just below a simmer.

2. Heat the olive oil in a large, deep skillet over medium heat. When the oil is hot, add the garlic and stir for 10 seconds. Add the shrimp and cook, stirring frequently, until pink and firm, about 3 minutes. Transfer the shrimp and garlic to a bowl and set aside.

3. Return the skillet to the stove and melt the butter over medium heat. Add the onion and cook, stirring often, until it is soft and fragrant, about 5 minutes.

4. Add the rice and stir for 1 minute. It should be well coated with butter. Add the wine and cook, stirring constantly, until the liquid is a mere glaze. Reduce the heat to medium-low.

5. Using a ladle, add enough stock to just cover the rice, and stir constantly until the stock is absorbed, 2 to 3 minutes. Continue to add stock in this manner, stirring constantly but slowly until each addition is fully absorbed, until the rice is creamy and *al dente* (tender but with some bite), about 20 minutes.

6. Add the shrimp and stir until it is evenly distributed and heated through. Season with salt and pepper.

7. Add the cheese and stir just until it melts and is well incorporated. Serve immediately.

CHARD AND SHRIMP RISOTTO When the rice is al dente, stir in 2 cups chopped Swiss chard. Cook until it is tender, about 5 minutes, then proceed as directed.

HERBED SHRIMP RISOTTO Add 2 teaspoons chopped rosemary and 2 teaspoons chopped oregano after the onion has softened.

PRESSURE-COOKER SHRIMP RISOTTO Cook the shrimp in a large skillet, as directed in the recipe; set aside. Cook the onions as directed in a pressure cooker with the lid off. Add the rice and stir as directed for 1 minute. Add the wine and all the stock. Cover the pressure cooker and cook according to the manufacturer's instructions at high pressure for about 6 minutes. Unlock the lid according to the manufacturer's instructions for quick release. Stir in the cheese and shrimp (and any herbs you desire) and simmer, uncovered, for 3 minutes, or until the shrimp are heated through.

SHRIMP RISOTTO MILANESE Crumble ¼ teaspoon saffron threads into the stock when you heat it, stirring to incorporate the saffron.

SHRIMP RISOTTO WITH PEAS Add 1 cup fresh or thawed frozen peas with the cheese. Simmer, stirring constantly, for 2 minutes.

Shrimp Rolls

THE MINUTE YOU CROSS the border into Maine, you start to see the shacks selling lobster rolls. Shrimp makes these Down East treats even easier—and more economical. Serve Shrimp Rolls with potato chips or a salad of apples, raisins, and arugula dressed with lemon juice and walnut oil. (Or slip them into your kids' lunch one week. They won't know what got into you!) **MAKES 2 ROLLS**

¾ pound small shrimp (more than 55 per pound), peeled and deveined

¼ cup mayonnaise (regular, low-fat, or fat-free)

1 teaspoon ketchup

1 teaspoon fresh lemon juice

1 teaspoon bottled horseradish

½ teaspoon Worcestershire sauce

Salt and freshly ground black pepper to taste

4 teaspoons unsalted butter, at room temperature

2 hot dog buns

1. Bring 2 quarts salted water to a boil in a large pan over high heat. Fill a large bowl halfway with ice water and set it aside. Add the shrimp to the boiling water and cook until pink and firm, 3 to 5 minutes. Transfer the shrimp to the ice water using a slotted spoon. Allow them to cool completely. Drain the shrimp and blot them dry with paper towels.

2. Coarsely chop the shrimp and place in a large mixing bowl. Add the mayonnaise, ketchup, lemon juice, horseradish, and Worcestershire sauce. Gently toss just until the shrimp pieces are well coated and the mixture is uniform. Season with salt and pepper. (The shrimp mixture can be prepared 24 hours in advance, covered, and refrigerated.)

3. Heat a heavy skillet over medium heat until hot. Butter the insides of the hot dog buns. Lay them open, buttered side down, in the pan. Cook until the insides are toasted.

4. Fill each bun with half the shrimp mixture, and serve immediately.

BASIL SHRIMP ROLLS Line each toasted hot dog bun with 2 large basil leaves before you add the shrimp mixture.

HEARTY SHRIMP ROLLS Reduce the shrimp to ½ pound. Add 2 hard-cooked eggs, coarsely chopped, to the shrimp mixture.

PICKLED SHRIMP ROLLS Stir 2 tablespoons pickle relish or hot chow-chow into the shrimp mixture.

SPICY SHRIMP ROLLS Omit the horseradish. Add 3 dashes Tabasco sauce, or more to taste, to the shrimp mixture.

TOMATO AND SHRIMP ROLLS Line each of the toasted hot dog buns with 2 thin tomato slices before you add the shrimp mixture.

TUNA AND SHRIMP ROLLS Reduce the shrimp to ½ pound. Stir ¼ cup drained canned tuna into the shrimp mixture.

Shrimp Salad

SHRIMP SALAD IS A SUMMER TREAT: crunchy, garden-fresh vegetables and tender shrimp in a flavorful dressing. (Keep in mind that this salad should not be left out in the heat because of the mayonnaise dressing. If you do take it to a picnic, make sure it is deep in the ice in your cooler.) Make an easy dinner by piling the salad into lettuce leaves and surrounding them with sliced ripe tomatoes sprinkled with a little coarse salt. **MAKES 4 SERVINGS**

1 pound small shrimp (more than 55 per pound), peeled and deveined, or precooked cold-water (or baby) shrimp, thawed

1 celery stalk, finely diced

1 small shallot, finely diced

3 sweet pickles, finely chopped, or 2 tablespoons sweet pickle relish

⅓ cup mayonnaise (regular, low-fat, or fat-free)

2 tablespoons sour cream (regular, low-fat, or fat-free)

Juice of ½ lemon

2 teaspoons chopped dill

2 dashes Tabasco sauce (optional)

Salt and freshly ground black pepper to taste

1. If you're using raw shrimp, bring 2 quarts salted water to a boil in a large pot over high heat. Fill a large bowl halfway with ice water and set it aside. Add the shrimp to the boiling water and cook until pink and firm, about 2 minutes. Remove the shrimp with a slotted spoon or strainer and place them in the ice water to cool. Drain the shrimp and blot them dry with paper towels. If you're using precooked shrimp, omit this step and skip to step 3.

2. Coarsely chop the cooked shrimp and set aside.

3. Combine the celery, shallot, pickles, mayonnaise, sour cream, lemon juice, and dill in a large bowl. Add the shrimp and stir until all the ingredients are well combined. Stir in the Tabasco sauce, if desired. Season with salt and pepper.

4. Serve immediately, or cover and refrigerate until you're ready to serve the salad. (The salad can be made up to 3 days in advance and kept tightly covered in the refrigerator.)

ALMOND AND SHRIMP SALAD Sprinkle the top of each serving with 1 tablespoon toasted slivered almonds.

CURRIED SHRIMP SALAD Increase the lemon juice to the juice of 1 lemon. Add 2½ teaspoons curry powder to the dressing.

DEVILED SHRIMP SALAD Increase the Tabasco sauce to 4 dashes, or more to taste. Add 1 tablespoon cider vinegar, 1 teaspoon ground cinnamon, ¼ teaspoon ground cloves, and ¼ teaspoon grated nutmeg to the dressing.

EGG AND SHRIMP SALAD Increase the mayonnaise to ½ cup. Add 3 hard-boiled eggs, coarsely chopped, to the dressing.

HERBED SHRIMP SALAD Add 1½ tablespoons minced marjoram and 2 teaspoons minced thyme to the dressing.

MEDITERRANEAN SHRIMP SALAD Increase the mayonnaise to ½ cup. Add 2 tablespoons capers, drained and rinsed, 3 chopped anchovy fillets, and 3 pimientos, thinly sliced, to the dressing.

MINTED SHRIMP SALAD Add 2 teaspoons chopped mint to the dressing.

Shrimp Salade Niçoise

FOR THIS COMPOSED SALAD, ingredients are arranged in the bowl in colorful patterns, then topped with the dressing. Traditionally, a Salade Niçoise includes tuna; shrimp reinvents this Mediterranean classic. **MAKES 4 TO 6 SERVINGS**

FOR THE SALAD

- ½ pound thin green beans (haricots verts, or string beans cut in half lengthwise)
- 1½ pounds large shrimp (12 to 15 per pound), peeled and deveined, or precooked cocktail shrimp, thawed and peeled
- 1½ pounds small new potatoes
- 8 baby artichokes (no more than 2½ inches long), halved
- Juice of ½ lemon
- 2 small heads lettuce (such as Bibb, red leaf, green leaf, or romaine)
- 2 medium tomatoes, cut into 6 wedges each
- 3 large hard-boiled eggs, peeled and quartered
- 16 large olives (black or green)

FOR THE DRESSING

- 1 tablespoon Dijon mustard
- 1 garlic clove, minced
- 1 tablespoon chopped dill
- Juice of ½ lemon
- ¾ cup extra virgin olive oil
- Salt and freshly ground black pepper to taste

1. Bring 4 quarts salted water to a boil in a large pot over high heat. Fill a large bowl halfway with ice water and set it aside. Add the green beans to the boiling water and cook only until they are tender but still slightly crisp, about 1 minute. Remove the beans with a slotted spoon and place them in the ice water to cool.

2. If you're using raw shrimp, bring the water back to a boil over high heat. Add the shrimp and cook until pink and firm, about 3 minutes. Remove the shrimp with a slotted spoon and add them to the beans in the ice water.

3. If you've used raw shrimp, discard the water in the pot, refill it with 4 quarts salted water, and bring it back to a boil over high heat. Add the potatoes. Reduce the heat to medium and boil the

potatoes until they are just tender when pierced with a knife's tip, about 15 minutes. Transfer the potatoes to a colander set in the sink, using a slotted spoon. Let cool completely.

4. Return the salted water to a boil. Meanwhile, carefully trim the baby artichokes by removing the first two lower rings of outer leaves. Cut off most of the stems, leaving about ½ inch. If there is any fuzzy material (the choke) in the center, gently pull it out.

5. Add the lemon juice to the boiling water, then add the artichokes. Reduce the heat and cook until the centers are tender when pierced with a knife's tip, about 7 minutes. Drain the artichokes in a colander and set aside.

6. Remove the beans and shrimp from the ice water and dry them on paper towels. Set aside.

7. Tear the lettuce into 3-inch pieces and wash under cold water, removing any grit. Dry in a salad spinner or with paper towels. Place the lettuce on a large platter and top with the green beans. Arranging them in quadrants, top the beans and lettuce with the potatoes, baby artichokes, and tomato wedges. Place the shrimp in a mound down the middle of the platter. Place the eggs on either side of them. Scatter the olives over the platter. (The salad can be composed up to 8 hours before you want to serve it and kept covered with plastic in the refrigerator.)

8. To make the dressing, place the mustard, garlic, dill, and lemon juice in a medium bowl. Whisk or mix with a fork until well combined. In a thin stream, whisk in the oil, beating constantly until the dressing is smooth and creamy, and season with salt and pepper. (The dressing can be made up to 2 days in advance and kept covered in the refrigerator. Bring back to room temperature before you use it.)

9. Serve the dressing on the side, or pour it over the top of the salad in a thin, even drizzle.

CHEESE AND SHRIMP SALADE NIÇOISE Sprinkle 1½ cups crumbled feta (about 6 ounces) over the top of the salad with the shrimp and the eggs.

CURRIED SHRIMP SALADE NIÇOISE Omit the dill in the dressing. Increase the lemon juice to ¼ cup and whisk 2 teaspoons curry powder into the mustard mixture.

SHRIMP SALADE NIÇOISE WITH TARRAGON DRESSING Omit the dill and lemon juice in the dressing. Whisk 1½ tablespoons white wine vinegar and 1 tablespoon minced tarragon into the mustard mixture.

Shrimp Satay with Peanut Sauce

ALTHOUGH WE OFTEN ASSOCIATE satay with Thailand, it's actually a Malaysian dish. Originally, paper-thin strips of tough water buffalo were marinated to improve their texture, seared over a fire, and dipped in nut oils to improve their taste. Fortunately, shrimp are not nearly so tough or tasteless as water buffalo! Because you need to sear the skewers at such a high heat, a cast-iron skillet is the best choice. The peanut dipping sauce for the satay is also good over salads, on roasted meats, or as a dip for vegetables. You might want to double the recipe, saving some for another occasion; it will keep covered in the refrigerator for up to 2 weeks. **MAKES 4 TO 6 SERVINGS**

FOR THE SHRIMP

2 pounds medium shrimp (35 to 40 per pound), peeled and deveined

¼ cup peanut oil

4 teaspoons curry powder

FOR THE PEANUT SAUCE

½ cup smooth peanut butter

¼ cup toasted sesame oil

¼ cup plus 2 tablespoons soy sauce

3 tablespoons rice wine vinegar

2 teaspoons sugar

2 teaspoons minced ginger

1 garlic clove, minced

2 teaspoons chili oil (optional)

½ teaspoon freshly ground black pepper

Sixteen 8-inch bamboo or wooden skewers, soaked in water for 20 minutes

1. To prepare the shrimp, combine the shrimp, oil, and curry powder in a large mixing bowl. Toss until the shrimp are well coated. Set them aside in a cool place to marinate for 30 minutes.

2. Meanwhile, prepare the Peanut Sauce: Combine the peanut butter, sesame oil, soy sauce, vinegar, sugar, ginger, garlic, chili oil, if desired, and pepper in a blender. Cover and pulse until the mixture is smooth. (The sauce can be made ahead and stored in the refrigerator, tightly covered, for up to 2 weeks. Allow the sauce to come back to room temperature before serving.)

3. To cook the shrimp, thread them onto skewers, allowing 4 to 6 shrimp per skewer.

4. Place a large cast-iron or heavy nonstick skillet over high heat until it is extremely hot, just smoking. Place only as many skewers into the hot pan as will fit without crowding. Cook the shrimp for 1½ minutes per side, or until they are lightly browned and firm. Set the cooked shrimp aside. Cover and keep warm while you cook the remaining shrimp. (You could also use more than one skillet at a time.)

5. Serve the skewers with the peanut dipping sauce on the side.

ALMOND SHRIMP SATAY Substitute almond butter for the peanut butter in the sauce.

BROCCOLI AND SHRIMP SATAY Increase the peanut oil to ½ cup. Marinate 1 cup broccoli florets in the oil with the shrimp, then thread them all onto the skewers.

CASHEW SHRIMP SATAY Substitute cashew butter for the peanut butter in the sauce.

MUSHROOM AND SHRIMP SATAY Add 12 button or cremini mushrooms, cleaned and halved, to the marinade with the shrimp. Thread them onto the skewers with the shrimp.

ONION AND SHRIMP SATAY Increase the peanut oil to ⅓ cup. Quarter 1 small red onion and marinate it in the oil with the shrimp. Thread them all onto the skewers.

SCALLOP AND SHRIMP SATAY Reduce the shrimp to 1 pound. Marinate 1 pound sea scallops in the oil with the shrimp, then thread them all onto the skewers.

TOMATO AND SHRIMP SATAY Add 24 cherry tomatoes to the marinade with the shrimp. Thread them onto the skewers with the shrimp.

Shrimp Scampi

THERE IS NO MORE quintessential Italian-American dish than Shrimp Scampi, a favorite in diners all across New Jersey. For this decadent treat, large shrimp are smothered in garlic and butter, then baked. Shrimp Scampi's ready in no time at all. Serve it alongside roasted potatoes, purchased coleslaw, or noodles tossed with poppy seeds. **MAKES 4 TO 6 SERVINGS**

1½ pounds large shrimp (12 to 15 per pound), peeled, leaving the final segment of the tail shell intact, and deveined

4 tablespoons (½ stick) unsalted butter, melted

½ cup olive oil

2 tablespoons sweet vermouth

1 tablespoon Worcestershire sauce

8 garlic cloves, coarsely chopped

½ teaspoon salt

¼ teaspoon freshly ground black pepper

1. Place the shrimp in a large bowl, add the melted butter, oil, vermouth, Worcestershire, garlic, salt, and pepper, and toss until well combined. Cover and set aside in a cool place for 30 minutes before cooking.

2. Preheat the oven to 450°F.

3. Remove the shrimp from the marinade and place them in a shallow baking dish, large enough to hold them comfortably in one layer. Pour the marinade over the shrimp. Bake for 15 minutes, or until the sauce is bubbling. Serve immediately.

GARLIC LOVERS' SHRIMP SCAMPI Increase the garlic to 14 cloves.

GRILLED SHRIMP SCAMPI Rather than baking the shrimp, grill them on a prepared barbecue for 2 minutes per side. Do not pour the marinade over them—use it to baste the shrimp as they cook.

HEART-HEALTHY SHRIMP SCAMPI Omit the butter and increase the olive oil to ¾ cup.

MARTINI SHRIMP SCAMPI Add ¼ cup gin and 1 tablespoon juniper berries to the marinade. Omit the berries before serving, and garnish the dish with a few green olives.

ROSEMARY SHRIMP SCAMPI Add 1 tablespoon chopped rosemary to the marinade. Lay 2 rosemary sprigs over the dish as it bakes; discard them before serving.

SAVORY SHRIMP SCAMPI Use dry vermouth instead of sweet, and add 2 tablespoons chopped parsley to the marinade.

SPICY SHRIMP SCAMPI Add 1 teaspoon red pepper flakes, or more to taste, to the marinade.

Shrimp Scorpio

THIS GREEK-AMERICAN FAVORITE COMBINES RICH, herbed tomato sauce with feta, the tangy white, slightly dry sheep's or goat's milk cheese so popular in the Cyclades. The shrimp are folded into the rich sauce, then baked. Serve this hearty dish with rice, couscous, or orzo, the tiny grain-shaped pasta. **MAKES 4 SERVINGS**

2 tablespoons olive oil

2 medium onions, finely chopped

1 garlic clove, minced

½ teaspoon red pepper flakes

2 teaspoons capers, drained

½ cup black olives, pitted and halved

Once 28-ounce can tomato purée

¼ cup finely chopped parsley

2 tablespoons chopped dill

1 teaspoon salt

Freshly ground black pepper to taste

1 pound medium shrimp (35 to 40 per pound), peeled and deveined

2 cups crumbled feta (about 8 ounces)

1. Preheat the oven to 350°F.

2. Heat the oil in a large ovenproof skillet over medium heat. Add the onions and cook, stirring often, until soft and translucent, about 4 minutes.

3. Add the garlic, red pepper flakes, capers, and olives; cook, stirring constantly, until the garlic is fragrant, about 1 minute. Add the tomato purée, parsley, and dill and bring to a simmer. Reduce the heat to low and cook, uncovered, until the mixture thickens to the consistency of spaghetti sauce, about 15 minutes. Add the salt and pepper.

4. Turn off the heat. Stir the shrimp into the sauce until they are well incorporated. Sprinkle the top evenly with the feta.

5. Place the skillet in the oven for 20 minutes, or until the shrimp are cooked through and the cheese is bubbling. Serve immediately.

BLUE CHEESE SHRIMP SCORPIO Reduce the feta to 1 cup. Mix 1 cup crumbled blue cheese (such as Gorgonzola; about 4 ounces) with the feta before sprinkling.

BUTTERY SHRIMP SCORPIO Substitute unsalted butter for the olive oil.

CLAM AND SHRIMP SCORPIO Top the dish with 12 small clams (such as pismo), scrubbed, 5 minutes before the shrimp are done.

GARLIC LOVERS' SHRIMP SCORPIO Increase the garlic to 4 cloves.

HERBED SHRIMP SCORPIO Add 1 tablespoon chopped oregano and 1 tablespoon chopped basil with the tomato purée.

MIXED SEAFOOD SCORPIO Reduce the shrimp to ½ pound. Add ½ pound whole baby octopus, cleaned by your fishmonger, and ½ pound squid, cleaned and cut into ½-inch rings, with the shrimp.

ROCK SHRIMP SCORPIO Substitute peeled and cleaned rock shrimp for the regular shrimp.

SCALLOP AND SHRIMP SCORPIO Reduce the shrimp to ½ pound. Add ¾ pound sea scallops, cut in half, with the shrimp.

Sesame Shrimp

IN THIS CHINATOWN FAVORITE, the shrimp are deep-fried, then stir-fried with vegetables in an aromatic sauce made from oil seasoned with chiles and ginger. Sesame seeds are available in bulk in Indian and Asian markets, and also in larger supermarkets. Serve the shrimp over white or brown rice—avoid aromatic rices like jasmine that will compete with the dish's flavors. **MAKES 4 SERVINGS**

1 tablespoon soy sauce

1 tablespoon black vinegar

1 tablespoon sweetened Chinese vinegar

1 tablespoon sugar

½ teaspoon chili oil

1 pound broccoli, large stems removed

1 large egg white

1 tablespoon dry sherry

1 pound medium shrimp (35 to 40 per pound), peeled and deveined

1 teaspoon cornstarch

¼ cup white sesame seeds

8¼ cups peanut oil

6 large dried red Asian chiles

One 3-inch piece ginger, thinly sliced

1. Whisk the soy sauce, black vinegar, sweet vinegar, sugar, and chili oil together in a small bowl. Set aside.

2. Break or cut the broccoli into medium florets, about the size of walnuts.

3. Bring 2 quarts of salted water to boil in a large pot over high heat. Add the broccoli and cook for 30 seconds. Drain the broccoli and set aside.

4. Combine the egg white and sherry in a large bowl and whisk until foamy. Add the shrimp and toss until coated. Add the cornstarch and sesame seeds and toss until the shrimp are well coated.

5. Combine ¼ cup of the peanut oil with the chiles and ginger in a wok or large skillet. Place the wok over very low heat to allow the flavors of the chiles and ginger to infuse the oil while you prepare the shrimp. If the oil begins to smoke, turn off the heat.

6. Pour the remaining 8 cups oil into a large saucepan at least 4 inches deep and 10 inches in diameter; the oil should be at least 1½ inches deep but reach no more than halfway up the sides of the pan. Alternatively, fill an electric deep fryer with oil according to the manufacturer's instructions. If you're using a pan, clip a deep-frying thermometer to the inside and place the pan over medium heat. Heat the oil to 375°F. Adjust the heat to maintain that temperature while you fry the shrimp. If you're using an electric deep fryer, set the temperature control to 375°F.

7. Add the shrimp to the oil and cook until they are lightly golden, about 2 minutes, turning occasionally with tongs. If necessary, cook the shrimp in two batches to avoid crowding the pan. Remove the shrimp with a slotted spoon and drain them on paper towels.

8. With a slotted spoon, remove the chiles and ginger from the oil in the wok; discard them. Raise the heat under the wok to high. After 1 minute, add the broccoli. Stir constantly for 30 seconds. Add the shrimp and stir and toss for 30 seconds more.

9. Stir in the soy sauce mixture. Allow the mixture to come to a boil, stirring constantly. When the sauce is thickened slightly, remove the wok from the heat. Serve immediately.

BLACK SESAME SHRIMP Use black sesame seeds instead of the white sesame seeds.

DOUBLE-GINGER SESAME SHRIMP Add 1 tablespoon minced ginger to the stir-fry with the shrimp.

EXTRA-HOT SESAME SHRIMP Increase the chili oil to 1 tablespoon and the dried chiles to 12.

HEART-HEALTHY SESAME SHRIMP Instead of deep-frying the shrimp, add them to the wok raw, and stir-fry them for an additional 2 minutes, or until pink and firm.

ORANGE SESAME SHRIMP Omit the ginger. Remove the zest from 1 orange in large strips with a vegetable peeler, and add to the ¼ cup oil with the chiles. Do not remove the orange zest from the oil before you stir-fry the shrimp.

SESAME SHRIMP WITH MIXED CHINESE VEGETABLES Add one 8-ounce can straw mushrooms, drained, and 1 can bamboo shoots, drained, to the stir-fry with the shrimp.

SESAME SHRIMP WITH SCALLIONS Add 4 scallions, chopped into 2-inch pieces, to the stir-fry with the shrimp.

SESAME SHRIMP WITH SNOW PEAS Omit the broccoli. Add 2 cups snow peas (about 4 ounces) to the stir-fry with the shrimp.

Shrimp Skewers

SHISH KEBAB, MOVE OVER. Shrimp skewered on rosemary sprigs will make your next barbecue a sensation. The heady smell of rosemary permeates the shrimp, and the presentation is quite dramatic. Serve them alongside some grilled vegetables, with a little Dijon mustard or purchased honey mustard dressing for a dipping sauce. Shrimp Skewers also make lovely appetizers, hot or at room temperature. For elegant finger food, use a pair of scissors to cut between the shrimp on the skewers. **MAKES 8 APPETIZER SERVINGS OR 4 MAIN-COURSE SERVINGS**

1½ pounds large shrimp (12 to 15 per pound), peeled and deveined

3 tablespoons olive oil

1 teaspoon grated lemon zest

1 tablespoon fresh lemon juice

2 garlic cloves, finely chopped

1 teaspoon salt

½ teaspoon cracked black peppercorns

4 to 6 sturdy rosemary sprigs (for skewers), each at least 6 inches long

1. Combine the shrimp, olive oil, lemon zest, lemon juice, garlic, salt, and pepper in a large bowl. Toss until all the ingredients are well blended and the shrimp are evenly coated. Cover and marinate the shrimp in the refrigerator for no more than 30 minutes.

2. Twenty minutes before you're ready to cook the shrimp, place the rosemary skewers in a large bowl and add water to cover them by 1 inch. Set aside to soak. Prepare the barbecue grill. Or, if you're cooking the shrimp on a gas grill or in the broiler, preheat it 5 minutes before you're ready to cook.

3. When the coals are glowing red with a thin covering of ash, place the rack on the barbecue.

4. Meanwhile, remove the shrimp from the refrigerator. Use a small sharp knife to puncture a small slit in the underside of the shrimp (where the little legs were), and gently push the knife through to the other side of the shrimp, keeping the slit as small as possible. Drain the rosemary skewers and thread 3 to 4 shrimp onto each skewer, starting at the woody stem end of the rosemary. Use the slits you made in the shrimp as your guide. Leave ½ inch between each shrimp so the rosemary flavor can permeate the shrimp.

5. Lay the shrimp skewers on the grill rack directly over the coals. Cook for 2 minutes, then turn, using tongs or a metal spatula. Cook for 2 more minutes, or until the shrimp are firm and pink. Or, if you're using the broiler, lay the shrimp skewers on a baking sheet and place them 4 inches from the flame. Cook for 2 minutes per side, or until firm and pink.

ASPARAGUS SHRIMP SKEWERS Add 1 tablespoon chopped rosemary or thyme to the shrimp marinade. Substitute narrow asparagus spears for the rosemary sprigs (omit the soaking). Thread the shrimp on from the stem end of the asparagus.

CINNAMON SHRIMP SKEWERS Omit the lemon zest and lemon juice. Add 1 tablespoon cider vinegar and 2 teaspoons Indian curry paste to the shrimp marinade. Substitute 6-inch cinnamon sticks, broken in half lengthwise, for the rosemary sprigs.

LEMONGRASS SHRIMP SKEWERS Omit the olive oil, lemon zest, and lemon juice. Add 3 tablespoons toasted sesame oil, 1 tablespoon rice wine vinegar, and 1 tablespoon finely minced ginger to the shrimp with the garlic. Skewer the shrimp onto thin lemongrass stalks instead of rosemary.

SIMPLE SHRIMP SKEWERS Omit the rosemary sprigs. Marinate the shrimp as directed and skewer them on wooden or bamboo skewers that have been soaked in water or metal skewers. You needn't cut a guide hole in each shrimp.

Shrimp Soufflé

SOUFFLÉ MEANS *"PUFFED UP"* in French—and in a very hot oven, that's exactly what happens to a soufflé. Despite any dire warnings you may have heard about how hard it is to make one, how liable it is to collapse, a soufflé is an easy elegant meal, great for company, expected or not. Serve Shrimp Soufflé hot, the moment it's ready, with a tossed green salad or steamed green beans. You can even top the soufflé with Szechwan Cold Garlic Sauce (page 194) or purchased honey mustard salad dressing.

MAKES 4 SERVINGS

3 tablespoons unsalted butter, plus additional for the soufflé dish

1 cup freshly grated Parmigiano-Reggiano (about 4 ounces)

6 large eggs, at room temperature

½ pound small shrimp (more than 55 per pound), peeled and deveined, or precooked cold-water (or baby) shrimp, thawed

¼ cup all-purpose flour

1¼ cups whole milk

¼ cup clam juice

2 teaspoons minced tarragon

1 teaspoon Dijon mustard

½ teaspoon salt

1. Preheat the oven to 400°F. Butter a 2-quart soufflé dish. Coat the inside of the dish with ¼ cup of the grated cheese. Set aside.

2. Separate the eggs, placing the yolks in a small bowl and the whites in a large mixing bowl or the bowl of a stand mixer.

3. If you're using raw shrimp, bring 1 quart salted water to a boil in a medium pot over high heat. Fill a medium bowl halfway with ice water and set it aside. Add the shrimp to the boiling water and cook until pink and firm, about 2 minutes. Using a slotted spoon or strainer, transfer the shrimp to the ice water and allow them to cool. Drain the cooled shrimp and blot dry with paper towels. If you're using precooked shrimp, skip this step.

4. Place the cooked shrimp in a food processor and pulse until they are finely ground—resembling crabmeat—but not puréed. Set aside.

5. Melt 3 tablespoons of the butter in a medium saucepan over medium heat. Add the flour and whisk until completely incorporated. Cook until the flour loses its raw white color but does not

brown, about 1 minute. Add the milk and clam juice and continue to whisk until the mixture comes to a simmer and thickens.

6. Remove the pan from the heat. Whisk ½ cup of the hot milk mixture into the reserved egg yolks until smooth, about 20 seconds. Then whisk the warmed egg yolk mixture back into the hot milk mixture. Whisk in the tarragon, mustard, salt, and the remaining ¾ cup Parmigiano-Reggiano. Add the ground shrimp and stir until well blended. Set aside.

7. Beat the reserved egg whites at medium-high speed until soft peaks form when the beater is lifted from the egg whites. With a wooden spoon, stir one-third of the egg whites into the ground shrimp mixture, mixing quickly to lighten the shrimp mixture.

8. Pour the shrimp mixture into the bowl with the remaining beaten egg whites, and very gently fold the two together, using large circular strokes with a rubber spatula, until the ingredients are well distributed but not necessarily fully combined. Do not overfold—streaks of egg white may still be visible.

9. Pour the soufflé mixture into the prepared dish and bake for 35 minutes, or until the soufflé is puffed up over the rim of the dish and the top is golden brown. Serve immediately.

ASIAN SHRIMP SOUFFLÉ Omit the tarragon and mustard. Add 1½ teaspoons minced ginger and ½ teaspoon wasabi paste to the egg yolk–milk mixture.

GARDEN SHRIMP SOUFFLÉ Omit the tarragon. Add 2 teaspoons minced chervil, 2 teaspoons minced parsley, and 1 teaspoon minced chives to the egg yolk–milk mixture.

SHRIMP CHEDDAR SOUFFLÉ Omit the Parmigiano-Reggiano. Coat the inside of the dish with ¼ cup grated Cheddar. Add ¾ cup grated Cheddar (about 3 ounces) to the egg yolk milk mixture with the ground shrimp.

SHRIMP DILL SOUFFLÉ Substitute 1 tablespoon chopped dill for the tarragon.

SHRIMP MARJORAM SOUFFLÉ Substitute minced marjoram for the tarragon.

SHRIMP THYME SOUFFLÉ Substitute 1 tablespoon minced thyme for the tarragon.

SPICY SHRIMP SOUFFLÉ Omit the Dijon mustard. Add 1 teaspoon bottled horse-radish and ½ teaspoon Tabasco sauce, or more to taste, to the egg yolk–milk mixture.

Southwestern Stewed Shrimp

THIS FIERY, SANTA FE–STYLE STEW is a fine blend of tequila, chiles, and cinnamon. The cornmeal will thicken the stew; stir often so it doesn't burn on the bottom of the pot. The stew is good over rice, couscous, or wilted greens. It's also excellent on its own, with warmed flour or corn tortillas served alongside. (You can even make a double batch so you're sure there will be leftovers for the next day.)

MAKES 6 SERVINGS

2 tablespoons cornmeal

2 tablespoons pure chile powder

1 teaspoon ground cumin

1 teaspoon ground cinnamon

3 tablespoons tequila

2 tablespoons honey

2 tablespoons vegetable oil

1 large red onion, finely chopped

2 garlic cloves, minced

3 pickled jalapeños, minced

2 cups canned or homemade chicken stock

Two 15-ounce cans Latin American black beans, drained and rinsed

1 teaspoon salt, or more to taste

Freshly ground black pepper to taste

1½ pounds medium shrimp (35 to 40 per pound), peeled and deveined

1. Preheat the oven to 350°F.

2. Combine the cornmeal, chile powder, cumin, cinnamon, tequila, and honey in a small bowl. Stir until well blended and a thick paste forms. Set aside.

3. Heat the oil in a large heavy ovenproof pot or Dutch oven over medium heat. When the oil is hot, add the onion and cook, stirring often, until it is completely softened and just begins to brown, about 6 minutes. Add the garlic and jalapeños and cook, stirring constantly, for 30 seconds. Add the cornmeal paste and cook, stirring constantly, for 1 minute.

4. Add the stock and stir until the mixture comes to a simmer and thickens slightly. Add the beans and salt, and return the mixture to a simmer.

5. Cover the pot and place it in the oven. Bake for 45 minutes, stirring occasionally to prevent the stew from burning on the bottom of the pan. If the stew begins to stick, lower the oven temperature to 300°F.

6. Add the shrimp to the pot and stir until they are well incorporated. Place the pot back in the oven for 15 minutes or until the shrimp are pink and firm and the sauce is bubbling; stir occasionally. Season with pepper and check for salt. Serve immediately.

MILD SOUTHWESTERN STEWED SHRIMP Omit the jalapeños.

SOUTHWESTERN BEER-STEWED SHRIMP Use two 12-ounce bottles dark beer instead of the stock.

SOUTHWESTERN FISH AND SHRIMP STEW Increase the chicken stock to 3 cups. Reduce the shrimp to 1 pound. Add 1 pound fish fillets (such as red snapper or orange roughy), cut into 2-inch cubes and picked over for bones, with the shrimp.

SOUTHWESTERN SHRIMP AND CORN STEW Omit the black beans. Add two 10-ounce packages frozen corn, thawed, to the stew before you bake it.

SOUTHWESTERN VEGETABLE AND SHRIMP STEW Increase the chicken stock to 3 cups. Add 1 cup sliced green beans and 1 cup sliced carrots with the black beans.

Steamed Shrimp

THIS IS BY FAR the easiest way to prepare shrimp. You can also steam any extra shrimp you happen to have on hand and then freeze them for later. Cool the cooked shrimp, blot them dry with paper towels, and place them in an individual layer on a cookie sheet in your freezer. Once they're frozen, dump them into a plastic bag. Then simply thaw them in your refrigerator, and you'll have your own precooked cocktail shrimp, ready for one of the easy recipes in this book. **MAKES 4 SERVINGS**

1½ pounds medium shrimp (35 to 40 per pound), deveined but not peeled

1. Place the shrimp in a bamboo steamer. (If all the shrimp do not fit in one steamer basket and allow you to still use the cover, steam them in batches or use stacking steamer trays, covering the uppermost basket.) Alternatively, you can use a conventional metal vegetable steamer.

2. Fill a large pot—one whose width matches the bamboo steamer or one that accommodates the vegetable steamer—with water to a depth of 1 inch. Or you can set the bamboo steamers in a wok filled with just enough water to reach to ½ inch below the bottom of the steamer basket. Bring the water to a boil over high heat.

3. Place the steamer basket(s) on top, cover, and cook until all the shrimp are pink and firm, about 5 minutes, or set the filled vegetable steamer in the pot, cover it, and steam for 5 minutes. Immediately remove the shrimp from the steamer. Be careful—the steam is very hot.

4. Serve the shrimp hot, at room temperature, or cold, alongside your favorite dipping sauce, a small dish of melted salted butter, or equal parts of soy sauce and rice wine vinegar whisked together.

STEAMED SHRIMP WITH ASPARAGUS Toss the raw shrimp with 8 asparagus spears, cut into 2-inch pieces. Steam the shrimp and asparagus together. (This is particularly good with Szechwan Cold Garlic Sauce, page 194.)

STEAMED SHRIMP WITH BAMBOO SHOOTS Toss the raw shrimp with one 8-ounce can sliced bamboo shoots, drained. Steam the shrimp and bamboo shoots together.

STEAMED SHRIMP WITH GINGER Toss the raw shrimp with ¼ cup shredded ginger. Steam the shrimp and ginger together. (This is particularly good with Peanut Sauce, page 166.)

STEAMED SHRIMP WITH SCALLIONS Toss the raw shrimp with 6 scallions, cut into 2-inch pieces. Steam the shrimp and scallions together. (This is particularly good with Szechwan Cold Garlic Sauce, page 194.)

STEAMED SHRIMP WITH SHIITAKE MUSHROOMS Toss the raw shrimp with 1 cup shiitake mushrooms, caps sliced into ½-inch strips. Steam the shrimp and shiitake mushrooms together.

STEAMED SHRIMP WITH SNOW PEAS Toss the raw shrimp with 1½ cups snow peas. Steam the shrimp and snow peas together.

STEAMED SHRIMP WITH WALNUTS Toss the raw shrimp with 1½ cups walnut halves. Steam the shrimp and walnuts together. (This is particularly good with Barbecue Sauce, page 26.)

STEAMED SHRIMP WITH WATER CHESTNUTS Toss the raw shrimp with one 8-ounce can sliced water chestnuts, drained. Steam the shrimp and water chestnuts together.

Shrimp Stroganoff

COUNT STROGANOV, A NINETEENTH-CENTURY Russian diplomat and heir to one of imperial Russia's largest fortunes, is credited with this opulent sauce usually served over beef (although we might also have to credit his long-forgotten chef as well). The rich mélange of butter, onions, and mushrooms is not truly Russian—the count was trying to show his western European cohorts that Russians could cook like the French. His dish lives on, a great way to make a satisfying one-plate meal, ready in minutes. **MAKES 4 SERVINGS**

10 ounces egg noodles

5 tablespoons unsalted butter

1 small onion, finely chopped

2 garlic cloves, minced

1½ cups thinly sliced button mushrooms (about 6 ounces)

1 pound medium shrimp (35 to 40 per pound), peeled and deveined

2 tablespoons all-purpose flour

1½ cups fish stock or clam juice

½ cup sour cream (regular or low-fat, but not fat-free)

3 tablespoons dry vermouth

1½ teaspoons salt

Freshly ground black pepper to taste

1. Bring 2 quarts salted water to boil in a large pot over high heat. Add the egg noodles and cook them according to the package's instructions until they are al dente, about 6 minutes. Drain the noodles in a colander, rinse them thoroughly, and return them to the pot. Add 1 tablespoon of the butter, toss, and cover the pot to keep the noodles warm.

2. Melt 2 tablespoons of the butter in a large heavy saucepan over medium heat. Add the onion and cook, stirring often, until soft and aromatic, about 2 minutes.

3. Add the garlic and mushrooms. Cook, stirring often, until the mushrooms give off their juices, about 3 minutes. Add the shrimp and cook, stirring often, until pink and firm, about 3 minutes. At this point, the liquid remaining around the shrimp should be slightly thick. If it is too thin, let it simmer for another minute or so, until it reduces and thickens slightly. Remove the pan from the heat and cover it to keep the shrimp warm while you prepare the sauce.

4. Melt the remaining 2 tablespoons butter in a large deep skillet over medium heat. Add the flour and whisk until it is completely incorporated. Whisk constantly for another 2 minutes to cook the mixture just until the flour loses its raw white appearance. Do not let the flour brown— reduce the heat if necessary.

5. Whisk the stock into the roux in a slow, thin stream. Keep whisking until the sauce is thick and smooth, about 1 minute. Reduce the heat to low and whisk in the sour cream, vermouth, and salt. Quickly add the shrimp, vegetables, and any accumulated juices, and stir until all the shrimp are well coated. Cook for 2 minutes at the lowest heat possible, just until the shrimp are warmed through. Do not allow the sauce to boil, or the sour cream will break and curdle. Season with pepper.

6. Serve the shrimp over the noodles, on a large platter or on individual plates.

BRANDIED SHRIMP STROGANOFF Omit the vermouth and add 3 tablespoons brandy with the sour cream. Be careful that it does not flame. If it does, cover the pan and remove it from the heat for 1 minute.

HEARTY SHRIMP STROGANOFF Add ½ cup diced pancetta with the onion. Stir 12 new potatoes, boiled and cut in halves or quarters, into the sauce with the cooked shrimp.

ROSEMARY SHRIMP STROGANOFF Add 3 rosemary sprigs and 2 tablespoons chopped parsley with the sour cream. Discard the rosemary sprigs before serving.

SHRIMP AND ASPARAGUS STROGANOFF Add 8 asparagus spears, cut into 2-inch pieces, with the mushrooms.

SHRIMP AND PEA STROGANOFF Add 1 cup fresh or thawed frozen peas with the mushrooms.

Stuffed Shrimp

WITH A LIGHT STUFFING of bread crumbs laced with crabmeat, these shrimp are a great addition to a picnic or a wonderful treat after a long day working in the yard. You can always double or even triple the recipe—and remember, many hands make light work. Have pitchers of your favorite drink handy, and get your family or friends involved in stuffing the shrimp—that way, your party will truly be a group effort! **MAKES 4 TO 6 SERVINGS**

¼ cup olive oil

1 garlic clove, minced

1 shallot, minced

1 celery stalk, minced

1 tablespoon minced oregano

1 tablespoon chopped basil

6 ounces lump crabmeat (about 1 cup), picked over for shells and cartilage

⅓ cup plain dry bread crumbs

¼ cup freshly grated Parmigiano-Reggiano (about 2 ounces)

½ teaspoon salt

Freshly ground black pepper to taste

1 large egg, lightly beaten

1 pound large shrimp (12 to 15 per pound), peeled, leaving the final segment of the tail shell intact, and deveined

1. Preheat the oven to 400°F. Oil a 9 x 13-inch baking pan and set it aside.

2. Heat the olive oil in a medium saucepan set over medium heat. Add the garlic, shallot, and celery; cook, stirring often, until soft and aromatic, about 3 minutes. Add the oregano and basil and cook for 10 seconds more. Transfer the vegetables to a mixing bowl.

3. Add the crabmeat, bread crumbs, cheese, and salt to the vegetables. Mix with a fork until well combined. Season with pepper.

4. Add the beaten egg to the crab-and-vegetable mixture, and stir until the egg is well incorporated. Set aside.

5. Butterfly the shrimp: Begin at the neck end of each shrimp and make a long slit with a paring knife down the back of the shrimp (opposite where the little legs were), about two-thirds of the way through, stopping just before the final tail segment. (You do not want to cut the shrimp in

half.) Gently open the slit with your fingers, remove any remaining parts of the vein, and flatten the shrimp by pressing cut side down onto the work surface, thereby creating a butterfly shape.

6. Hold a shrimp cut side up in one hand and place 1 heaping tablespoon of stuffing in the shrimp. Closing your hand slightly, bring the sides of the shrimp up and press them lightly into the stuffing. Lay the shrimp in the prepared baking pan and repeat with the remaining shrimp.

7. Bake, uncovered, for 25 minutes, or until the stuffing is lightly browned. Serve immediately.

CHEESY STUFFED SHRIMP Substitute ⅓ cup grated aged Manchego, a sheep's milk cheese from Spain (about 3 ounces), for the Parmigiano-Reggiano.

CRAWFISH STUFFED SHRIMP Substitute chopped cooked crawfish for the crabmeat.

LOBSTER STUFFED SHRIMP Substitute chopped cooked lobster for the crabmeat.

SPICY STUFFED SHRIMP Add 5 dashes Tabasco sauce, or more to taste, to the filling with the egg.

STUFFED ASIAN SHRIMP Omit the celery, oregano, and salt. Add 2 tablespoons chopped cilantro, 1 tablespoon soy sauce, and 1½ teaspoons minced ginger to the filling with the crabmeat.

STUFFED GREEK SHRIMP Omit the basil. Add 1 tablespoon drained capers, chopped, and 1 teaspoon grated lemon zest to the filling with the crabmeat.

STUFFED THAI SHRIMP Omit the oregano and salt. Increase the basil to 2 tablespoons. Add 2 teaspoons fish sauce to the filling with the crabmeat.

Shrimp Stuffed Grape Leaves

JARRED GRAPE LEAVES are packed in brine and must be rinsed before use. Include both big and small leaves—pick through them carefully and save the large intact ones for stuffing; use the torn and smaller leaves to layer the pan when you are ready to cook the stuffed ones. **MAKES ABOUT 3 DOZEN STUFFED LEAVES**

FOR THE FILLING

½ cup olive oil

1 large onion, finely chopped

1¼ cups long-grain white rice

¾ cup finely chopped parsley

1 teaspoon salt

½ teaspoon freshly ground black pepper

¾ cup clam juice

½ pound small shrimp (more than 55 per pound), peeled and deveined

FOR THE GRAPE LEAVES

2 tablespoons prepared tomato sauce

2 cups canned or homemade vegetable stock or chicken stock

¼ cup fresh lemon juice

One 18-ounce jar grape leaves

1. To prepare the filling, heat the oil in a medium saucepan over medium heat. Add the onion, reduce the heat to low, and cook, stirring often, until golden, about 10 minutes.

2. Add the rice and cook, stirring constantly, for 3 minutes. Add the parsley, salt, and pepper. Cook for 1 minute, stirring often. Add the clam juice and bring to a simmer. Cover and cook for 10 minutes. Remove the pan from the heat; the rice will be only partially cooked. Allow the mixture to cool for 10 minutes.

3. Meanwhile, finely chop the shrimp.

4. Add the shrimp to the rice mixture and mix until well combined. Set aside.

5. To prepare the grape leaves, whisk together the tomato sauce, stock, and lemon juice in a small bowl. Set aside.

6. Drain the grape leaves. Rinse the leaves under cold water to remove the brine. Be very careful—the leaves tear easily. Pick through them to find the largest, most intact ones. Cut off any stems from the largest leaves with a sharp paring knife or kitchen shears. Reserve the smaller and torn leaves.

7. Lay 1 of the largest leaves, vein side up, on the counter with the points of the leaf facing away from you. Place 1 heaping tablespoon of filling in the middle of the leaf. Pull the sides of the leaf over to cover the filling, then roll the leaf up away from you, creating a sealed bundle that resembles a small egg roll. Set aside, seam side down, and repeat with the remaining large leaves until all the filling is used.

8. Oil the bottom of a medium Dutch oven or covered flameproof casserole. Lay about two-thirds of the reserved small and torn leaves in the bottom of the pot. Place a layer of stuffed leaves over the leaves in the pot, so that the stuffed leaves just touch but are not packed tight. Cover with the remaining small and torn leaves. Add another layer of the remaining stuffed leaves. (Do not make more than two layers, or the stuffed leaves will not be submerged in the braising liquid.)

9. Pour the reserved stock mixture over the leaves. Place a small heatproof plate on top to weight down the leaves while they cook. Place the pot over low heat and bring the liquid to a simmer. Cover and cook for 1 hour and 15 minutes. The loose leaves on the bottom will dry out—but lower the heat if they begin to scorch.

10. Remove the pot from the heat and allow the leaves to cool before removing them from the pot. Serve at room temperature or cold. The stuffed leaves will keep for up to 1 week tightly covered in the refrigerator.)

FETA SHRIMP STUFFED GRAPE LEAVES Add ¼ cup crumbled feta (about 2 ounces) to the filling with the shrimp.

OUZO SHRIMP STUFFED GRAPE LEAVES Reduce the stock to 1½ cups. Add ½ cup ouzo (anise-flavored Greek liqueur) with the tomato juice.

SHRIMP AND PINE NUT STUFFED GRAPE LEAVES Add ⅓ cup toasted pine nuts to the filling with the shrimp.

Shrimp Stuffed Mushroom Caps

STUFFED MUSHROOM CAPS ARE great appetizers, picnic bites, or lunch treats. Buy white button or cremini mushrooms that are sold individually, rather than prepackaged, so you can choose mushrooms whose caps are two or more inches in diameter. Avoid any mushrooms whose gills (the black spore chambers) are showing under the cap. **MAKES 12 STUFFED MUSHROOMS**

½ pound small shrimp (more than 55 per pound), peeled and deveined

12 large mushrooms (about ¾ pound), cleaned

4 teaspoons olive oil, plus additional for the baking dish

1 large shallot, minced

1 garlic clove, minced

1½ teaspoons minced oregano

1 teaspoon minced thyme

2 tablespoons sweet vermouth

½ teaspoon salt

Freshly ground black pepper to taste

2 tablespoons plain dry bread crumbs

1 tablespoon finely chopped parsley

3 tablespoons freshly grated Parmigiano-Reggiano

1. Preheat the oven to 400°F. Lightly oil a baking dish large enough to hold the mushrooms in one layer, such as a 9 × 13-inch or 10-inch square dish. Set aside.

2. Finely chop the shrimp. Set them aside.

3. Pull the stems from the mushroom caps. Set the caps aside. Finely chop the stems.

4. Heat 2 teaspoons of the olive oil in a medium skillet (preferably nonstick) over medium heat. Add the shallot and garlic; cook, stirring constantly, until the shallot is barely softened, about 1 minute. Add the chopped mushroom stems. Cook, stirring often, until they have given off their juices, about 4 minutes. Continue to cook, stirring occasionally, until the pan is almost dry, about 3 minutes more.

5. Add the chopped shrimp, oregano, and thyme to the skillet and cook, stirring constantly, until the shrimp is pink, about 2 minutes. Break up any clumps of shrimp with a wooden spoon as you cook.

6. Add the vermouth and salt; cook, stirring often, until the vermouth has evaporated, about 1 minute. Transfer the mixture to a large mixing bowl. Season with pepper.

7. Add the bread crumbs, parsley, 1 tablespoon of the Parmigiano-Reggiano, and the remaining 2 teaspoons of olive oil to the bowl and mix until well blended.

8. With a small spoon, fill 1 mushroom cap with 1 teaspoon (or slightly more) of the stuffing mixture. Sprinkle the cap with a pinch of grated cheese, and place it in the oiled baking dish. Repeat with the remaining caps.

9. Bake for 30 minutes, or until the stuffing is lightly browned. The mushrooms will release some of their juices as they bake, but most of the liquid should evaporate. Serve hot or at room temperature.

BASIL SHRIMP STUFFED MUSHROOM CAPS Omit the oregano and thyme. Add 2 teaspoons chopped basil to the sautéed mushrooms with the shrimp.

CORN BREAD SHRIMP STUFFED MUSHROOM CAPS Substitute crumbled day-old corn bread for the bread crumbs.

JALAPEÑO SHRIMP STUFFED MUSHROOM CAPS Omit the thyme. Add 1½ teaspoons minced seeded pickled or fresh jalapeño pepper to the stuffing with the bread crumbs.

LEMON SHRIMP STUFFED MUSHROOM CAPS Omit the oregano. Add 1½ teaspoons grated lemon zest to the sautéed mushrooms with the shrimp.

OLIVE SHRIMP STUFFED MUSHROOM CAPS Add ¼ cup minced pitted green olives to the stuffing.

SPICY SHRIMP STUFFED MUSHROOM CAPS Add 3 dashes Tabasco sauce, or more to taste, to the sautéed mushrooms with the shrimp.

TARRAGON SHRIMP STUFFED MUSHROOM CAPS Omit the oregano and thyme. Add 2 teaspoons minced tarragon to the sautéed mushrooms with the shrimp.

WASABI SHRIMP STUFFED MUSHROOM CAPS Omit the oregano, thyme, salt and cheese. Increase the bread crumbs to 3 tablespoons, and add 1 teaspoon wasabi paste and 2 teaspoons soy sauce to the stuffing with the bread crumbs.

Shrimp Sushi

TRADITIONALLY, SHRIMP SUSHI (*NIGIRI*) is made with tiny raw shrimp, laid over sea-soned rice. These shrimp, *amaebi*, are not readily available in North American markets—and there are some health concerns about eating raw shrimp. This sushi, therefore, is made with cooked medium shrimp. Sushi rice is available in Asian markets or by mail-order (see Source Guide, page 239). The rice mixture you'll create is called *sushi meshi* in Japanese. It takes a bit of practice, but once you learn, you'll be making sushi for every party you throw. Serve Shrimp Sushi with the dipping sauce and pickled ginger, accompanied by a cold beer or cold sake, or cold spring water. **MAKES 35 TO 40 PIECES**

1 pound medium shrimp (35 to 40 per pound), peeled and deveined

FOR THE SUSHI

¾ cup rice wine vinegar

½ cup water

1½ teaspoons sugar

½ teaspoon salt

5 cups just-cooked short-grain sushi rice (about 2½ cups raw rice, cooked according to the package directions), still hot

3 tablespoons wasabi paste, or more to taste

½ cup soy sauce

½ cup pickled sliced ginger

About forty 6-inch bamboo or wooden skewers

1. To prepare the shrimp, thread each onto a skewer, starting at the neck of the shrimp, pushing the skewer through the shrimp the long way until it comes out of the tail. (This will keep the shrimp from curling up while it cooks.)

2. Bring 3 quarts salted water to a boil in a large saucepan over high heat. Fill a large bowl halfway with ice water and set it aside. Add as many shrimp skewers to the boiling water as will fit and still allow the shrimp to be submerged, and cook until the shrimp are pink and firm, about 2 minutes. Using tongs, transfer the shrimp to the ice water. Repeat with any remaining shrimp. Allow the shrimp to cool, then remove from the skewers.

3. Using a paring knife, cut through the underside of each shrimp from the tail end to the neck. Leave just enough flesh at the bottom of your cut to hold the shrimp together when you open it up.

4. To assemble the sushi, whisk ½ cup of the rice wine vinegar and the water together in a small bowl. Set aside.

5. In a second small bowl, whisk together the remaining ¼ cup rice wine vinegar, the sugar, and salt, whisking until the sugar and salt are completely dissolved.

6. Spread the hot rice on a large flat surface (such as an 11 × 17-inch lipped baking sheet or a 12 to 15-inch round shallow casserole). Sprinkle the sugared vinegar evenly over the rice. Using a rubber spatula or flat wooden spoon held in one hand, gently toss the rice, flattening it out after each toss. This will evenly distribute the flavored vinegar while cooling the rice. Be sure to reach the corners and include all the rice in your tossing and spreading. If possible, use your other hand to fan the rice with a magazine or hand-held fan. The rice should be tossed, spread, and fanned until it is at room temperature and slightly sticky.

7. Moisten your fingers with the reserved vinegar and water mixture and pick up a small amount of rice (about the size of a golf ball) in your left hand. Making a loose fist, squeeze the ball into an oval about 3 inches long. Open your fist and flatten the long sides of the rice ball, using the fingers of your right hand. Press firmly so that the rice will hold its shape, but not so firmly that it loses its cylindrical oblong shape. (You may reverse hands, of course, if you are left-handed.)

8. Using your forefinger, spread a scant ¼ teaspoon of the wasabi paste onto the flat surface of the shaped rice. Place 1 shrimp cut side down on top of the wasabi. Set on a serving platter or individual plates. Repeat with the remaining rice and shrimp.

9. Whisk the soy sauce and the remaining wasabi paste together in a small bowl. Taste and add more wasabi if you desire a hotter sauce.

10. Serve the sushi immediately with the wasabi dipping sauce and the pickled ginger on the side.

Sweet-and-Sour Shrimp

THERE'S NO MORE CLASSIC Chinese-American dish than Sweet-and-Sour Shrimp. The tangy sauce, laced with chunks of pineapple, has roots that date back to the ancient Chinese culinary techniques of blending fruits with roasted meat to create a harmonic balance. Traditionally, this dish was more sour than its modern incarnation, which tends to emphasize the salty and sweet aspects of the sauce; you can return the dish to its more ancient roots by increasing the vinegar and decreasing the sugar according to taste. Serve the shrimp over bowls of white or brown rice. **MAKES 4 SERVINGS**

FOR THE SAUCE

¼ cup packed light brown sugar

2 tablespoons minced ginger

2 garlic cloves, minced

⅔ cup canned or homemade chicken stock

¼ cup cider vinegar

1 tablespoon soy sauce

½ teaspoon salt

1 green or red bell pepper, cored, seeded, and cut into 1-inch chunks

2 cups canned pineapple chunks, drained

1 tablespoon cornstarch, dissolved in 1 tablespoon water

FOR THE SHRIMP

8 cups peanut oil

½ cup all-purpose flour

2 tablespoons cornstarch

1 teaspoon baking powder

1 teaspoon salt

⅔ cup water

1 teaspoon toasted sesame oil

1 pound medium shrimp (35 to 40 per pound), peeled and deveined

1. To prepare the sauce, combine the brown sugar, ginger, garlic, chicken stock, vinegar, soy sauce, and salt in a large saucepan. Place over medium heat and stir until the sugar is completely dissolved and the mixture comes to a boil.

2. Add the bell pepper chunks and pineapple to the sauce, reduce the heat to low, and let the sauce simmer, uncovered, for 5 minutes. Remove the sauce from the heat and set it aside.

3. To prepare the shrimp, pour the oil into a large saucepan at least 4 inches deep and 10 inches in diameter; the oil should be at least 1½ inches deep but reach no more than halfway up the sides of the pan. Alternatively, fill an electric deep fryer with oil, according to the manufacturer's

instructions. If you're using a pan, clip a deep-frying thermometer to the inside and place the pan over medium heat. Heat the oil to 375°F. Adjust the heat to maintain that temperature while you prepare the shrimp. If you're using an electric deep fryer, set the temperature control to 375°F.

4. Combine the flour, cornstarch, baking powder, and salt in a large mixing bowl. Whisk gently until well combined. Gradually whisk in the water and sesame oil until the batter is completely smooth.

5. Dip a shrimp into the batter until it is completely coated. Let the excess batter drip off, then gently slide the shrimp into the hot oil. Repeat with the remaining shrimp, dipping and frying only as many shrimp at a time as will fit in the pan in one layer without crowding. Fry the shrimp until they are lightly golden, 1 to 2 minutes, turning occasionally with tongs. Remove the shrimp from the oil and drain them on paper towels.

6. To finish the dish, place the sauce over high heat and bring to a boil. Restir and add the cornstarch mixture, stirring constantly until the sauce thickens, about 1 minute.

7. Immediately add the shrimp to the sauce and toss until all the shrimp are well coated. Serve immediately.

FIERY SWEET-AND-SOUR SHRIMP Add 6 dried red Asian chiles to the sauce with the bell pepper chunks. Swirl 1 teaspoon chili oil into the sauce with the cornstarch mixture.

HEART-HEALTHY SWEET-AND-SOUR SHRIMP Omit the batter and don't deep-fry the shrimp. Instead, add them to the sauce once it is thickened with the cornstarch mixture, and simmer for 1 minute, stirring constantly. Remove the pan from the heat, cover it, and let stand for 5 minutes, or until the shrimp are pink and firm. Serve immediately.

SWEET-AND-SOUR SHRIMP AND BROCCOLI Reduce the shrimp to ½ pound. Dip 2 cups broccoli florets into the batter and fry them as you do the shrimp.

SWEET-AND-SOUR SHRIMP AND MUSHROOMS Reduce the shrimp to ½ pound. Dip ½ pound button or cremini mushrooms, cleaned, into the batter and fry them as you do the shrimp.

SWEET-AND-SOUR SHRIMP AND SCALLOPS Reduce the shrimp to ½ pound. Dip ½ pound scallops into the batter and fry them as you do the shrimp.

Szechwan Cold Garlic Shrimp

MAKE A DOUBLE BATCH of this cold garlic sauce—it's great over all sorts of meats and vegetables, not just these ginger-and-garlic infused shrimp. You could also serve this simple dish over cold soba noodles, sliced cucumbers, or even ramen noodles. **MAKES 4 APPETIZER SERVINGS OR 2 MAIN-COURSE SERVINGS**

FOR THE SHRIMP

One 6-inch piece ginger, peeled and sliced into ½-inch-thick rounds

6 scallions, white part only, cut into quarters

6 peeled garlic cloves

4 cups water

1 cup clam juice

1 pound large shrimp (12 to 15 per pound), peeled, leaving the final segment of the tail shell intact, and deveined

FOR THE SZECHWAN COLD GARLIC SAUCE

2 tablespoons soy sauce

1 tablespoon clam juice

1 tablespoon black vinegar

1 tablespoon toasted sesame oil

1 tablespoon chili oil

1 tablespoon sugar

¼ cup chopped cilantro

1 scallion, minced

4 garlic cloves, minced

2 celery stalks, cut into 2-inch lengths and julienned

1. To prepare the shrimp, place the ginger, scallions, garlic, water, and the clam juice in a large pot. Place over high heat and bring to a boil. Reduce the heat to low and simmer for 15 minutes.

2. Raise the heat to high and bring the broth back to a rolling boil. Add the shrimp, cover the pot, and immediately remove it from the heat. Let stand for 10 minutes. (The shrimp will cook in the hot liquid.)

3. Pour the shrimp and liquid into a large bowl and refrigerate until the shrimp are cold, about 4 hours.

4. To prepare the Szechwan Cold Garlic Sauce, whisk together the soy sauce, clam juice, black vinegar, sesame oil, chili oil, sugar, cilantro, scallion, and garlic in a large bowl. Cover and set aside.

5. To finish the dish, remove the cold shrimp from the broth with a slotted spoon and blot them dry with paper towels. Place them on a large plate with a lip. Pour the sauce over the shrimp and top them with the celery. Serve immediately.

PEPPERY SZECHWAN COLD GARLIC SHRIMP Add 3 tablespoons Szechwan peppercorns to the sauce.

SZECHWAN COLD GARLIC SHRIMP AND BEAN THREAD NOODLES Pour boiling water over two 2-ounce packages dried bean thread noodles in a large bowl. Soak for 15 minutes, or until the noodles turn transparent, then drain them. Toss the noodles with the drained shrimp; then pour the sauce over them.

SZECHWAN COLD GARLIC SHRIMP AND BROCCOLI Toss 1 cup cooked and chilled broccoli florets with the cooked shrimp in the sauce.

SZECHWAN COLD GARLIC SHRIMP AND PEPPERS Toss 1 cup 1-inch chunks red or green bell pepper with the cooked shrimp in the sauce.

SZECHWAN COLD GARLIC SHRIMP AND UDON NOODLES Omit the celery. Toss the drained shrimp with 8 ounces udon noodles, cooked and drained. Top the dish with sliced cucumbers.

Shrimp Tacos

TACOS HAVE BECOME AS American as apple pie. They're easy, light, and fun, as satisfying as any sandwich. If you'd like, set out all the ingredients and let your guests—or your kids—make their own shrimp Tacos. **MAKES 6 SERVINGS**

2 tablespoons vegetable oil

1 pound small shrimp (more than 55 per pound), peeled and deveined

2 tablespoons pure chile powder

1 tablespoon ground cumin

6 taco shells

3 cups shredded iceberg lettuce (about ⅓ medium head)

¾ cup shredded Cheddar (about 3 ounces)

2 medium tomatoes, seeded and cut into ¼-inch dice

1 small red onion, finely chopped

½ cup sour cream (regular, low-fat, or fat-free)

¼ cup finely chopped cilantro

1. Heat the oil in a large skillet over medium heat. Add the shrimp and cook, stirring often, until pink and firm, about 2 minutes. Add the chile powder and cumin and stir for 10 seconds, or until the shrimp are well coated. Remove the pan from the heat and cover to keep the shrimp warm.

2. Heat the taco shells according to the package instructions, using the microwave or a conventional oven. Set the warmed shells on your work surface.

3. Place 8 to 12 small shrimp (depending on their size) in each shell. Top each with ½ cup lettuce, 2 tablespoons Cheddar, 1 to 2 tablespoons tomatoes, 1 to 2 teaspoons onion, a dollop of sour cream, and a sprinkle of cilantro. Serve immediately.

BARBECUED SHRIMP TACOS Omit the chile powder and cumin. Pour ½ cup Barbecue Sauce (page 26) over the shrimp in the skillet once they're cooked, and stir to coat the shrimp thoroughly.

FANCY SHRIMP TACOS Omit the Cheddar. Add 1 tablespoon crumbled soft goat cheese to each taco. (You'll need about 6 ounces in total.) Sprinkle 1 tablespoon pepitás (pumpkin seeds, available in Latin American and gourmet markets) over the top of each taco.

FIERY NEW ORLEANS SHRIMP TACOS Fill the taco shells with Butterfly Fried Shrimp (page 50), and dust the shrimp in each shell with a pinch of cayenne pepper and garlic salt. Pour 1 tablespoon purchased French dressing over the shrimp before adding the fresh ingredients.

HOT SHRIMP TACOS Add 2 to 3 sliced jalapeño rings, fresh or pickled, to each taco.

TEXAS SHRIMP TACOS Omit the sour cream. Pour 1 tablespoon salsa and 1 tablespoon purchased Thousand Island dressing over the shrimp in each taco before topping with the fresh ingredients.

Shrimp Tamale Pie

E VERY TEXAS CHILD KNOWS Tamale Pie, a school-lunch staple. But it's not just for kids. It's old-fashioned comfort food, a hot, cheesy casserole with a rich sauce loaded here with shrimp. Masa harina is made from roasted corn kernels that are first soaked in limewater, then pulverized into meal—the same meal that makes corn tortillas. You can find it in most supermarkets or in any Latin American or Mexican market. Serve Tamale Pie with a tossed green salad or mango slices splashed with a little balsamic vinegar. **MAKES 6 TO 8 SERVINGS**

FOR THE FILLING

- ¼ cup vegetable oil
- 1 pound small shrimp (more than 55 per pound), peeled and deveined
- 1 small onion, finely chopped
- 2 medium tomatoes, chopped
- 2 teaspoons pure chile powder
- 1 teaspoon minced oregano
- 1 teaspoon minced thyme
- 1 teaspoon ground cumin
- 2 cups fresh or thawed frozen corn kernels
- ¼ cup clam juice
- ½ teaspoon salt
- Freshly ground black pepper to taste

FOR THE MASA

- 1½ cups masa harina
- ⅓ cup chilled vegetable shortening, or 6⅓ tablespoons cold unsalted butter
- ½ teaspoon baking powder
- ½ teaspoon salt
- ¼ cup half-and-half or light cream
- 1 cup vegetable stock, or as needed

Unsalted butter for the pan

- 1 cup shredded Cheddar (about 4 ounces)

1. To prepare the filling, heat 2 tablespoons of the vegetable oil in a large heavy skillet over medium heat. Add the shrimp and cook, stirring often, until pink and firm, about 2 minutes. Transfer the shrimp to a plate or bowl and set aside.

2. Add the remaining 2 tablespoons oil to the skillet and set the pan back over medium heat. Add the onion and cook until soft and translucent, about 3 minutes.

3. Add the tomatoes, chile powder, oregano, thyme, and cumin. Cook, stirring constantly, until the tomatoes break down, release their juices, and begin to reduce slightly, about 4 minutes. Add the corn, clam juice, and salt; stir until everything is well combined. Season with black pepper. Remove the pan from the heat and allow the sauce to cool.

4. Pour half the cooled sauce over the cooked shrimp. Mix until the shrimp are well coated. Set the coated shrimp and the remaining sauce aside. (The shrimp filling and sauce can be made up to 12 hours ahead and kept covered in the refrigerator.)

5. Combine the masa harina, shortening, baking powder, and salt in a food processor. Pulse 3 or 4 times, until the mixture is well combined and resembles coarse meal. With the machine running, pour the half-and-half though the feed tube. Process until the mixture is smooth, about 1 minute.

6. With the machine running, pour the broth through the feed tube in a thin, steady stream. Process just until a soft dough forms around the blade (it should resemble very thick cake frosting). Depending on the day's humidity and your kitchen's temperature, you may or may not use all the stock.

7. To assemble the pie, preheat the oven to 350°F. Butter a 9-inch square baking dish.

8. Spread two-thirds of the masa evenly in the bottom of the prepared baking dish, pressing it halfway up the sides. Spread the shrimp over the masa. Cover with the remaining masa, sealing the edges completely. Top the casserole with the reserved sauce. Cover the sauce with the cheese.

9. Bake for about 35 minutes, or until the cheese is bubbling and the masa is slightly firm. Serve hot or at room temperature.

FIERY SHRIMP TAMALE PIE Add 1 jalapeño pepper, chopped and seeded, to the filling with the tomatoes.

GARLIC LOVERS' SHRIMP TAMALE PIE Add 3 garlic cloves, minced, to the filling with the tomatoes.

SHEPHERD SHRIMP TAMALE PIE Make only half the masa dough. Top the casserole with mashed potatoes, and cover them with the cheese and sauce.

Tandoori Shrimp

ASSOCIATED WITH EAST INDIAN COOKING, the tandoor oven is actually a Middle Eastern invention: a ceramic oven, often in one piece like a huge pot. They've even been unearthed at Babylonian archeological digs. In 1948 a fashionable restaurant in New Delhi installed a tandoori oven, and Indian jet-setters began eating there. The media picked up the story, and the craze went around the world so fast, that tandoori cooking is now almost exclusively associated with India. The meat is first rubbed with a spiced yogurt marinade, then cooked at high heat. Since most of us don't have a tandoori oven at home, a barbecue can be a simple stand-in. Serve this simple dish with *naan* (an Indian flatbread, available in speciality markets) or perhaps tortillas, along with mango chutney, sliced tomatoes, and Cucumber Raita (recipe follows). **MAKES 6 TO 8 APPETIZER SERVINGS OR 4 MAIN-COURSE SERVINGS**

⅔ cup yogurt (regular or low-fat, but not fat-free)

1 tablespoon vegetable oil

1½ teaspoons pure chile powder

1 teaspoon ground coriander

1 teaspoon ground ginger

2 garlic cloves, minced

1 teaspoon salt

1 lemon, cut in half

2 pounds large shrimp (12 to 15 per pound), peeled, leaving the final segment of the tail shell intact, and deveined

Cucumber Raita (recipe follows)

1. Combine the yogurt, vegetable oil, chile powder, coriander, ginger, garlic, salt, and juice of half of the lemon in a large mixing bowl and stir until well combined. Add the shrimp and stir to coat. Cover and refrigerate for at least 30 minutes, but no more than 1 hour.

2. Light the coals in the barbecue at least 20 minutes before you're ready to cook the shrimp. Or if using a gas grill or the broiler, preheat it 5 minutes before you're ready to cook.

3. When the coals are glowing red with a thin covering of ash, place the rack on the barbecue. Remove the shrimp from the marinade and scrape away the excess. Lay the shrimp on the rack directly over the coals and cook for 2 minutes. Turn them with tongs or a metal spatula and cook for 2 more minutes, or until pink and firm. Remove them from the grill.

Or, if you're using a broiler, lay the shrimp on a baking sheet and place them 4 inches from the flame. Cook for 2 minutes per side, or until firm and pink. Remove them from the heat and transfer to plates.

4. Before serving, squeeze the juice of the remaining lemon half over the shrimp. Serve the raita alongside.

Cucumber Raita

1 large cucumber, peeled, seeded, and finely chopped

3 cups yogurt (regular, low-fat, or fat-free)

1 teaspoon minced mint

½ teaspoon salt

¼ teaspoon freshly ground black pepper

Stir the cucumber, yogurt, mint, salt, and pepper in a large bowl until well combined. (The raita can be made ahead and stored covered in the refrigerator for up to 2 days. Stir to reincorporate before serving.)

The raita can be varied endlessly by substituting other fruits and vegetables for the cucumber, such as . . .

1 cup canned crushed pineapple, drained • 1 large mango, peeled, seeded, and finely chopped • 2 medium bananas, finely chopped • 2 stalks celery, minced

Shrimp Tempura

TEMPURA IS THE FAVORITE way of deep-frying in Japan, for the thin batter makes an extraordinarily lacy, crunchy crust. The keys to success are rice flour (available in most Asian markets and in health food stores) and ice water. You might even want to try making the batter with water and shaved ice. The tiny ice particles explode when they hit the hot oil: stand back—it's very messy—but the result is unbelievably light and airy. Serve tempura the moment it's out of the fryer, with a dipping sauce—several versions follow the recipe. **MAKES 6 TO 8 SERVINGS**

8 cups vegetable oil

½ cup all-purpose flour

½ cup rice flour

1 teaspoon baking powder

1 large egg white, beaten until frothy

1½ cups ice water

2 pounds medium shrimp (35 to 40 per pound), peeled and deveined

1. Pour the oil into a large saucepan at least 4 inches deep and 10 inches in diameter; the oil should be at least 1½ inches deep but reach no more than halfway up the sides of the pan. Alternatively, fill an electric deep fryer with oil according to the manufacturer's instructions. If you're using a pan, clip a deep-frying thermometer to the inside and place the pan over medium heat. Heat the oil to 375°F. Adjust the heat to maintain that temperature while you prepare the shrimp. If you're using an electric deep fryer, set the temperature control to 375°F.

2. Combine the all-purpose flour, rice flour, and baking powder in a large mixing bowl; gently whisk until they are well blended. Whisk in the egg white until just combined. Add the ice water and whisk until smooth. Work quickly so the batter stays very cold; tiny ice particles can be left whole in the batter.

3. Dip a shrimp into the batter, then slide it into the hot oil. Stand back—the batter will pop. Repeat with the remaining shrimp, dipping and frying only as many shrimp at a time as will fit in the pan without crowding. Fry the shrimp until crisp and barely colored, not browned, about 2 minutes, turning occasionally with tongs. Remove each shrimp from the oil when it's done, and drain on paper towels. Sprinkle with salt and serve immediately.

DIPPING SAUCES

Tentsuyu (a traditional Japanese dipping sauce)

¼ cup soy sauce

1 tablespoon mirin (sweetened
   rice wine, available in Asian
   and some gourmet markets)

¼ teaspoon dashi concentrate
   (a soup base, available in Asian
   and some gourmet markets)

Whisk the soy sauce, mirin, and dashi concentrate together in a medium bowl until well blended.

Simple Japanese Dipping Sauce

¼ cup soy sauce

1 tablespoon rice wine vinegar

1 teaspoon sugar

Whisk the soy sauce, rice wine vinegar, and sugar together in a medium bowl until the sugar is dissolved.

Sesame Dipping Sauce

¼ cup soy sauce

2 tablespoons toasted sesame oil

½ teaspoon fresh lemon juice

Whisk the soy sauce, sesame oil, and lemon juice together in a medium bowl until well blended.

Tequila Grilled Shrimp

PERFECT FOR A BARBECUE or a cocktail party, these shrimp are redolent of agave—the plant used in making tequila—and lime. Serve them with tortillas and salsa, or toss them into a green salad with a light vinaigrette or purchased Thousand Island dressing. **MAKES 6 TO 8 APPETIZER SERVINGS OR 4 MAIN-COURSE SERVINGS**

1 cup high-quality tequila
(preferably 100% blue agave)

Juice of 3 limes

2 tablespoons grated orange
zest

2 pounds large shrimp (12 to 15
per pound), peeled, leaving the
final segment of the tail shell
intact, and deveined

1½ tablespoons kosher salt

1. Combine the tequila, lime juice, and orange zest in a large mixing bowl. Add the shrimp and toss to coat. Cover and refrigerate for no more than 30 minutes.

2. Light the coals in the barbecue at least 20 minutes before you're ready to cook the shrimp. Or if using a gas grill or the broiler, preheat it 5 minutes before you're ready to cook.

3. When the coals are glowing red with a thin covering of ash, place the rack on the barbecue. Lay the shrimp on the rack directly over the coals and cook for 2 minutes. Turn the shrimp with tongs or a metal spatula, and cook for another 2 minutes, or until pink and firm.

   Or, if using a broiler, lay the shrimp on an oiled lipped baking sheet or broiler pan and place them 4 inches from the flame. Cook for 2 minutes per side, or until firm and pink. Cook them in batches if necessary.

4. Place the shrimp on a large platter and sprinkle them with the kosher salt.

CAIPIRHINA GRILLED SHRIMP Omit the orange zest. Substitute 1 cup cachaça (Brazilian sugarcane rum) for the tequila. Sprinkle the finished shrimp with the salt, or omit it depending on your taste.

COSMOPOLITAN GRILLED SHRIMP Omit the tequila, and mix ½ cup cranberry juice and ½ cup vodka with the lime juice. Sprinkle the finished shrimp with the salt, or omit it, depending on your taste.

DAIQUIRI GRILLED SHRIMP Omit the orange zest. Substitute gold rum for the tequila and add 1 teaspoon sugar. Sprinkle the finished shrimp with the salt, or omit it, depending on your taste.

WHISKEY SOUR GRILLED SHRIMP Substitute high-quality whiskey for the tequila, and add 2 teaspoons sugar. Sprinkle the finished shrimp with salt, or omit it, depending on your taste.

Shrimp Teriyaki

IN JAPANESE, *TERI* MEANS gloss or sheen, and *yaki* refers to something grilled. Shrimp Teriyaki is indeed a glossy grilled dish, and it's also an easy meal—set the shrimp to marinate when you walk in from work, get changed and pour a drink, and dinner is almost ready. And this version is far better than any made with store-bought teriyaki sauces, which are loaded with preservatives and MSG. You can serve Shrimp Teriyaki with plain white rice, or you can dress up the rice by stirring ½ cup unsweetened coconut milk and 1 cup diced mango into it once it's cooked. **MAKES 6 TO 8 APPETIZER SERVINGS OR 4 MAIN-COURSE SERVINGS**

1 cup soy sauce

¼ cup plus 1 tablespoon sugar

1 small shallot, minced

1 tablespoon minced ginger

2 pounds large shrimp (12 to 15 per pound), peeled, leaving the final segment of the tail shell intact, and deveined

1. Combine the soy sauce, sugar, shallot, and ginger in a large mixing bowl. Stir until the sugar is completely dissolved. Stir the shrimp into the mixture, cover, and refrigerate for at least 30 minutes, but no more than 1 hour.

2. Light the coals in the barbecue at least 20 minutes before you're ready to cook the shrimp. Or if using a gas grill or the broiler, preheat it 5 minutes before you're ready to cook.

3. When the coals are glowing red with a thin covering of ash, place the rack on the barbecue. Lay the shrimp on the rack directly over the coals and cook for 2 minutes. Turn the shrimp with tongs or a metal spatula and cook for 2 more minutes, or until the shrimp are golden and firm.

Or, if using the broiler, lay the shrimp on a baking sheet and place them 4 inches from the flame. Cook for 2 minutes per side, or until golden and firm. Serve immediately.

APPLE SHRIMP TERIYAKI Omit the sugar. Add ¼ cup apple juice concentrate to the marinade.

GARLIC LOVERS' SHRIMP TERIYAKI Add 2 garlic cloves, minced, to the marinade.

LEMON SHRIMP TERIYAKI Add 1 teaspoon minced lemon zest to the marinade.

ORANGE SHRIMP TERIYAKI Add 2 tablespoons orange juice concentrate to the marinade.

PINEAPPLE SHRIMP TERIYAKI Omit the sugar. Add ¼ cup pineapple juice concentrate to the marinade.

SHRIMP TERIYAKI SKEWERS Skewer the shrimp on 6 large metal skewers or 6 bamboo skewers that have been soaked in water: thread 4 shrimp, 4 pineapple chunks, and 4 chunks of green bell pepper on each. Brush the skewers with the teriyaki marinade, cover, and refrigerate for 1 hour.

SPICY SHRIMP TERIYAKI Add 1 teaspoon cayenne pepper to the marinade.

Shrimp Thai Hot-and-Sour Soup

THIS IS AN EASY version of *tomm yumm goong,* a Thai soup that's made all across Southeast Asia in spicier and milder variations. You can add more chiles to the soup, but be warned: it will become super-hot. For a quick meal, this dish would be good with Shrimp Thai Sticky Rice (page 210), or with a flavorful salad of sliced seeded papaya and cucumber in a light vinaigrette. **MAKES 4 TO 6 SERVINGS**

1 tablespoon peanut oil

3 stalks lemongrass, bruised with the side of a chef's knife or with a small pot

1 pound medium shrimp (35 to 40 per pound), peeled and deveined, shells reserved

6 cups fish stock, or 3 cups chicken stock plus 3 cups clam juice

3 serrano chiles, seeded and thinly sliced

Grated zest of 1 lime

2 cups canned straw mushrooms, drained

3 tablespoons fish sauce

¼ cup fresh lime juice

¼ cup chopped cilantro

1. Place a large pot over medium heat and heat it until it is hot but not smoking. Add the peanut oil and swirl it around the pot. Add the bruised lemongrass and the reserved shrimp shells and stir until the shells turn pink, about 2 minutes.

2. Add the stock and bring to a boil. Reduce the heat to low, cover, and simmer for 15 minutes.

3. Strain the soup into a second large pot. Place the pot over high heat, add the chiles and lime zest, and bring back to a boil.

4. Reduce the heat to low, cover, and simmer the soup for 15 minutes. (The soup can be prepared to this point up to 24 hours ahead of time and kept covered in the refrigerator. Bring back to a simmer before continuing.)

5. Add the shrimp and mushrooms; cook until the shrimp are pink and firm, about 3 minutes. Remove the pot from the heat, stir in the fish sauce, lime juice, and cilantro. Serve immediately.

BANGKOK HOT-AND-SOUR SOUP Add 1 teaspoon sugar with the chiles.

COCONUT THAI HOT-AND-SOUR SOUP Add 1 cup unsweetened coconut milk with the fish sauce.

GINGER THAI HOT-AND-SOUR SOUP Add 2 tablespoons minced ginger with the chiles.

THAI HOT-AND-SOUR FISH SOUP Reduce the shrimp to ½ pound. Add ½ pound sliced fish fillets (such as red snapper or turbot), cut into 1-inch cubes and picked over for bones, with the shrimp.

THAI HOT-AND-SOUR SCALLOP SOUP Reduce the shrimp to ½ pound. Add ½ pound sea scallops, cut in half, with the shrimp.

Shrimp Thai Sticky Rice

THIS TRADITIONAL THAI DISH is a sticky medley of rice and shrimp—and the only basic recipe in this book to call exclusively for dried shrimp. To make this dish, you'll need a sticky-rice steamer (an urn-like pot with a V-shaped bamboo basket), available in Asian markets or by mail-order. Sticky rice, which isn't sticky until you cook it, is sometimes called *Thai sweet rice*, or *kao neuw* in Thai. It's available in most Southeast Asian markets and from outlets listed in the Source Guide (page 239). Thai sticky rice is traditionally eaten with your fingers—you scoop some out of the steamer basket, squeeze it into a small ball, and dip it in a sauce. Try it with Simple Japanese Dipping Sauce (page 203), Peanut Sauce (page 166), or even Barbecue Sauce (page 26). **MAKES 4 SERVINGS**

> **2 cups Thai sticky rice**
> **¼ cup dried shrimp (about ¼ ounce)**

1. Place the rice in a large bowl and add water to cover by at least 2 inches. Soak the rice for at least 4 hours, but preferably overnight.

2. Add enough water to the base of a sticky-rice steamer to reach 1 to 2 inches below the bottom of the bamboo basket. Bring the water to a boil over high heat.

3. Drain the rice and rinse it thoroughly in a fine-mesh sieve. Toss the rice with the dried shrimp until the shrimp are well distributed.

4. Place the rice into the V-shaped bamboo steamer basket and set it over the boiling water. Cover with a lid or heatproof plate that will fit inside the bamboo basket and rest at least 1 inch above the rice. Reduce the heat to medium-low and steam for 30 to 40 minutes, until the rice is tender and very sticky. Be very careful when you remove the lid—the steam is very hot.

5. The rice can be kept warm, covered, in the bamboo basket over barely simmering water for up to 1 hour. It can also be placed in a large bowl, cooled, then tightly covered with plastic wrap, and refrigerated for up to 48 hours. Resteam it for 5 minutes to reheat, or serve it cold or at room temperature.

SHRIMP THAI STICKY RICE WITH CHERRIES Add ½ cup dried cherries to the rice with the dried shrimp.

SHRIMP THAI STICKY RICE WITH CHESTNUTS Add ½ cup drained and coarsely chopped canned chestnuts to the rice with the dried shrimp.

SHRIMP THAI STICKY RICE WITH PEANUTS Add ½ cup coarsely chopped peanuts to the rice with the dried shrimp.

SHRIMP THAI STICKY RICE WITH SAUSAGE Add ½ cup crumbled cooked pork sausage to the rice with the dried shrimp.

SHRIMP THAI STICKY RICE WITH SCALLIONS Add 2 scallions, thinly sliced, to the rice with the dried shrimp.

SHRIMP THAI STICKY RICE WITH SIX TREASURES Add 2 tablespoons *each* of the following to the rice with the dried shrimp: dried cherries, minced cooked pork sausage, drained and coarsely chopped canned chestnuts, coarsely chopped peanuts and chopped orange zest.

Shrimp Thermidor

LOBSTER THERMIDOR WAS A 1960s symbol of the good life. It's sadly out of fashion, but perhaps Shrimp Thermidor will bring the dish back in vogue. The shrimp are cooked in their shells for more flavor, then peeled when they become part of the *gratinée*—that is, when they are topped with the cheese-and-wine sauce and broiled to a golden brown. Serve Shrimp Thermidor with poached asparagus spears or chilled green beans tossed in a light vinaigrette. **MAKES 4 SERVINGS**

1 pound large shrimp (12 to 15 per pound), deveined but not peeled

2 tablespoons vegetable oil

¾ cup dry white wine or dry vermouth

⅔ cup fish stock or clam juice

1 shallot, minced

1 tablespoon unsalted butter

1 tablespoon all-purpose flour

1 cup milk (whole, 2%, or 1%, but not fat-free)

1 tablespoon Dijon mustard

¼ cup heavy cream

2 large egg yolks

Salt and freshly ground black pepper to taste

¼ cup grated Gruyère or Swiss cheese (about 2 ounces)

1. Preheat the broiler.

2. Toss the shrimp with the oil in a large bowl until well coated.

3. Place the shrimp on the broiler rack or a lipped baking sheet. Broil 4 inches from the heat source for 2 minutes, then turn with tongs or a metal spatula. Broil for 2 more minutes, or until the shells turn a light brown and the meat inside is firm. Set the shrimp aside to cool.

4. Combine the wine, stock, and shallot in a small saucepan and place it over high heat. Bring to a boil and cook until the liquid is reduced to a thick glaze, about 10 minutes. Set aside.

5. Melt the butter in a large heavy skillet over medium heat. Whisk in the flour until it is completely incorporated. Cook for 1 minute, but do not allow the flour to brown.

6. Add the milk and whisk constantly until the mixture is bubbling, smooth, and thick, about 3 minutes. Whisk in the mustard and the reduced wine mixture. Reduce the heat to low and leave the sauce at the slowest simmer, just a bubble or two at a time.

7. In a medium bowl, lightly whisk the cream with the egg yolks until just combined. Slowly whisk a small amount (perhaps one small ladle) of the hot white sauce into the egg yolk mixture. (This will heat the eggs without scrambling them.) Add the egg mixture to the pan with the remaining white sauce, whisking constantly. Cook without boiling for 30 seconds to thicken the sauce, still whisking constantly; do not boil. Season with salt and pepper, then cover the pan and turn off the heat.

8. Preheat the broiler again.

9. Peel the cooked shrimp. Place them in a 1½- to 2-quart gratin dish or baking dish. Cover the shrimp with the cream sauce. Sprinkle the top with the grated cheese. Place the pan under the broiler for 2 minutes or until the top is brown and bubbly. Remove from the broiler and let stand for 3 minutes, then serve.

DILL SHRIMP THERMIDOR Add 2 tablespoons chopped dill with the mustard.

MADEIRAN SHRIMP THERMIDOR Substitute dry Madeira for the wine. Stir ½ cup fresh or thawed frozen peas into the white sauce before pouring it over the shrimp.

PARSLEY SHRIMP THERMIDOR Add 2 tablespoons finely chopped parsley with the mustard.

SAFFRON SHRIMP THERMIDOR Add ¼ teaspoon saffron threads, crumbled, to the wine mixture.

SPICY SHRIMP THERMIDOR Add 1 teaspoon Tabasco sauce with the mustard.

TARRAGON SHRIMP THERMIDOR Add 2 tablespoons minced tarragon with the mustard.

Shrimp Toast

THESE APPETIZERS SHOW UP on Chinese-American menus everywhere. They've even recently made a splash in Paris, where Chinese-American food is suddenly hyper-hip. Shrimp Toast is made by spreading a shrimp paste onto slices of bread, then deep-frying it. The best are made with a firm white bread, like Pepperidge Farm. You can also leave the bread out on the counter, uncovered, overnight, so it gets slightly stale. **MAKES 6 TO 8 APPETIZER SERVINGS**

½ cup Japanese bread crumbs (*panko*), or plain dry bread crumbs

8 cups plus 1 tablespoon peanut or vegetable oil

1 pound small shrimp (more than 55 per pound), peeled and deveined

2 large egg whites

4 teaspoons minced ginger

4 teaspoons soy sauce

4 shallots, minced

8 slices dense white bread, crusts removed

Salt to taste

1. Place the bread crumbs on a small plate. Set aside.

2. Pour 8 cups of the oil into a large saucepan at least 4 inches deep and 10 inches in diameter; the oil should be at least 1½ inches deep but reach no more than halfway up the sides of the pan. Alternatively, fill an electric deep fryer with oil according to the manufacturer's instructions. If you're using a pan, clip a deep-frying thermometer to the inside and place the pan over medium heat. Heat the oil to 375°F. Adjust the heat to maintain that temperature while you prepare the shrimp toasts. If you're using an electric deep fryer, set the temperature control to 375°F.

3. Combine the remaining 1 tablespoon oil, shrimp, egg whites, ginger, soy sauce, and shallots in a food processor. Process until a smooth paste is formed.

4. Divide the paste equally among the 8 slices of bread, spreading it evenly to the edges. Cut each slice diagonally into 4 triangles.

5. Dip each triangle, shrimp side down, into the bread crumbs. Press down lightly so that the crumbs adhere to the shrimp. Fry the toasts in the hot oil, adding only as many at a time as will fit without crowding the pan, until golden brown on both sides, about 2 minutes, turning them with tongs or a metal spatula once or twice. Remove the toasts from the oil and drain on paper towels. While they are still hot, sprinkle the toasts with salt. Serve immediately.

HERBED SHRIMP TOAST Add 1 garlic clove, minced, 2 teaspoons minced parsley, and 1 teaspoon grated lemon zest to the food processor with the shrimp.

PECAN SHRIMP TOAST Substitute ½ cup pecans, finely chopped in a food processor, for the bread crumbs.

SESAME SHRIMP TOAST Substitute white sesame seeds for the bread crumbs.

SPICY SHRIMP TOAST Omit the extra 1 tablespoon peanut oil, and add 2 teaspoons chili oil to the food processor with the shrimp.

WALNUT SHRIMP TOAST Substitute ½ cup walnut pieces, finely chopped in a food processor, for the bread crumbs.

Shrimp Tortilla Casserole

THIS HEARTY, TEX-MEX CASSEROLE is a one-dish meal. It can be assembled ahead of time and refrigerated for up to a day or frozen for several weeks. Tomatillos are sometimes called Mexican green tomatoes, but their papery husks reveal that they are actually cousins to gooseberries. Both tomatillos and poblano chiles can be found in the produce section of large supermarkets and gourmet stores, as well as in Latin American and Mexican markets. **MAKES 8 SERVINGS**

FOR THE TOMATILLO SAUCE

3 poblano chiles

2 tablespoons olive oil

3 garlic cloves, minced

1 large onion, minced

10 tomatillos, husks removed, washed, and coarsely chopped

¼ cup water

2 cups sour cream (regular, low-fat, or fat-free)

1 cup packed cilantro leaves, chopped

1½ pounds small shrimp (more than 55 per pound), peeled and deveined

6 tablespoons olive oil

18 corn tortillas

1½ cups shredded Cheddar (about 6 ounces)

½ cup grated Monterey Jack (about 2 ounces)

1. To prepare the tomatillo sauce, roast the chiles directly over a high flame on top of the stove, turning them with long-handled tongs as necessary, until they are charred all over. Alternatively, you can place the chiles under the broiler about 3 inches from the heat source, turning them as necessary until the skin is blackened. Place the charred chiles in a paper bag. Seal the bag by folding it down several times and let the peppers sit for 30 minutes.

2. Meanwhile, place a large skillet over medium heat. When it's hot but not smoking, add the olive oil and swirl it around to coat the pan well. Add the garlic and all but ¼ cup of the onion and cook, stirring constantly, until the onion is soft and translucent, about 4 minutes.

3. Add the chopped tomatillos and water. Cook for 5 minutes, or until the tomatillos begin to soften and the mixture is bubbling. Reduce the heat to low, cover, and cook for 10 minutes. Remove the pan from the heat and allow the mixture to cool slightly.

4. Remove the charred skin from the peppers with your hands (be careful not to touch your face or eyes while handling the peppers). Rinse your hands as necessary, but avoid rinsing the peppers, as they will lose some of their flavor. Remove as much charred skin as you can—a few specks may remain. Cut off the stems of the peppers, then cut open the peppers. Remove the seeds and white membranes with your fingers.

5. Finely chop the peppers and add them to the tomatillo mixture, along with the sour cream, chopped cilantro, and reserved ¼ cup onion. Stir until well combined. (The sauce can be made ahead and kept covered in the refrigerator for up to 24 hours.)

6. To assemble the casserole, preheat the oven to 350°F. Oil a 9 × 13-inch baking dish.

7. Bring 2 quarts salted water to a boil in a large pot over high heat. Add the shrimp and cook until pink and firm, about 3 minutes. Drain and set aside.

8. Place a small skillet over high heat and add 1 teaspoon of the olive oil. When it is hot but not smoking, add 1 tortilla. Cook for 10 seconds, then flip the tortilla over and cook for another 10 seconds, or just until it softens slightly. Transfer the tortilla to a plate and repeat with the remaining tortillas and olive oil. Alternatively, you can brush the tortillas with the oil, stack them on a plate, cover with plastic wrap, and microwave on high for 2 minutes.

9. Place 6 tortillas in the prepared baking dish, overlapping them so that the entire bottom of the dish is covered. Top with one-third of the tomatillo sauce, half of the shrimp, and half of the Cheddar. Repeat with 6 more tortillas, another one-third of the sauce, and the remaining shrimp and Cheddar. Top with the last 6 tortillas and the remaining tomatillo sauce, and sprinkle with the Monterey Jack. (The casserole can be made up to this point and frozen, well wrapped, for up to 1 month. Defrost completely in the refrigerator before baking.)

10. Bake the casserole for 45 minutes, or until lightly browned and bubbling. Let it stand 10 minutes before serving.

EASY SHRIMP TORTILLA CASSEROLE Instead of making the tomatillo sauce from scratch, use three 6-ounce cans tomatillo sauce (available in Latin American markets and most large supermarkets).

MILD SHRIMP TORTILLA CASSEROLE Use 3 green bell peppers instead of the poblano chiles.

Tuscan White Bean Shrimp

INSPIRED BY THE SIMPLE bean salads served in Tuscany on warm summer days, this one is redolent of olive oil, fresh vegetables, and shrimp—and makes a terrific dish for weekend company, since you can prepare it ahead of time and serve it chilled or at room temperature. **MAKES 4 TO 6 SERVINGS**

¾ pound small shrimp (more than 55 per pound), peeled and deveined, or precooked cold-water (or baby) shrimp, thawed

One 14-ounce can cannellini beans, drained and rinsed

1 small shallot, minced

1 celery stalk, minced

1 tablespoon minced sage

1 teaspoon anchovy paste

1½ tablespoons cider vinegar

¼ cup olive oil

½ teaspoon salt

Freshly ground black pepper to taste

1. If you're using raw shrimp, bring 1 quart salted water to a boil in a medium pot over high heat. Fill a medium bowl halfway with ice water and set it aside. Add the shrimp to the boiling water and cook until pink and firm, about 2 minutes. Transfer the shrimp to the ice water using a slotted spoon or a strainer and allow them to cool. Drain the shrimp and blot dry with paper towels. Cut the shrimp in half or thirds, so that each piece is about the size of a bean. If you're using precooked cold-water shrimp, skip this step.

2. Combine the cooked shrimp, beans, shallots, celery, and sage in a medium bowl. Toss until well combined.

3. In a small bowl, combine the anchovy paste and vinegar, stirring with a fork until well blended. Slowly beat in the oil, using the fork or a small whisk, until the mixture is emulsified and slightly thickened. Whisk in the salt.

4. Pour the dressing over the shrimp and bean mixture and gently toss until well combined. Season with pepper. Cover the salad and refrigerate for at least 1 hour to allow the flavors to meld. Serve cold or at room temperature. (The salad will keep for up to 3 days tightly covered in the refrigerator.)

TUSCAN RAW VEGETABLE SHRIMP Add any or all of the following to the salad, in ½-cup portions: thinly sliced carrots, sliced green beans, chopped watercress, and/or shaved fennel bulb.

TUSCAN RED BEAN SHRIMP Use red kidney beans instead of the white beans.

TUSCAN SPINACH AND WHITE BEAN SHRIMP Add one 10-ounce package frozen chopped spinach, cooked according to the package directions, drained, cooled, and squeezed of excess water, to the salad with the beans.

TUSCAN WHITE BEAN SHRIMP OVER GREENS Stem and wash 4 cups spinach, mustard greens, turnip greens, or watercress. Wilt the greens in 1 tablespoon olive oil or butter in a large saucepan over medium heat for 4 minutes. Serve the salad over the warm wilted greens.

Shrimp Twice-Baked Potatoes

TWICE-BAKED POTATOES BECAME A hit in the U.S. in the '70s, when certain national restaurant chains turned the dish from a side into dinner itself. Stuffed with cheese and shrimp, these potatoes are meals in themselves, perfect at the end of a long day. You can even bake the potatoes up to a day in advance and have them ready and waiting for the heavenly filling. **MAKES 4 SERVINGS**

4 large baking potatoes (about ¾ pound each), scrubbed

1 pound small shrimp (more than 55 per pound), peeled and deveined

2 tablespoons unsalted butter, softened

¼ cup finely chopped parsley

2 tablespoons chopped dill

2 large eggs

¼ cup milk (whole or 2%, but not 1% or fat-free)

½ teaspoon salt

Freshly ground black pepper to taste

1 cup plus 2 tablespoons shredded Cheddar (about 5 ounces)

1. Preheat the oven to 400°F.

2. Bake the potatoes on a lipped baking sheet until they are feel soft when pierced with a sharp knife or skewer, about 1 hour.

3. Meanwhile, coarsely chop the shrimp.

4. Melt the butter in a large skillet over medium heat. Add the shrimp and cook, stirring constantly, until pink, about 2 minutes. Break up any clumps of shrimp with a wooden spoon as you cook them. Remove the skillet from the heat and set it aside.

5. When the potatoes are done, remove them from the oven and allow them to cool until they are easy to handle. Maintain the oven temperature.

6. Cut the top third off each potato the long way. Using a spoon, scoop the inside of both the larger section of the potato and its "lid" into a large mixing bowl, leaving a ⅛-inch layer of potato in the shell. Discard the lids.

7. Add the parsley, dill, eggs, milk, salt, and pepper to the potato "insides." Using a hand mixer, beat the mixture until it is smooth. Add 1 cup of the Cheddar and the shrimp to the bowl. Stir with a wooden spoon until well blended.

8. Fill the hollowed-out potatoes evenly with the filling. Top each with ½ tablespoon of the remaining Cheddar. Place the potatoes on a baking sheet and bake for 30 minutes, or until they are lightly browned and puffed on top. Serve immediately.

BLUE CHEESE–SHRIMP TWICE-BAKED POTATOES Reduce the Cheddar to ½ cup plus 2 tablespoons. Add ½ cup crumbled blue cheese (such as Roquefort; about 2 ounces) to the filling with the Cheddar.

EXTRA-RICH SHRIMP TWICE-BAKED POTATOES Substitute heavy cream for the milk.

HERBED SHRIMP TWICE-BAKED POTATOES Omit the Cheddar and dill. Add 1 tablespoon chopped oregano, 2 teaspoons chopped rosemary, and 1 cup freshly grated Parmigiano-Reggiano (about 4 ounces) to the filling. Top each potato with 2 teaspoons grated Parmigiano-Reggiano.

ROCK SHRIMP TWICE-BAKED POTATOES Substitute peeled and cleaned rock shrimp for the regular shrimp.

Shrimp Vatapa

VATAPA IS A BRAZILIAN SHRIMP STEW, thickened with coconut milk. A heady mixture of beer and ground peanuts adds a wonderful grainy, salty taste to the final dish. Vatapa can be made in advance—if it thickens up too much in the refrigerator, thin it out with a little water. Serve with a dense, dark bread, such as pumpernickel. **MAKES 4 TO 6 SERVINGS**

3 tablespoons peanut oil

1 medium onion, coarsely chopped

4 garlic cloves, minced

1 fresh jalapeño pepper, seeded and minced

1 tablespoon minced ginger

One 28-ounce can peeled tomatoes

One 12-ounce bottle beer (such as Bass or Heineken)

1 cup water

1½ pounds medium shrimp (35 to 40 per pound), peeled and deveined

½ cup unsalted peanuts

1 cup unsweetened coconut milk

½ cup finely chopped parsley

½ cup finely chopped cilantro

1 teaspoon salt

Freshly ground black pepper to taste

1 lime, halved

1. Heat the peanut oil in a large pot or Dutch oven over medium heat. Add the onion and garlic and cook until the onion is translucent, about 3 minutes.

2. Add the jalapeño and ginger and cook, stirring constantly, for 1 minute. Pour the tomatoes, with their liquid, into the pot and break them up with the back of a wooden spoon. Add the beer and water. Bring to a boil, cover, reduce the heat to low, and simmer for 20 minutes.

3. Meanwhile, place the peanuts in a food processor and process until finely ground, like coarse meal. Be careful not to turn them into peanut butter. Transfer the ground nuts to a medium bowl and add the coconut milk. Stir to combine well. Set aside.

4. Add the shrimp to the simmering stew, stirring to make sure all the shrimp are submerged in the hot liquid. Cover and cook for 5 minutes.

5. Add the peanut mixture to the soup. Cook, stirring constantly, until the soup returns to a simmer and thickens slightly, about 3 minutes.

6. Stir in the parsley, cilantro, salt, and pepper. Squeeze the lime juice into the pot and stir—or squeeze some juice over individual servings. Serve immediately.

DILLED SHRIMP VATAPA Omit the parsley and cilantro. Stir ½ cup minced dill into the stew.

DOUBLE PEANUT SHRIMP VATAPA Swirl 2 tablespoons peanut butter into the coconut milk before adding the ground peanuts.

DOUBLE SHRIMP VATAPA Add 2 tablespoons dried shrimp with the raw shrimp.

EXTRA-HOT SHRIMP VATAPA Use 2 serrano peppers, seeded and sliced, or more to taste, instead of the jalapeño pepper.

GARLIC LOVERS' SHRIMP VATAPA Omit the ginger. Increase the garlic to 8 cloves.

Shrimp Vegetable Stir-fry

THIS SIMPLE STIR-FRY IS a good workday meal. Put the rice on first, then prep the vegetables, and you'll have dinner in minutes. With precooked cocktail shrimp, it's even faster. Crisp vegetables and sweet shrimp make a warm, comforting dish. What makes this stir-fry extraordinary is the pickled Szechwan cabbage available in 10-ounce jars in many Chinese markets or by mail-order (see Source Guide, page 239). **MAKES 4 SERVINGS**

3 tablespoons soy sauce

2 tablespoons dry sherry or
   dry vermouth

2 teaspoons sugar

3 tablespoons peanut oil, or 1
   tablespoon peanut oil, if using
   precooked shrimp

1 pound medium shrimp (35 to 40
   per pound), peeled and
   deveined, or precooked
   cocktail shrimp, thawed and
   peeled

2 tablespoons minced ginger

1 garlic clove, minced

One 15-ounce can straw
   mushrooms, drained

One 8-ounce can baby corn,
   drained

One 8-ounce can sliced bamboo
   shoots, drained

¼ cup Szechwan pickled cabbage,
   drained

1 teaspoon cornstarch, dissolved
   in 2 teaspoons water

1. Whisk together the soy sauce, sherry, and sugar until the sugar is dissolved. Set aside.

2. Heat a large heavy saucepan or wok over medium heat until it is hot but not smoking. Add 2 tablespoons of the peanut oil and swirl to coat the pan. Add the raw shrimp, if using, and cook, stirring and tossing constantly, until pink and firm, about 3 minutes. Transfer the shrimp to a bowl and set aside.

3. Add 1 tablespoon peanut oil to the pan and raise the heat to high. Add the ginger and garlic; toss and stir for 10 seconds. Add the straw mushrooms, baby corn, bamboo shoots, and pickled cabbage; toss and stir for 1 minute. Add the soy sauce mixture. Continue to toss and stir the mixture until the sauce is bubbling, about 30 seconds.

4. Add the cooked shrimp to the pan. Toss and stir until everything is well blended and the shrimp are heated through, about 1 minute.

5. Add the cornstarch mixture and stir vigorously. The sauce will thicken immediately. Remove it from the heat at once and serve.

SHRIMP BROCCOLI STIR-FRY Add ½ cup broccoli florets with the mushrooms.

SHRIMP CABBAGE STIR-FRY Omit the baby corn. Add ½ cup shredded Napa cabbage with the bamboo shoots.

SHRIMP PEA STIR-FRY Add ½ cup fresh or thawed frozen peas with the mushrooms.

SHRIMP SNOW PEA STIR-FRY Omit the mushrooms. Add ⅔ cup snow peas with the baby corn.

SHRIMP WATER CHESTNUT STIR-FRY Omit the bamboo shoots. Add one 8-ounce can sliced water chestnuts, drained, with the mushrooms.

SPICY VEGETABLE SHRIMP STIR-FRY Add 8 dried Asian red chiles with the ginger.

Vietnamese Spring Rolls Shrimp

CHINESE SPRING ROLLS ARE deep-fried and traditionally served on the first day of Chinese New Year. Vietnamese Spring Rolls are never fried and are eaten all year, a taste of spring even in the dead of winter. They are wrapped in edible rice-paper, made from a dough of rice flour, water, and salt, rolled out to paper-thin sheets, and dried in the sun on bamboo mats (thus, the beautiful crosshatch designs). They must be soaked before use. The delicate wrappers can be stored tightly covered in a cool, dark place for up to 3 months. Serve the spring rolls with hoi sin sauce for dipping or Peanut Sauce (page 166) or even a light vinaigrette. **MAKES 12 ROLLS**

12 large shrimp (12 to 15 per pound), peeled and deveined

2 ounces dried bean thread noodles

12 rice paper wrappers (8- to 10-inch circles), plus a few extra in case some tear

12 sprigs cilantro

24 mint leaves

3 scallions, green part only, cut into 2-inch pieces

½ cup hoi sin sauce

12 bamboo or wooden skewers

1. Thread 1 shrimp onto a skewer, starting at the neck end of the shrimp and pushing the skewer through the shrimp the long way until it comes out of the tail. (This will keep the shrimp from curling while it cooks.)

2. Bring 2 quarts salted water to a boil in large pot over high heat. Fill a large bowl halfway with ice water and set it aside. Add as many shrimp skewers to the boiling water as will fit while keeping all the shrimp submerged. Cook until the shrimp are pink and firm, about 2 minutes. Using tongs, transfer the shrimp to the ice water to cool. Repeat with any remaining shrimp.

3. Meanwhile, cover the bean thread noodles with boiling water in a large bowl and let them soak until they are soft, about 15 minutes. Drain the noodles and run them under cold water until they're cool. Squeeze out any excess water with your hands. Set the noodles aside.

4. Drain the cooled shrimp. Remove them from the skewers and blot dry with paper towels.

5. Fill a baking dish large enough to hold a rice paper sheet without crimping its edges with 1 to 2 inches warm water. Place a rice paper sheet in the warm water and soak only until it is soft, about 30 seconds. Remove the sheet from the water and carefully place it on your work surface. Set 1 shrimp in the middle of the sheet. Top the shrimp with 1 heaping tablespoon bean thread noodles, 1 cilantro sprig, 2 mint leaves, and 2 or 3 pieces of scallion. Fold the sides of the rice paper sheet over to cover the filling. Fold the bottom of the sheet up and slightly over the filling, and roll the bundle up to create a small sealed package. Set aside seam side down. Repeat the process with the remaining ingredients to form 12 rolls in all. (The rolls can be covered tightly with plastic wrap and refrigerated for up to 2 hours.)

6. To serve, place the hoi sin sauce in a small bowl and serve it with the rolls as a dipping sauce.

BEER-SOAKED VIETNAMESE SHRIMP SPRING ROLLS Soak the rice paper rounds in beer rather than water. This is a traditional Vietnamese technique.

LEMONGRASS-SOAKED VIETNAMESE SHRIMP SPRING ROLLS Remove the tough outer leaves from 1 stalk lemongrass and pound the stalk gently with a mallet or a small saucepan to bruise it and release its flavor. Place the lemongrass in a bowl and cover it with boiling water; allow the water to cool completely. Discard the lemongrass. Soak the rice paper in the lemongrass-infused water.

SPICY VIETNAMESE SHRIMP SPRING ROLLS Add a dash of chili oil to the filling in each spring roll.

SUGAR-SOAKED VIETNAMESE SHRIMP SPRING ROLLS Dissolve 1 teaspoon sugar in the water used for soaking the rice paper; this is also a traditional Vietnamese technique.

VIETNAMESE SHRIMP AND BEAN SPROUT SPRING ROLLS Omit the cilantro. Using 3 ounces bean spouts in all, add 2 or 3 bean sprouts to the filling in each spring roll.

VIETNAMESE SHRIMP AND PEANUT SPRING ROLLS Add 4 or 5 peanuts, salted or unsalted, to the filling in each spring roll. Or carefully spread a scant 1 teaspoon peanut butter in the center of each roll before you add the shrimp.

Vietnamese Sugarcane Shrimp

THIS TRADITIONAL SNACK, a favorite at open-air markets across Vietnam, is made by shaping shrimp paste around quartered stalks of sugarcane. Sugarcane is available year-round in supermarkets in the South, and is often available in gourmet markets everywhere in the fall. If you can't find fresh sugarcane, you can always use canned—buy two 15-ounce cans, drain them thoroughly, and cut the sections in half (not into quarters, since they are too soft). Vietnamese Sugarcane Shrimp is often served with a spicy vinegary dipping sauce, such as the widely available bottled Tiger Sauce. You could also use Barbecue Sauce (page 26) or Peanut Sauce (page 166). **MAKES 4 SERVINGS**

Four 8-inch pieces sugarcane

¼ cup plus 2 tablespoons rice flour

1 pound small shrimp (more than 55 per pound), peeled and deveined

2 tablespoons minced pork fat or lard

1 large shallot, minced

1 tablespoon fish sauce

1. Split each piece of sugarcane lengthwise into quarters; set aside. Place ¼ cup of the rice flour on a large flat plate; set aside.

2. Preheat the broiler.

3. Combine the shrimp, pork fat, the remaining 2 tablespoons rice flour, shallot, and fish sauce in a food processor. Process until the mixture is a smooth paste, about 1 minute, scraping down the sides of the bowl as necessary. Transfer to a medium bowl. Wet your hands and carefully scoop out a golf-ball–sized portion of shrimp paste. Wrap it around the middle of 1 sugarcane piece, squeezing and spreading the paste to a thickness of about ¼ inch; only 3 to 5 inches of cane should be covered. Roll the shrimp paste wrapping in the rice flour, and set the sugarcane piece on a broiler tray or cookie sheet. Repeat with the remaining shrimp paste and sugarcane.

4. Broil the coated sugarcane for about 4 minutes, turning occasionally, until the paste turns pink on all sides and is firm. Serve hot with your favorite dipping sauce.

BARBECUED VIETNAMESE SUGARCANE SHRIMP Light the coals in the barbecue. When they are coated with ash, after about 20 minutes, place the rack on the barbecue, or preheat the gas grill for 5 minutes. Lay the wrapped sugarcane pieces on the grill and cook for about 4 minutes, turning them often, until the shrimp paste is pink and firm.

VIETNAMESE LEMONGRASS SHRIMP Use 16 stalks of lemongrass, tops trimmed and outer leaves removed, instead of the sugarcane.

VIETNAMESE SCALLION SHRIMP Use 16 scallions, root ends trimmed and green tops trimmed so that each scallion is about 8 inches long, instead of the sugarcane.

Shrimp Vindaloo

A SOUTHERN INDIAN DISH with colonial roots, vindaloo has come to mean the hottest curry imaginable. Its roots stretch back to Goa, once a Portuguese trading post, where it was originally a hearty pork stew made with wine (*vinho*) and garlic (*alhos*). Over the years, Indian cooks added their own spices to the colonialists' favorite dish, converting it into a spicy, heady mélange that the colonialists could barely tolerate—a kind of cultural payback, perhaps. Serve Shrimp Vindaloo over rice. **MAKES 4 SERVINGS**

1 teaspoon ground turmeric

1 teaspoon salt

1 teaspoon freshly ground black pepper

1 teaspoon red pepper flakes

1 teaspoon ground coriander

½ teaspoon ground cumin

½ teaspoon dry mustard

½ teaspoon ground cinnamon

½ teaspoon ground ginger

¼ teaspoon ground cloves

¼ teaspoon ground cardamom

1½ tablespoons cider vinegar

3 tablespoons vegetable oil

1 large onion, finely chopped

2 garlic cloves, minced

One 28-ounce can peeled tomatoes, drained and finely chopped

1½ pounds large shrimp (12 to 15 per pound), peeled and deveined

1 tablespoon fresh lemon juice

1. In a small bowl, combine the turmeric, salt, black pepper, red pepper flakes, coriander, cumin, mustard, cinnamon, ginger, cloves, cardamom, and vinegar and mix until a smooth paste is formed. Set aside.

2. Heat the oil in a large saucepan set over medium heat. Add the onion and garlic and cook, stirring often, until the onion is translucent, about 4 minutes.

3. Add the spice paste to the pan and stir for 20 seconds. Immediately add the tomatoes and stir well, scraping up any brown bits from the bottom of the pan. When the mixture begins to simmer, reduce the heat to low, cover, and cook for 15 minutes, stirring often.

4. Add the shrimp and stir until they are well coated with the sauce. Raise the heat to medium and cook, stirring often, until the shrimp are firm and pink, about 3 minutes. Stir in the lemon juice and serve immediately.

ROCK SHRIMP VINDALOO Substitute peeled and cleaned rock shrimp for the regular shrimp.

SHRIMP AND CLAM VINDALOO Reduce the shrimp to 1 pound. Add 12 medium clams (such as cherrystone or Pacific littleneck), scrubbed, with the shrimp. Cook for an additional 4 minutes, or until the clams have opened.

SHRIMP AND SCALLOP VINDALOO Reduce the shrimp to ¾ pound. Add ¾ pound sea scallops, cut in half, with the shrimp.

TAMARIND SHRIMP VINDALOO Add 1 tablespoon tamarind concentrate (available in Indian and Asian markets and some gourmet stores) to the spice paste.

Shrimp Wild Mushroom Soup

AT FIRST GLANCE, this soup seems to be a wintry dish. Mushrooms and spices are combined elegantly with shrimp for a comforting, come-in-from-the-cold meal. But during the warm spring or hot summer, you'll yearn for it again—and sure enough, you'll discover it's good any time of year. **MAKES 4 TO 6 SERVINGS**

¼ cup olive oil

1 large onion, thinly sliced

¾ pound mixed wild mushrooms (such as porcini, portabello, or cremini—but not shiitake), cleaned and thinly sliced

½ cup dry vermouth

3 tablespoons tomato paste

4 cups fish stock, or 3 cups vegetable stock plus 1 cup clam juice

2 teaspoons minced thyme

¾ pound small shrimp (more than 55 per pound), peeled and deveined

¼ cup chopped parsley

Salt and freshly ground black pepper to taste

1. Heat 2 tablespoons of the oil in a large pot over medium heat. Add the onion and cook, stirring often, until soft and aromatic, about 4 minutes.

2. Add the remaining 2 tablespoons oil and allow it to heat for 30 seconds. Add the mushrooms and cook, stirring often, until they give off their juices, about 2 minutes. Continue to cook, stirring occasionally, until the juices are reduced to a glaze and the pan is nearly dry. Add the vermouth. Cook until the pan is nearly dry again.

3. Add the tomato paste and stir until well combined. Stir in the stock and thyme, raise the heat to high, and bring the soup to a boil.

4. Add the shrimp. Immediately turn the heat to low, and simmer the soup for 4 minutes, or until the shrimp are pink and firm. Stir in the parsley. Season with salt and pepper. Serve immediately.

CHUNKY TOMATO AND SHRIMP WILD MUSHROOM SOUP Omit the tomato paste. Reduce the stock to 2 cups (use only fish or vegetable stock). Add one 28-ounce can peeled tomatoes, drained and chopped, after the vermouth is reduced.

DILLED SHRIMP WILD MUSHROOM SOUP Substitute chopped dill for the parsley.

FENNEL AND SHRIMP WILD MUSHROOM SOUP Remove the upper stalks and fronds from a fennel bulb, leaving only the white portion. Slice off the bottom, and pull off the tough outer leaves. Chop the fennel bulb into 1-inch chunks. Add to the pot with the onion.

SAGE AND SHRIMP WILD MUSHROOM SOUP Substitute 1 tablespoon chopped sage for the thyme.

SWEET SHRIMP WILD MUSHROOM SOUP Use sweet vermouth instead of the dry vermouth.

WINE AND SHRIMP WILD MUSHROOM SOUP Do not add the vermouth after the mushrooms have given off their juices—instead, add it just before serving.

Shrimp Wild Rice Salad

WILD RICE ISN'T RICE AT ALL—it's the seed of a marsh grass that's been cultivated in the Upper Great Lakes for centuries by Native American tribes. Before cooking it, soak the rice in water a few minutes, stirring it once or twice to see if any hulls float to the surface, then cook according to the package instructions. This simple salad, which can be prepared up to 3 days in advance, makes a lovely, easy lunch or dinner, whether at home or al fresco, under the trees in the local park. **MAKES 6 LARGE SERVINGS**

1 teaspoon salt

½ teaspoon cayenne pepper

¾ pound medium shrimp (35 to 40 per pound), peeled and deveined

¾ cup plus 3 tablespoons extra virgin olive oil

¾ cup chopped walnuts

3 cups cooked wild rice (follow the package instructions), cooled

2 scallions, thinly sliced

1 red bell pepper, cored, seeded, and cut into ¼-inch pieces

2 medium tomatoes, coarsely chopped

½ cup golden raisins

½ cup finely chopped parsley

1 tablespoon chopped thyme

3 tablespoons fresh lemon juice

Salt and freshly ground black pepper to taste

1. Combine the salt and cayenne pepper in a medium bowl. Add the shrimp and stir until they are well coated with the spices. Set aside.

2. Heat a medium skillet over high heat until it is hot but not smoking. Add 3 tablespoons of the oil and swirl to coat the pan with oil. Add the shrimp and cook, stirring constantly, until pink and firm, about 3 minutes. Transfer the shrimp to a large mixing bowl.

3. Add the walnuts to the pan and lower the heat to medium. Cook the nuts, tossing occasionally, until they are lightly toasted and smell nutty, about 1 minute. Add the walnuts to the bowl with the shrimp. Allow them both to cool.

4. Add the rice, scallions, bell pepper, tomatoes, raisins, parsley, thyme, lemon juice, and the remaining ¾ cup olive oil to the shrimp and nuts. Toss until well combined. Season with salt and pepper. Cover the salad and refrigerate for at least 2 hours before serving. (The salad will keep for up to 3 days covered in the refrigerator.)

CASHEW AND CURRANT SHRIMP WILD RICE SALAD Add ¾ cup chopped cashews and ¾ cup dried currants instead of the walnuts and raisins.

HAZELNUT AND CHERRY SHRIMP WILD RICE SALAD Add ¾ cup chopped hazelnuts and ½ cup dried cherries instead of the walnuts and raisins.

PECAN AND CRANBERRY SHRIMP WILD RICE SALAD Add ¾ cup chopped pecans and ½ cup dried cranberries instead of the walnuts and raisins.

PISTACHIO AND BLUEBERRY SHRIMP WILD RICE SALAD Add ½ cup shelled pistachios and ½ cup dried blueberries instead of the walnuts and raisins.

SWEET-AND-SOUR SHRIMP WILD RICE SALAD Stir 3 tablespoons sweetened Chinese vinegar into the finished salad.

VINEGARY SHRIMP WILD RICE SALAD Stir 2 tablespoons balsamic vinegar into the finished salad.

Shrimp Wraps

A TORTILLA WRAP IS now a favorite lunch across the U.S. No wonder—it's an easy sandwich, the filling rolled up in a neat package. You can seal these wraps individually in wax paper, then plastic wrap, so they can travel with you and your kids. **MAKES 4 WRAPS**

1 pound large shrimp (12 to 15 per pound), peeled and deveined, or precooked cocktail shrimp, thawed and peeled

4 large soft flour tortillas (10 to 12 inches)

4 large green leaf lettuce leaves

1 large ripe Hass avocado, peeled, pitted, and thinly sliced

½ cup salsa (mild, medium, or hot)

1 small red onion, thinly sliced and separated into rings

¼ cup coarsely chopped cilantro

1. If you're using raw shrimp, bring 2 quarts salted water to a boil in a medium pan over high heat. Fill a large bowl halfway with ice water and set it aside. Add the shrimp to the boiling water and cook until pink and firm, 3 to 5 minutes. Transfer the shrimp to the ice water using a slotted spoon. Allow to cool completely. Drain the shrimp and blot dry with paper towels. If you're using precooked shrimp, skip this step.

2. Lay the tortillas out on your work surface. Place 1 lettuce leaf in the middle of each tortilla. Lay 3 or 4 shrimp over each lettuce leaf and top with one-quarter of the avocado slices, 2 tablespoons salsa, a few onion rings, and 1 tablespoon cilantro. Fold the sides of the tortilla over toward the center. (The sides may not meet to cover the filling.) Fold the bottom over the filling. Roll the tortilla away from you, keeping it as tight as possible.

3. Serve immediately, or wrap each sandwich tightly in wax paper, then in plastic wrap. Refrigerate until ready to serve. (The wraps can be made up to 8 hours in advance.)

SHRIMP WRAPS WITH CORN RELISH Add 1 tablespoon corn relish to each sandwich before rolling it up.

SHRIMP WRAPS WITH MANGO CHUTNEY Add 1 tablespoon mango chutney to each sandwich before rolling it up.

SHRIMP WRAPS WITH MAYONNAISE Spread 1 tablespoon mayonnaise on each tortilla before adding the lettuce.

SHRIMP WRAPS WITH SALSA Add 1 tablespoon tomato or fruit salsa to each sandwich before rolling it up.

SHRIMP WRAPS WITH WASABI Spread ¼ to ½ teaspoon wasabi paste on each tortilla before adding the lettuce.

XO Shrimp

WITH THE SUCCESS OF the TV show *Iron Chef,* spicy Szechwan XO sauce is something of a legend. Its oily taste blends perfectly with the sweetness of shellfish. XO sauce comes in a hot version (extremely hot) and a mild one (still fairly spicy). Premium brands, which will give this dish a more aromatic touch, contain dried scallops, dried shrimp, oyster sauce, and chiles. XO sauce can be found in Chinese markets or ordered by mail (see Source Guide, page 239). It's quite expensive, but the stir-fry you'll create will be authentic and delicious. Have bowls of white or brown rice standing by. **MAKES 4 SERVINGS**

1½ pounds medium shrimp (35 to 40 per pound), peeled and deveined

2 tablespoons oyster sauce

1 teaspoon toasted sesame oil

2 tablespoons peanut oil

3 scallions, thinly sliced

2 garlic cloves, minced

3 tablespoons XO sauce (hot or mild)

1. Combine the shrimp, oyster sauce, and sesame oil in a medium bowl, stirring until the shrimp are well coated. Set aside for 15 minutes.

2. Heat a large wok or skillet (preferably nonstick) over high heat. When it is very hot, add the peanut oil and swirl it around to coat the pan. Add the shrimp and cook, stirring and tossing constantly, until pink and firm, about 3 minutes.

3. Add the scallions and garlic; stir and toss for 30 seconds. Add the XO sauce and cook, stirring and tossing constantly, for 30 seconds, or until the sauce is bubbling. Serve immediately.

XO SHRIMP WITH LOBSTER Reduce the shrimp to 1 pound. Add ½ pound cooked lobster meat, coarsely chopped, with the scallions.

XO SHRIMP WITH SCALLOPS Reduce the shrimp to 1 pound. Add ½ pound sea scallops, cut in half, to the shrimp in the marinade.

XO SHRIMP WITH SNOW PEAS Add 1 cup snow peas to the pan with the shrimp.

SOURCE GUIDE

Boyajian
349 Lenox Street
Norwood, MA 02062
1-800-419-4677
www.boyajianinc.com

Boyajian produces a wide range of flavored oils and vinegars, including the most fragrant peanut oil on the market. Although many of these products are available at supermarkets and gourmet stores, you'll find the entire collection of high-quality oils and vinegars on Boyajian's website.

Central Market
4001 N. Lamar
Austin, TX 78756
1-512-206-1000

Perhaps the finest gourmet market in the United States, Central Market stocks more specialty and international foods than anyplace else we know. They are incredibly helpful on the phone and will ship almost anything.

Kalustyan's
123 Lexington Avenue
New York, NY 10016
1-212-685-3451
www.kalustyans.com

This Indian market is really an international warehouse of specialty foods, including herbs, nuts, tamarind syrup, rice noodles, rice wrappers, rice flour, flavored oils, and many of the Asian and Indian ingredients used in this book.

Kam Man Food Products
200 Canal Street
New York, NY 10013
1-212-571-0330

At one of New York's finest Asian grocery and cookware stores, you'll find all sorts of canned and dried Chinese vegetables—from the standard bamboo shoots, baby corn, and straw mushrooms to more exotic Szechwan pickled vegetables, dried shrimp, and dozens of varieties of dried mushrooms. They also carry a comprehensive line of Asian oils, vinegars, sauces, and dried noodles.

Pacific Rim Gourmet
www.pacificrim-gourmet.com
1-800-618-7575

This online gourmet resource has a full range of Asian ingredients and kitchenware.

Penzeys Spices
P.O. Box 933
West 19362 Apollo Drive
Muskego, WI 53150
1-800-741-7787
www.penzeys.com

This purveyor of fine spices carries a delicious variety of Vietnamese cinnamon.

Shrimp.com™
www.shrimp.com
Gulf Coast Specialties
PMB 250, 16211 Clay Road, Suite 106
Houston, TX 77084
1-888-5-SHRIMP

Can't get to the store? Five-pound bags of individually quick frozen shrimp are just a click or phone call away. Shrimp.com sells shrimp that range from 41 to 50 per pound all the way down to 6 to 12 per pound.

ThaiGrocer
2961 N. Sheridan Rd.
Chicago, IL 60657
1-773-988-8424
www.thaigrocer.com

The first and one of the most complete Thai online grocers, this site offers sauces, condiments, chili pastes, noodles, oils, and vinegars, as well as rice flour, Thai sticky rice, rice noodles, and rice paper wrappers.

Uwajimaya
519 6th Ave South
Seattle, WA 98104
1-206-624-6248
www.uwajimaya.com

This enormous Asian grocery store has three retail outlets in Washington State. The website has plenty of information on the store, but doesn't indicate just how extensive their inventory is.

The Wok Shop
718 Grant Avenue
San Francisco, CA 94108
1-888-780-7171
www.wokshop.com

In the heart of San Francisco's Chinatown, this store carries a huge assortment of woks, rice steamers, bamboo steamers, cleavers, sushi mats, and other Asian cooking equipment. Nearly everything is available online. The staff is extremely friendly, offering advice and recipes with even the smallest order.

www.quickspice.com
1-800-553-5008

This is one of the most exhaustive online resources for Asian ingredients and equipment. Their inventory includes sushi rice, nori, wakame, miso, Japanese bread crumbs (*panko*), fish sauce, oyster sauce, XO sauce, coconut milk, dried Chinese black beans, rice paper wrappers, and rice noodles, as well as sushi mats, bamboo steamers, and sticky rice steamers.

www.ultimatecook.com

At the Ultimatecook website, you'll find extra recipes and information on all the Ultimate books, as well as a complete list of links to our favorite food mail-order sources.

INDEX

frittata, shrimp, 88–89
fritters, shrimp, 90–91

garden shrimp soufflé, 177
garlic:
  bread shrimp, 47
  sauce popcorn shrimp, 145
  sauce shrimp, 92–93
  shrimp, Szechwan cold,
    194–95
  shrimp balls, 25
  shrimp paprikash, 129
  shrimp scampi, 169
  shrimp Scorpio, 171
  shrimp tamale pie, 199
  shrimp vatapa, 223
gazpacho shrimp cocktail, 63
General Tsao's shrimp, 94–95
gin, shrimp penne à la, 135
ginger, gingery, 12
  double-, sesame shrimp, 173
  peel and eat shrimp, 133
  shrimp balls, 25
  shrimp curry, 67
  steamed shrimp with, 181
  Thai hot-and-sour soup, 209
goat cheese:
  shrimp enchiladas, 79
  shrimp Parmesan, 131
grape leaves, shrimp stuffed,
    186–87
Greek-American shrimp Scorpio,
    170–71
Greek-style dishes:
  deviled shrimp, 69
  shrimp bread pudding, 43
  shrimp chiffon ring, 57
  shrimp dip, 73
  shrimp phyllo pillows, 139
  stuffed shrimp, 185
greens, Tuscan white bean
    shrimp over, 219
grilled shrimp:
  honey, 98–99
  scampi, 169

tequila, 204–5
teriyaki, 206–7
gulf shrimp, 3
gumbo, shrimp, 96–97

ham and Portuguese shrimp, 147
hazelnuts:
  and cherry shrimp wild rice
    salad, 235
  Portuguese shrimp with, 147
herb, herbed, 12
  lemon shrimp, 107
  popcorn shrimp, 145
  shrimp bisque, 35
  shrimp cakes, 53
  shrimp Diane, 71
  shrimp dumplings, 77
  shrimp fra diavolo, 85
  shrimp frittata, 89
  shrimp mousse, 117
  shrimp risotto, 159
  shrimp salad, 163
  shrimp Scorpio, 171
  shrimp toast, 215
  shrimp twice-baked potatoes,
    221
herbal deviled shrimp, 69
hoi sin sauce, 12
hollandaise sauce, easy blender,
    117
honey:
  barbecued shrimp, 27
  grilled shrimp, 98–99
hot-and-sour:
  shrimp noodle soup, 123
  soup, shrimp Thai, 208–9
hummus shrimp bruschetta, 47
Hungarian-style dishes:
  hot shrimp bisque, 35
  shrimp paprikash, 128–29

Iberian stewed shrimp, 100–101
Indian-style dishes:
  butterfly fried shrimp, 51
  shrimp Bengalese stew, 32–33

shrimp frittata, 89
shrimp vindaloo, 230–31
tandoori shrimp, 200–201
ingredients, 8–16
island coconut shrimp, 65
Italian-American-style dishes:
  shrimp Alfredo, 20–21
  shrimp cioppino, 60–61
  shrimp fra diavolo, 84–85
  shrimp lasagne, 104–5
  shrimp Parmesan, 130–31
  shrimp scampi, 168–69
Italian-style dishes:
  butterfly fried shrimp, 51
  shrimp bruschetta, 46–47
  shrimp chiffon ring, 57
  shrimp chowder, 59
  shrimp dressing, 75
  shrimp frittata, 88–89
  shrimp penne à la vodka,
    134–35
  shrimp pesto, 136–37
  shrimp risotto, 158–59
  Tuscan white bean shrimp,
    218–19

jalapeño pepper shrimp stuffed
    mushroom caps, 189
Japanese-style dishes:
  bread crumbs, 12
  butterfly fried shrimp, 51
  shrimp, mussel, and clam stew,
    119
  shrimp dip, 73
  shrimp maki, 110–11
  shrimp noodle soup, 122–23
  shrimp puffs, 153
  shrimp sushi, 190–91
  shrimp tempura, 202–3
  shrimp teriyaki, 206–7
  simple dipping sauce, 203
  tentsuyu, 203

kabas, barbecued shrimp-and-
    vegetable, 27

Key West honey grilled shrimp, 99
kung pao shrimp, 102–3

lasagne, shrimp, 104–5
lemon:
  popcorn shrimp, 145
  shrimp, 106–7
  shrimp stuffed mushroom caps, 189
  shrimp teriyaki, 207
lemongrass, 13
  shrimp, Vietnamese, 229
  shrimp skewers, 175
  -soaked Vietnamese shrimp spring rolls, 227
lettuce cups, shrimp pesto in, 137
lobster:
  and shrimp bread pudding, 43
  and shrimp cioppino, 61
  and shrimp fra diavolo, 85
  and shrimp Newburg, 121
  and shrimp paella, 127
  stuffed shrimp, 185
  XO shrimp with, 238
lo mein, shrimp, 108–9
Louisiana-style dishes:
  Bayou shrimp gumbo, 97
  New Orleans shrimp bisque, 35
  New Orleans shrimp chowder, 59
  New Orleans shrimp tacos, 197
  shrimp cakes, 53
  shrimp étouffée, 80–81
  shrimp fajitas, 83
  shrimp gumbo, 96–97
  shrimp rémoulade, 156–57

Madeira, Madeiran:
  shrimp, 147
  shrimp Thermidor, 213
  stewed shrimp, 101
maki, shrimp, 110–11

Malaysian-style dishes:
  black pepper caramel shrimp, 39
  shrimp satay with peanut sauce, 166–67
mango:
  black bean shrimp, 37
  chutney, shrimp wraps with, 237
Manhattan shrimp chowder, 59
martini shrimp scampi, 169
mayonnaise, shrimp wraps with, 237
Mediterranean shrimp salad, 163
Mexican-style dishes:
  butterfly fried shrimp, 51
  coconut shrimp, 65
  shrimp chiffon ring, 57
  shrimp mole, 112–15
Milanese, shrimp risotto, 159
mole, shrimp, 112–15
Moroccan deviled shrimp, 69
mousse, shrimp, with hollandaise, 116–17
mushrooms:
  caps, shrimp stuffed, 188–89
  garlic sauce shrimp and, 93
  kung pao shrimp and, 103
  lemon shrimp and, 107
  shiitake, steamed shrimp with, 181
  shrimp Alfredo with, 21
  shrimp dumplings, 77
  shrimp fried rice, 87
  shrimp frittata, 89
  and shrimp paprikash, 129
  straw, 14
  straw, cashew shrimp and, 55
  sweet-and-sour shrimp and, 193
  wild, shrimp soup, 232–33
mussels, 9
  Iberian stewed shrimp with clams and, 101
  and Portuguese shrimp, 147
  shrimp and clam stew, 118–19
  shrimp bisque with, 35

and shrimp chowder, 59
  and shrimp paella, 127
mustard shrimp cocktail, 63

Newburg, shrimp, 120–21
New England:
  shrimp curry, 67
  shrimp frittata, 89
noodle dishes:
  garlic sauce shrimp and noodles, 93
  shrimp and noodle soup, 122–23
  shrimp lo mein, 108–9
  shrimp pad Thai, 124–25
  Szechwan cold garlic shrimp and udon noodles, 195
  see also pasta
nutty:
  coconut shrimp, 65
  shrimp balls, 25
  shrimp curry, 67
  shrimp penne à la vodka, 135

okra and shrimp fritters, 91
olives:
  and Portuguese shrimp, 147
  shrimp stuffed mushroom caps, 189
onion and shrimp satay, 167
orange:
  sesame shrimp, 173
  shrimp Diane, 71
  shrimp teriyaki, 207
ouzo shrimp stuffed grape leaves, 187
oyster:
  sauce, 13
  and shrimp Newburg, 121

pad Thai, shrimp, 124–25
paella, shrimp, 126–27
paella pan, 16
pancetta, 13
paprika, 13